Workers Without Weapons

The South African Congress of Trade Unions
and
The Organization of the African Workers

by

Edward Feit

ARCHON BOOKS / 1975

Library of Congress Cataloging in Publication Data

Feit, Edward.
    Workers without weapons.

    Bibliography: p.
    Includes index.
    1. South African Congress of Trade Unions—History.
    2. Trade-unions—Africa, South. I. Title.
    HD8799.S72S584   331.88'0968   75-5738
    ISBN 0-208-01496-9

Workers

without

Weapons

Contents

Preface

The failure of organizations is often as fascinating as their success. Yet it is the latter that mainly occupies the attention of social scientists. While many studies explain why one or other policy or organization succeeded, few explain why others did not. The reason is, perhaps, that we all want our own ventures to succeed, and look to other examples of success for encouragement. Yet the pathology of failure can tell us as much or more of our prospects. This book is written in the belief that a discussion of the dynamics of failure, the failure of an African trade union organization in South Africa, can teach us much about African organization in that country and elsewhere. Apart from causes of failure, the story has an interest of its own, for there is no other detailed study of the South African Congress of Trade Unions (SACTU). Where other authors have mentioned it, they have given it a page or two or have lumped it with what is known as the "Congress Alliance."

SACTU was intended to be a vehicle to mobilize large numbers of Africans, most of whom were workers feeling themselves to be exploited, against the South African "establishment"—the government and the employers. It was allied to the most significant of the African resistance groups as well as with those of other races. It appealed on an issue that would seem unassailable—higher wages. Yet, for all that, it seemed unable to generate mass support on a significant scale. Why? The story, as set out here, helps make this clear. It explores how SACTU was made to fail: through official attack, through legislative and executive action against it, through the deficiencies of the leaders and in the organization of SACTU, and through SACTU'S failure to raise the political consciousness of actual or potential members. The reasons for the failure emerge in these pages.

The story of SACTU, as is true of most African organizations, cannot be told completely. There is much evidence missing. As is also true for many, however, there is a great enough fund of evidence to at least present the story convincingly. The book concentrates on what is known, relying on documentary materials, original material produced by SACTU both for internal and external consumption, records made available by the International Confederation of Free Trade Unions (ICFTU), the newspapers in which the SACTU line was made public (mainly the *New Age*), and in available literature. In addition, transcripts of interviews, recorded verbatim, were made available to the author. These transcripts added little to what was shown in the documentation and were full of inaccuracies, and tended therefore to reinforce the author's doubts of the value of interviews on subjects where recall of a contested part is in question. The study ends with a conclusion in which some analysis is essayed, although, because the story speaks for itself so often, and because it is so little known, a minimum of theory is introduced.

However, to tell the story has meant providing at least some historical background, and this is done largely from secondary sources. The first chapter, thus, treats of the first of the mass African trade unions—the Industrial and Commercial Workers' Union —and the fate that overtook it. The last chapter deals with the present developments and prospects for African trade unionism on a number of dimensions and seeks to draw some inferences for the future.

Very little has appeared that considers African trade unions in any depth, particularly since the demise of the Industrial and Commercial Union in the late 1930s. This volume may, therefore, fill a gap, but again no claim is made for completeness. It is not, nor can it be, a history in which each "i" is dotted and every "t" crossed; it does nonetheless, I believe, convey something of the flavor, the hopes, and the frustrations of African trade unions in South Africa.

As with every book, thanks is owed to more people than can be named. I am particularly grateful to Mr. P. H. de Jonge of the International Confederation of Free Trade Union in Brussels who made much documentation available to me. I owe a particular debt to the late Benjamin Seligman of the Labor Relations and Research Center of the University of Massachusetts, Amherst, and to his successor Harvey Friedman for their financial and moral support, and to Christian Potholm of Bowdoin College who made some useful suggestions. I, of course, am alone responsible for all that is written here.

Edward Feit

Amherst, Massachusetts

AATUF	All African Trade Union Federation
ANC	African National Congress
CAS	Central Administrative Services
CMBU	Confederation of Metal and Building Unions
CNETU	Council of Non-Eurpoean Trade Unions
FOFATUSA	Federation of Free African Trade Unions
GWU	General Workers' Union
ICU	Industrial and Commercial Workers' Union (see also ICWU below)
ICFTU	International Confederation of Free Trade Unions
ICWU	Industrial and Commercial Workers' Union (earlier designation of ICU though sometimes retained later as well).
IWA	Industrial Workers of Africa
NCC	National Coordinating Committee (SACTU)
NEC	National Executive Committee (SACTU)
NUSWEL	National Union of Students' Welfare Organization
PAC	Pan-Africanist Congress
POQO	(not an acronym—the African word for "pure") the violent arm of the PAC.
SACOD	South African Congress of Democrats
SACOL	South African Confederation of Labour
SACTU	South African Congress of Trade Unions
SATUC	South African Trade Union Council (see TUCSA)
SEIFSA	Steel and Engineering Industrial Federation of South Africa
TLC	Trades and Labour Council
TUCSA	Trades and Labour Council of South Africa
UTP	United Training Project (Johannesburg)
WFTU	World Federation of Trade Unions

Introduction

The Origin
of African Trade Unions

African trade unions in South Africa were, by their nature, trade unions of the poorest and least skilled workers. The industrial development of the country was based on a pattern of labor differentiated by color that originated in the gold mines.[1] The pattern that emerged, and largely continues to exist, confined Africans to the lowest rungs of the economic ladder. Above them were Indians and Coloureds, some of whom were semiskilled workers but most of whom worked alongside the Africans as unskilled laborers. Whites were at the apex of the pyramid.[2] Because such unions Africans were able to organize were often short-lived, poorly organized, and kept few records, their story has not often been recorded. The few books that have been written are the work of men and women who were often personally involved and who propagate a particular viewpoint.[3] It is difficult to reconstruct the workings of African trade unions in South Africa, and this will be evident in this chapter dealing with the earlier African trade unions. The information must be based largely on secondary sources which are often incomplete and sometimes in conflict with each other both as to interpretation and fact. It is also impossible to give full credit to individuals or organizations and their relation to events in this brief overview. The story needs, nonetheless, to be told if the accomplishments and failures of the

South African Congress of Trade Unions (SACTU)—our pro-
tagonists—is to be fairly assessed.

Herbert Blumer's model of racial stratification under conditions of industrialization provides the best starting point, for it
fits South Africa particularly well, at least until the early 1960s.[4]
Blumer begins by rejecting some of the established notions re-
garding the effects of industrial development on ethnically stratified societies. Industrialization does not, he argues, through
its inherent rationality ensure that racial stratification will be
abandoned. Stratification can be readily encompassed within the
structure of a growing industrial system. Economic rationality may
reinforce the racial order instead of contributing to its dissolution.
Industrial managers who might be willing to hire workers of the
subordinate racial group and employ them according to their
abilities may refrain from doing so in order to avoid difficulties
with other workers. This, as Blumer points out, is a *rational* decision.[5] Nor is racial tension likely to be a solvent. Members of
the subordinate group move from ascribed positions in the
countryside to ascribed positions in towns. Where boundaries
are undefined, they are quickly established "under the overbridg-
ing sway of traditional views of the appropriate positions of the
races." The wisdom of Blumer's analysis emerges clearly when
the history of South African labor is examined in the perspective
of time.

The modern development of South Africa from a largely backward and rural country to one that today is highly developed can
almost be dated to begin with the mineral discoveries of the nineteenth century. The discovery of diamonds in 1865 and particularly that of gold in 1886 produced, in Professor Richard's
words; "the first halting steps towards industrialization, population concentration, advanced communications, national mar-
kets, and participation in world trade and world problems."[6] The
lure of mineral wealth attracted adventurers at first, but as the
levels grew deeper, the mines drew capital, administrators, engin-
eers, and artisans from abroad. The artisans, mainly from England
and Wales, brought two kinds of exclusiveness with them: national
exclusiveness as Britishers and so superior to other whites, and
racial exclusiveness which put whites above all men of color. Such
conceptions were not, of course, confined to one European nation

at that time, but were very much the property of all. At the same time the British artisans brought trade unionism and the ideal of a universal socialism. Ideas that were to conflict, although the socialist ideal was confined largely to rhetoric. Like the whites, Africans were drawn into the cities and towns by dreams of betterment. These were not, of course, the only reasons. The mines, as hungry for Black labor as the farms had been, succeeded in securing that Africans were required to pay taxes in cash, and cash was to be earned only in the cities. The African thus went, partly willingly and partly against his will, into the money economy. Africans were then, and many still are, migrants alternating between town and countryside, although increasing numbers settled permanently in the cities and towns, breaking more or less completely with their rural origins.[7]

The division of labor that emerged mirrored the pattern that had characterized the rural economy. Africans supplied the muscle and whites the skills. Although African workers were essential to the economy, at no time was the African worker accepted as an equal at the workplace. White workers did not want to do the same work as Africans, labor which was regarded as "Kaffir work" and beneath the dignity of a white man, at the same time whites did not tolerate Africans doing the same work as their own. Whites demanded and received higher wages than Africans and saw their higher living standards threatened by black encroachment. White workers saw themselves fighting a rearguard action to protect their statuses and wages against black competition, and directed their activities to obtaining legal protection —pleas successive South African governments rejected until 1924. The election of the "Pact Government"—based on an electoral pact between the Afrikaner Nationalist party and the English-speaking South African Labour Party—secured the first industrial color bar legislation, applicable first to the mines and later copied in industry. From that time no South African government could ignore the wishes of white workers who claimed to be threatened by non-white competition, and employers reacted as Blumer has indicated. The labor market became increasingly stratified.[8] A result has been to make skilled labor scarce and to enable the unions to push wages of white workers to unjustifiably high levels.[9] White workers were understandably reluctant to change this condition. It is against this background that the rise of African trade unions must be viewed.

The Formation and Early Years of the ICU

African trade unions date from after the First World War. Before the war Africans had been spectators in the industrial struggle between white workers and white employers.[10] The war itself helped blacks but little, for they were faced with rising prices and were without the protection of a cost-of-living allowance. Sparks of protest appeared here and there in strikes and demonstrations, but these were sporadic and easily crushed by troops or police. Some rudimentary efforts at organization of African unions had been attempted by militant left-wing socialists of the International Socialist League who formed the Industrial Workers of Africa (IWA) in imitation of the Industrial Workers of the World in the United States. The organization issued a few leaflets but organized no strikes. Indeed a strike by African sanitary workers in 1918 seems to have caught them unawares, and when a general strike of African workers in sympathy was proposed, the IWA leadership opposed it as "premature." The leaders were nonetheless arrested, and though acquitted were unable to reestablish the Industrial Workers. Interestingly enough, in the light of later history, the African National Congress (then the South African Native National Congress) was at that time reluctant to involve itself in militant protest by African workers and remained unsympathetic to their organizing as workers rather than as Africans.

Through a chance meeting, apparently, the first African trade union of consequence was established in Cape Town, a city that had been free of demonstrations. Clements Kadalie, an educated African from Nyasaland (now Malawi) had been pushed by a white policeman and was supported in his complaint by a passing white who, it turned out, was A. F. Batty, a candidate of the South African Labour Party. Batty, who was running for election in a racially-mixed district, enlisted Kadalie to support his campaign, and though Batty failed to get elected, urged Kadalie to form a non-white trade union. The union, named the Industrial and Commercial Union (ICU), held its formative meeting on January 17,

1919, with twenty-four members—the majority of whom were coloured—duly enrolled.

In an effort to outflank Kadalie's union, the Industrial Workers of Africa branch was established in Cape Town, and was, like the ICU, intended to organize dock workers. The IWA branch had a short life, soon being absorbed into the ICU for reasons to be explained below.

The ICU was given its opportunity by the anger of white dock workers over the export of food to Europe in the face of rising food prices in South Africa. The white unions planned to refuse to handle cargoes of foodstuffs destined overseas and invited the ICU to participate. Kadalie seized the opportunity to plan a strike of non-white dock workers for higher wages which, after having obtained the promise of cooperation from white unions, was launched on December 17, 1919. Thousands of dock workers left their jobs, and the government was forced to promise that no more food would be shipped to Europe. Employers, the stevedoring companies, made no move on African wages, and the white workers, in violation of their pledge, returned to work. Two weeks later, their funds exhausted, and harried by the police, the ICU called off the strike. Although the ICU had failed in its strike objectives, a wage increase—very small but an increase nonetheless—was granted African dock workers. In addition, the strike brought Kadalie before a national audience.

Together with Selby Msimang and Sam Masabalala, Kadalie was present at the first national conference of non-white trade unions which met in Bloemfontein, in the Orange Free State, on July 20, 1920. Interestingly enough, given its growing importance, there were no delegates from Transvaal. The conference agreed on a constitution, and the Industrial and Commercial Workers' Union (ICWU) of South Africa was founded. It was to be a nationwide, non-white trade union organization which would perform traditional union functions, with its main foes capitalists and protectionist White unions. Political action was not contemplated, for this conflicted with the work of the African National Congress.

The organization was barely established when it was split by a leadership conflict. Kadalie, who had apparently expected to be elected general-secretary, was defeated by a delegate from Kimberly. Kadalie then withdrew with his delegation, returning to Cape

Town to resume work among the dock workers. The question of where the Cape Town ICU stood in relation to the ICWU was unresolved. Nevertheless, Kadalie scored another success in his efforts for betterment of the dock workers' wages. An approach to the stevedoring companies led to the most powerful of them meeting with Kadalie and raising wages, after which all firms in this line raised their wages in turn. Kadalie won an important victory.

Matters did not go as smoothly in Port Elizabeth as in Cape Town. Masabalala returned to his home town and won some 4,000 workers for the ICWU out of a total of about 20,000 in the area. He was also able to gain a small increase in wages of about seven cents (at present exchange rates), which brought the minimum African wage to about fifty-five cents per day. Encouraged, Masabalala called for a minimum wage of $1.40 per day—an increase of about 250 percent. The police arrested Masabalala, and his followers demonstrated, demanding his release. These events,, on October 23, 1920, led to rioting and to an armed confrontation between whites and Africans in which one white and twenty-three Africans died. A Commission of Inquiry eventually held white vigilantes largely responsible for the tragedy, but the ICWU suffered, despite a further small wage gain it was able to win.

Despite this setback the ICWU seems to have expanded throughout the country. A second conference held in Cape Town in July, 1921, had a majority of delegates from the Cape Province with only one delegate present from Johannesburg. Although stressing the same grievances as the first conference, the shadow of Port Elizabeth fell heavily on the meeting. The delegates were very keen not to offend the authorities, discouraged "wild talk," and under the guidance of Msimang gave priority to organization. Kadalie, a delegate from the Cape, kept his own counsel, did not speak, and was not elected to any office. Although it is impossible to be sure on this point, it seems that he already was preparing to take over the machinery of the ICWU.

Kadalie's springboard was the anniversary of the Port Elizabeth disturbances. Visiting that city late in 1921, he called a conference of the ICWU, and under his leadership it elected a coloured as President of the ICWU, Kadalie its general-secretary, and Masabalala national-organizer-in-chief. A number of resolutions were passed, one that the ICWU was a trade union without political ambitions which dissociated itself from any political body. Kadalie already began to look to associations overseas, and demanded that delegates be sent to other countries to represent the interests of the non-white workers. The name of the organization remained as it was, but the acronym ICU was adopted, by which it became known to both white and black in South Africa.

In 1922 scattered strikes by white workers, directed against the mineowners who wished to reduce wages and to replace white labor with black, grew into a general strike. The white trade unions were committed to a color bar, and individual strikers vented their wrath in attacks on Africans. Early in March the government declared martial law and used troops to repress the strike. Given its racial overtones, the ICU had opposed the strike and expressed sympathy with the government's stand. As a result of their support, Kadalie was the first African trade unionist given an interview by the Minister of Mines and Industries in which, though the minister promised nothing, the mere fact of the interview gave Kadalie and the ICU new respectability.

The stage was thus set for the conference from which the ICU emerged as a significant national entity. Meeting in Cape Town in January, 1923, without any delegates from Johannesburg or the Orange Free State but with some coloured delegates present, Kadalie's leadership was confirmed. Reelected to the key position of general-secretary Kadalie firmly denied that the ICU had any linkage with the Communist Party and affirmed that it was independent of political involvement. The demands formulated then were largely economic, and political issues such as the "pass laws" were avoided, though the continuing hostility of white unions were viewed with concern. To strengthen its position the union decided to buy a printing press and to issue its own paper, which appeared in May of 1923 as *The Workers' Herald*. More important, perhaps, was that the ICU, came from the meeting a centralized and not a federal body now seeing to expand throughout the whole of South Africa.

THE Growth of ICU

In chronicling the ICU, 1924 seems a "lost year." The standard sources say little about what was done and so one can only conclude either that this was a year of quiet consolidation or that little was effected.[11] This cannot be said of 1925, which seems to have been a year of considerable progress. Until that year the ICU had mainly been confined to the Cape, but following some rioting and a clash between Africans and police in April, African anger swelled the ranks of the ICU. The ICU now put forward minimum wage demands in Bloemfontein, which though unsuccessful won the ICU public recognition from the South African Trades Union Congress. It was in this year also that the headquarters were moved to Johannesburg, which had the largest concentration of African workers, and its 1925 conference was held there. Moving the headquarters had advantages and disadvantages that were to tell later. The move deprived the ICU, which depended on the skill and experience of Coloured workers of much of their influence.

Among the gains were fresh support from established African leaders, one of whom, A. W. G. Champion of Durban, was to play a significant role in the ICU.[12] After this time, too, the ICU became increasingly political and less of a strictly trade union movement.

The year 1926 was one of leadership crisis in the ICU, for Kadalie seemed set on abandoning his past militancy and breaking with the Communists in his union. There were two possible reasons for his action, the first is the influence of white liberals, both South African and British, the second and perhaps more important was the threat of the Communists to expose the "disgraceful misappropriation and squandering of funds" by Kadalie and other of the ICU funtionaries.[13] Although Simons and Simons deny that the Communists were planning a takeover, and indeed that they were caught by surprise by Kadalie's moves against them, their argument seems unconvincing.[14] What seems more likely is that Kadalie got wind of a Communist coup in preparation and beat them to the punch. The events of that time can be briefly set forth, and a fuller explanation, from different viewpoints, is to be found in the literature cited.

In essence the argument was over the thrust of ICU policy: was it to be *hamba kahle* (the African for "go slowly") or was it to be militancy? By 1925 the ICU had expanded greatly but had done little. Something clearly had to be done if the organization was to survive. Thousands had joined and paid their subscriptions, and money had flowed into the Union's coffers; money was being freely spent without result. Nothing had been gained for the membership since the dock strikes, no attempt had been made to initiate direct action. The spread of ICU had, in fact, something artificial to it. As people grew disillusioned in one district and the organization atrophied, organizers moved to another district, as yet untouched. At the time the ICU was flourishing in the Transvaal it was dying in the Cape.[15]

As Simons and Simons show, the quick growth of the movement probably accounted in part for the financial irregularities, autocratic rule, and inefficiency:[16]

> Estimates based on enrolment figures or sheer guesswork credited the union with 30,000 members in 1925; 40,000 in 1926; from 80,000 to 120,000 in 1927; and 70,000 in 1928; but the number in financial compliance with the rules was usually less than half the reputed membership. Kadalie told the Economic and Wage Commission in September 1925 that about half the members were in financial standing: La Guma's figure for 1926 was 28,000; Bunting estimated 30,000 in 1927; and Ballinger* 12,500 in February 1929.

Managing a large organization always requires considerable administrative skill, but the ICU would have called for the most consummate of managerial techniques. The ICU was a broad and undifferentiated body mainly of unskilled workers but also of others. Chiefs had, for instance, led their entire tribes into, and been accepted by, the ICU.[17] Their numbers were augmented by recruits gained by untrained officials who enrolled new members and collected their subscriptions. Falsification and peculation were inevitable.

Ignorance of bookkeeping may have accounted for some of the thefts which, La Guma reported, ran as high as £500 per year (about $1,200) through the inefficiency and dishonesty of union officials. Although inefficiency would have to be tolerated, he continued, dishonesty should be severely punished. La Guma also blamed Kadalie for ignoring constitutional procedures and for using the ICU's funds for union projects without consulting its

*J. A. La Guma was General-Secretary of the ICU and a Communist Party member. S. P. Bunting was a solicitor and well-known Socialist. W. G. Ballinger was a trade union organizer sent out to help in the affairs of the ICU who figures importantly later in the chapter.

appropriate bodies. Kadalie probably saw in this the beginnings of the Communist offensive and led him to attack first. Indeed, the "dictatorial rule" of Kadalie was one basis for the attack on him. Needless to say, the problems of the ICU were problems of new trade unions everywhere. The situation was worse in South Africa, for unlike European unions Africans in South Africa could look to no other unions, already established, for aid. They had to face not only the hostility of the government but also that of white labor.[18]

The militants, led by the Communists, had four members on the National Executive Committee of ICU and demanded a change in internal organization. They wanted control of finance and stricter supervision of the organizational cadres. The issue on which the battle was fought was whether the ICU should send a delegate to the League Against Colonial Oppression which was to meet in Brussels. Kadalie maintained that the Brussels meeting was that of a Communist front, and that he had come to the meeting determined to see a definite stand taken on communism. Arguments that non-Communist organizations such as the (white) South African Trade Union Congress had accepted an invitation merely enraged Kadalie who became abusive and stormed out of the conference. Forced to apologize, Kadalie returned, but it soon became apparent that he had regrouped his forces for a direct attack on the Communists. A resolution was passed, that "no member of the ICU shall be a member of the Communist Party." Communist members of the ICU had now either to renounce the party or the union. With the exception of a few who first resigned and then returned, the Communists dropped from the ICU leadership.[19]

The sequel came at a meeting in Port Elizabeth on the following Sunday when the Communists asked to be heard at an ICU meeting and were refused. They called a meeting of their own on a nearby hill and hundreds of Africans came to attend. A resolution was passed by all those present demanding the reinstatement of the Communists.[20] This was, it must be said, a characteristic Communist tactic that they were to later employ in their dealings with other African organizations. Meetings would be held and resolutions passed without reference as to the qualifications of those present as members or nonmembers of the organization.[21] The question of the Communist drive for control remains debated. Simons and Simons point to the ease with which Kadalie took on the Communist leadership and their failure to resist expulsion.[22] They admit, though, that Kadalie could well have taken La Guma's strictures as a threat to his leadership.[23] Be that as it may, Roux, after describing the great influence and support the Communists had in the ICU, admits that membership increased after the split with the Communists, and this also emerges in the Simons' figures quoted earlier. The loss of experienced and devoted, if doctrinaire, officials did not diminish the drive for members but doubtless hindered organization.

The ICU reached its highest point in 1927, without resolving the question of what was to be done. Kadalie used the Annual Conference of that year to consolidate his position against the Communists by getting a resolution adopted which endorsed the action of the National Council in expelling the Communists and which stated that "ordinary members of the ICU be not allowed to identify themselves in any way with the Communist Party."[24] This did not, however, heal the split between the left and right wings of the ICU. The left consisting of one time Communists who had remained with the Union, urged strong action both in strikes and in resistance to the hated "Pass Laws." They were opposed to further petitions to the government which they said were not only useless but likely to emasculate the movement. Kadalie opposed them with militant talk and barren proposals. He urged that the pass laws be tested in the courts; this met with little enthusiasm as few members felt the courts could help them. They were weary of petitioning. In the matter of strikes, Kadalie proposed a "day of prayer," and when that was turned down, a "day of protest." The left argued that the workers were ready to strike, but this was rejected. Several reasons have been adduced for Kadalie's failure to act. The first and most obvious is that there were few avenues open to Africans for action which would not be severely repressed. The second was that Kadalie was bidding for respectability both among his white liberal friends and for recognition of his union by the government and by white unions. The third, which is closely related to the second, is that Kadalie was looking to the international trade unions to help, an old chimera with him. Indeed, the decision to send Kadalie to Europe was, perhaps, the most momentous the ICU took at the Conference.[25]

The visit was due to a resolution of the ICU Annual Congress that a black worker should go to the International Labor Organization Conference in Geneva in 1927. Kadalie was, thus, to go to Geneva and speak for the African workers who were "the victims of merciless exploitation of both capitalism and the white labour Pact Government."[26] He was also to visit labor leaders in Britain, France, and the United States. Although welcomed by the leading trade unionists in England, the British Trades Union Congress would not let him attend its annual conference as a fraternal delegate for fear of offending the white South African trades unions.[27] Kadalie was profoundly influenced by what he saw, and began to visualize the ICU as an orthodox union with a bureaucratic structure. To bolster his prestige in South Africa, and perhaps to achieve the organizational end, he appealed to the British unions to send someone prominent to South Africa. This was eventually done, with results Kadalie could not have foreseen.[28]

Events were moving in Kadalie's absence. Spontaneous strikes—not the work of the ICU—were breaking out among Africans in the Transvaal and Natal. The ICU tried to stick with constitutional methods which jibed ill with the mood of the workers. Neither the strike of 1,500 African dock workers nor the strike at the Johannesburg railway goods yard had the support of the ICU. The opposite was indeed the case, with ICU organizers urging the workers to return to work. Yet, this did not help the ICU either with the government or with white farmers or employers who continued to regard the ICU with continued enmity.[29]

The Fall of the ICU

The absence of Kadalie encouraged local leaders to entrench themselves in their own bases of power. This was especially true in Durban, Natal, which was the most active branch, it had what is more, continued to grow as the other branches in the Transvaal and Orange Free State declined. The leader of the ANC, Champion, had not entered the ICU until its success had seemed assured, as he was not the man to voluntarily adopt a revolutionary role. But with the stengthening of his branch it was obvious that he now was Kadalie's rival for the leadership of the ICU. Because of Champion's accretion of strength in Kadalie's absence, the 1928 Congress of the ICU was hardly harmonious.

The circumstances of Champion's removal would seem strange were it not for his challenge to Kadalie. A leadership conflict had grown within the Durban organization itself, and to get rid of *his* rival Champion had accused him of misuse of the union's funds. A member of the Durban executive then issued a pamphlet stating that Champion too had acted similarly, and Champion brought a libel suit against his accuser. Champion lost the case and was censured by the president judge for the way in which the union's finances were handled. The apparent issue, then, was whether Champion should be expelled from the ICU.[30] This was, of course, only the apparent issue; if financial peculation were to be held against the union's officers, expulsions would have been widespread. It nonetheless served Kadalie in his attempt to hold on to the Durban branch without retaining Champion's services.

The conflict with Champion was intensified because of the very disintegration of the ICU. Much time at the conference that was to remove Champion was spent in wrangles over the credentials of different representatives who, it was claimed, came from defunct or "dud" branches.[31] Nevertheless, a tribunal appointed by the ICU Executive removed Champion from his post as Secretary for Natal pending the next Annual Congress. Champion did not wait for that meeting but, rallying the Natal branches behind him, left the ICU to found the ICU *yase* Natal as a completely independent organization. From this point it has a separate history that will be only touched on in this volume.

The secession of Natal removed the only flourishing branch of the ICU at a stroke. It also meant the loss of much of the union's paying membership, and to make things worse more splintering followed. Local leaders declared their independence and secretaries bolted with such cash as remained. The ICU head office's furniture had to be sold to pay lawyers' fees.[32]

Before the fateful Congress, and during its course, Kadalie was trying another trump card: affiliation to the South African Trades Union Congress, a largely white body. The African workers had friends in the TUC who were prepared to help, but Kadalie's lack of negotiating skill made this impossible. He applied for membership in the TUC for his 100,000 members, or rather the members he *claimed* to have. As the TUC had a total membership of less than 30,000, granting Kadalie's request would have meant subordinating the white unions to the ICU, a position none of the white unionists would accept. Kadalie was advised to apply on the basis of 5,000 members, but Kadalie insisted on his point. The application of the ICU was therefore rejected, and joint meetings for the two bodies to discuss mutual problems, were offered as an alternative. The door to the TUC remained closed, though Kadalie said that he would continue to knock until it opened.[33] The later collapse of the ICU made this a moot point.

In the midst of the breakup of the ICU the British trade union organizer, to whom Kadalie had looked in hope, arrived in South Africa. William Ballinger was a Glasgow-born member of the Motherwell trades council and his mission was to shape the ICU along the lines of British trade unions with which he was so familiar.[34] Ballinger, though he tried to the end, found the financial mess in the ICU unmanageable. The faulty accounts, missing records, and lack of documents formed an impenetrable thicket against any attempt at rational organization. Indeed, the union's deficit grew to £1,500, the union's furniture was seized for a debt of £100, and an appeal had to be made to the Independent Labour Party in England for the funds to pay Ballinger himself.[35]

Nor was Ballinger more successful in his role of "adviser" or, more properly, actual leader of the ICU. Ballinger had no experience of South African conditions on arriving in the country and was surprised and somewhat hurt by the storm of objections he met from the white community. Ballinger, in his speeches, stressed that the ICU was not revolutionary, and that it was being reorganized on saner lines and would live down its bad past. The errors of leaders who had made rash promises and wasted the union's resources would be corrected. Ballinger's attacks on the leadership of the ICU weakened confidence in Kadalie without appeasing the ICU's enemies. It also alienated these leaders and forced Kadalie into a more militant stance to hold such influence he still possessed.[36]

For a time Ballinger and Kadalie worked in uneasy partnership, but soon quarrels broke into the open. Ballinger had tried to reunite the Natal ICU with the main ICU, but despite the cordial talks the attempt was abortive. The quarrels attendant on this failure and Kadalie's general dissatisfaction led to a breach between the Britisher and the African that became final. Kadalie left the ICU taking the bulk of the remaining membership with him. Ballinger was left with what remained of the ICU organization, its newspaper, and the debts.[37] He continued for a while to sort the records and to attempt settlement of the debts, but the ICU was finished. "The veld fire had burned itself out. It was useless to blow on the ashes."[38] Ballinger turned his attention to journalism, research into African economic conditions, and to other matters such as organizing an African cooperative society in the Transvaal.

In Easter 1929, Kadalie gathered his followers at Bloemfontein and formed the Independent ICU, which after his attempts to obtain funds from white organizations failed, he directed once more to militancy and to the left. He applied to the League against Imperialism, which in 1927 he had denounced as Communist, and asked for £200 with which to build a huge and militant trade union. This was refused. In East London, where Kadalie retired with his followers, the Independent ICU's fire flickered for the last time. A general strike of railway and harbor workers was initiated on January 16, 1930. Kadalie cabled to overseas organizations for funds and urged the white unions not to scab. Although blackleg labor was brought in from a variety of sources, the strike spread, so that, at the end of the week, the strike committee could claim that ninty-six percent of the workers were out. As the strike lasted, however, African workers suffered and as funds were unavailable for their succour, they began returning to work on January 24, and Kadalie and the IICU leadership were arrested. From prison Kadalie ordered the workers to return to work. The net result was that wages rose by six pence per day, and workers who had not struck were paid somewhat more. Some strikers lost their jobs and the whole matter damaged the prestige of the IICU. "Thus," as Roux writes, "its leaders overawed, its ranks split into numerous sections, its membership practically gone, the ICU faded out from the revolutionary movement in South Africa."[39]

Perhaps the most fitting epitaph is that of A. Lerumo in the official Communist history. Lerumo points to the many reasons explaining the decline of the ICU. Its formlessness and all-embracing structure hindered organization on a factory or industrial basis; Kadalie and other leaders tended to substitute revolutionary platform oratory for mass mobilization and mass action; there was also the influence of white liberals, and Kadalie's rift with the

Communist Party, and his "misguided attempts to transform the organization from a revolutionary organ of the masses into a sort of respectable and bureaucratic machine which had developed among the white workers and in Britain."[40] These factors were of important, as Lerumo points out, but they overlook the massive machinery of the government ready to be unleashed against any African organization constituting a threat to white power.[41] As we shall see in the following chapters, the Communist attempt to build such a body, a political trade union organization, met with little more success for the very reason of the power as well as the organizational problem Lerumo adumbrates. Whether militant or operating within a framework of law it is unlikely that the ICU could have succeeded in its objectives.

The Communist Trades Unions

Both the Industrial Workers of Africa and the ICU had been loosely organized political parties rather than trade unions in the strict sense of the word. They had made little effort to organize Africans according to particular trades or industries and had accepted all comers. The Communist leadership, expelled from the ICU, moved to prepare African unions along more orthodox lines. Among the main sources of inspiration were Ben Weinbren who organized the Native Laundry Workers' Union [Native was, at that time, the term for an African. European is (or was) the term for a White]. Other small unions among African bakery workers, mattress workers, and furniture workers were quickly added to the list early in 1927.[42] Five unions were formed with a membership claimed to be 10,000, which were combined into the South African Federation of Non-European Trade Unions early in 1928.[43] The aim of the Federation was declared to be to promote a united front of all non-European organizations for equality in every sphere as a step to non-racial unions.

It is at this point that the Comintern intervened fatally in the budding organizations. A resolution in Moscow in 1928 called for the establishment of a "Native Republic," which meant closing the gates of the Communist Party to white workers. White Communist leaders objected that the decision was premature, but Moscow insisted on its way. A purge of the party followed in which the most able white leaders were expelled, including Ben Weinbren. Some unions broke away from the Communist Party, but with the onset of the Great Depression many dwindled from the scene between 1929 and 1932. Two remained: the Native Laundry Workers' Union and the Native Clothing Workers' Union.[44] The end of the depression brought fresh opportunities with it. The nucleus of a new union body under African leadership surfaced after 1933 owing largely to the intervention of a Trotskyist white unionist, Max Gordon. Gordon, according to Roux, had the flexibility to subordinate doctrinaire considerations to the needs of workers' organizations and was responsible for training a number of Africans who later became prominent trade union leaders.[45] An important and stable union was organized among store clerks and warehousemen, and the bakers and printing unions were reorganized. By 1937 Gordon was secretary of four flourishing African unions. Jealousy of Gordon among African subordinates served, however, to undo much of the work that had been done. Africans, they urged, should be secretaries of the unions, a wish that Gordon conceded though arguing that more training was needed. Gordon's work was eased with the establishment in 1938 of a Joint Committee of Gordon's unions and three new unions— the dairy, chemical, and general workers' unions. In 1939 the Joint Committee decided that all of its unions should have their own secretaries and that Gordon should be secretary for the group as a whole. Gordon's position was further weakened with his internment as a "safety measure" in the war during 1940. A new secretary was needed and a very capable white was proposed and rejected. Gordon tried to influence the unions from his internment camp but failed. The unions began languishing and some broke away from the Joint Committee. At its zenith the Committee had had some 23,000 members, most of which were lost though the Commercial and Distributive Workers' Union remained both permanent and stable.[46]

Leftist organizers tried to expand African unionism to all parts of the country. In the Cape, Ray Alexander, a young Communist, organized at least a dozen unions on an interracial basis though most of the members were non-white with Coloured or African secretaries. Among the most notable was the Non-European Railway and Harbor Workers' Union with a membership claimed to be over 20,000, though this claim was not substantiated. Other Leftist organizers were active in Natal creating new industrial unions.[47] A result was a wave of strikes at the end of 1942 mainly in the Transvaal but also in Natal. Some of these were spontaneous, a protest against low wages and rising prices; others were organised by the unions. The government's response was War Measure 145 which made strikes by African workers illegal in all circumstances. Recognition was denied African trade unions. In spite of all this, a few illegal strikes did take place between 1942 and 1944 but the measure did make the operation of African unions in the war years largely impracticable.

The growth of African trade unions had, however, been beyond denial. A Council of Non-European Trade Unions took place in 1942 with eighty-seven delegates representing twenty-nine affilated unions claiming to have some 150,000 organized African workers. The unions differed in vital respects. Politically they could be grouped as follows:[48]

1. Communist controlled unions
2. Unions controlled by the Workers' International League (Trotskyist)
3. A group of independent unions first led by Gana Makabeni who cooperated closely with the Communists in the war years but fell out of favor with them in 1945 and was replaced by a Communist, J. B. Marks as chairman of the Council of Non-European Trade Unions.
4. A group of unions originally Trotskyist but claiming, in 1945, to be without political affiliations.

The position early in 1950, as nearly as can be determined, was that there were at least fifty-two African trade unions in existence. Their paid up membership was approximately 34,551. In computing these figures, however, African trade unions run by the government-owned railways are included; if their number is removed, the membership of the remaining unions was 17,296. In addition there were some twelve mixed unions with some 3,700 paid-up African members.[49]

Conclusions

African unions were at all times from the end of the first world war living entities. They varied in success and strength to a great degree with their leadership, much of which was from the left-wing of the political spectrum—often the only people who seriously cared about the African and his needs. Membership of the unions fluctuated greatly, often from week to week or day to day depending on circumstances, and these unions did not have the sympathy and support of government, employers, or, often, much of the white unions or workers.

Organizing an African union on a small scale was not difficult, and *de facto* recognition could sometimes be obtained from employers or the authorities. The organizers could, as Roux points out, approach workers, hold meetings, set forth the advantages of trade unionism, and begin to recruit members.[50] Even if small they could make representations to individual employers, give evidence before government Wage Boards, draw the attention to labor inspectors of infringements of government regulations on wages and conditions, and could in this way secure benefits for their members and also for African workers in the industry who may not have joined the union. The workers affected would, then, in turn become convinced of the value of union organization and enter the union's ranks. A union might thus grow and in time become truly representative of the workers in the industry. A few African unions have followed this course, and will be more fully treated in the final chapters. The greater part, however, fell by the wayside, afflicted as they were with a variety of difficulties, some due to the opposition of the forces arrayed against African unionism, and some from the nature of the unions that developed.

Among the greatest difficulties were the related issues of funds and securing the services of efficient and honest union organisers. Dues could not be collected by the employer, and as a result organizers often found it difficult to find their members on pay-days at their workplaces, and employees themselves were often unwilling to make the payments. The result was that members often fell into arrear; for instance, of 6,651 members of African unions cited by the Legislation Commission only 2,645 were in good financial standing.[51] Lack of adequate funds was, thus, one part of a vicious circle. Officials who served the unions could not be properly paid for their services, and therefore tended to be men or women without the knowledge or ability to conduct the union's affairs. The originator of the union was often an individual with great powers of oratory not necessarily matched by organizing skills, and who became head of the union because of his role in forming it. This worked disadvantageously for the membership. Nevertheless, a proportion of African unions were well conducted and have lasted to the present day.

Since an African trade union cannot be registered in terms of the Industrial Conciliation Act, it cannot formally negotiate for its members, but only act informally. Yet African trade unions, often in cooperation with white unions, have accomplished results for their members and for African workers generally in the teeth of great hardships. As many of these hardships are of political origin, African unions have always been tempting to those who wish to see Africans engage in political action. This books deals with one such attempt.

Chapter I

The Formation
and First Year of SACTU

It is a truism that Africans are the major component of the South African labor force. Without their toil, their sweat, and their muscle, life in South Africa would grind to a halt. Africans made up some fifty-four percent of the industrial work force in 1962, and this proportion has been rising steadily at the rate of one percent each year. The phenomenal progress of South African economy, often called the "South African economic miracle," is borne on black backs. Clearly, a section of a population so vital to the continued prosperity of all has considerable political potential. The problem for opponents of the South African regime has always been to somehow tap this potential, and that of the South African Government to prevent the African labor force from being mobilized against it. The South African Congress of Trade Unions (SACTU) was one instrument by which opponents essayed the effort. It is important not only for this reason but also because it illuminates some of the difficulties of trade union organization in a hostile environment.

SACTU was an attempt by the Congress Alliance to mobilize the African work force. The Congress Alliance consisted of Congresses of Africans, whites, Indians, and Coloureds.[1] Of these, the African National Congress, the oldest African political organization, with an estimated membership of between 30,000 and 100,000, was the strongest and the most important. Next in importance was the Indian Congress with an estimated membership of some 2,000. The other Congresses were small and weak in numbers but of very significant influence. It was often said thay they in fact controlled the African National Congress. As the relationship of these organizations to each other has been extensively discussed elsewhere, it would be pointless to restate them here.[2] Suffice it to say that the aim of organizing SACTU was political. Leon Levy, later to be president of SACTU, has set the goals out clearly:

> SACTU recognized that the organizing of this great mass of [African] workers was linked inextricably with their struggle for political rights and liberation from all oppressive laws. Every attempt by the [African] workers to organize themselves was hampered by general legislation affecting their right of movement, domicile and political representation. Every effort for higher wages, better working conditions or the reinstatement of unjustly dismissed fellow workers was immediately met by the full force of the state.[3]

Although somewhat exaggerated, the statement is essentially true. Africans were, and still are, hemmed in by a network of laws that set a ceiling on their aspirations. They are prevented from seeking relief from such laws by others making such a search illegal. The Africans were indeed "workers without weapons"—they were denied all the weapons workers have traditionally used to better their lot.

SACTU was founded in 1954 to forge such weapons from the limited means that came to hand. It did not do so very well, and no doubt circumstances were against its doing better. Ten years later SACTU had virtually ceased to function, having fallen victim to government harassment and to its own shortcomings. SACTU's failure and the futility of some of its efforts should not blind us to the utility of studying it. Failure can often teach more than success, and the causes of failure in what might have been a powerful movement are certainly significant. Political trade unionism, an appeal to both pride and pocket, should on the face of things have a powerful appeal for Africans in South Africa. Economic gain could be harnessed to African resentment of constant repression. The story of SACTU shows why an oppressed people is difficult to organize, and how governments prevent organization. The story, furthermore, has fascination of its own and is worth the telling, not because SACTU was so important or so powerful, but because of what it did and what it tried to do.

Although intended as a multiracial trade union coordinating center, SACTU was largely a multiracial head on an African body. Men and women of all races made up the leadership, but the membership of the forty-seven unions that SACTU claimed as affiliated to it was mainly African. The published roster of memberships, which is unreliable, cites the number of members as 498 whites, 12,384 Coloureds, 1,650 Asians, and 38,791 Africans in 1960.[4] On this basis there were more than two Africans to members of all other races, and Africans outnumbered the next largest group, the Coloureds, by more than three to one. The unions of other races were, in addition, founded before SACTU, and entered into it on foundation. Many of the later unions were SACTU creations among Africans. One can, in discussing SACTU, think of its activities largely among Africans.

The intention of SACTU, as already explained, was to be a political trade union, to harness workers demands for economic amelioration to a political cause. Political trade unionism has many pitfalls because of these divided aims. To gain its long-term political ends the union must bring its members economic advantages in the short term. If overtly political decisions compromise immediate gain, the leadership risks alienating its followers, yet failure to take political action may compromise the long-range goals.

The problem is intensified by the trade union's need for political allies within the existing political system. The demands of trade unions are always in some sense political. Employers organizations lobby for legislative support, and labor organizations must likewise. Yet political allies expect repayment in support, and this means, in effect, support for the existing political system. SACTU's allies were denied all except extra-legal political activity. The Congress Alliance aimed at radically changing the political system, first by peaceful and later by violent means. Yet, to negotiate with employers, as it sought to do, SACTU had to work within the limits of the system. It had both to face the intransigeant opposition of the government and to depend on the goodwill of employers. This inherent contradiction was to remain unresolved to the end.

SACTU is a complex organization. To make clear its working this chapter deals with its foundation, and its first steps. Later chapters deal with the activities of the various SACTU organs. The conclusion summarizes and evaluates the part SACTU has played in the politics of South African opposition.

The Breakdown of the Trades and Labour Council and the Emergence of SACTU

Several streams, both African and non-African, merged into SACTU. Of these, the unions that met to form SACTU out of the wreckage of the Trades and Labour Council are among the most important. The Trades and Labour Council broke apart because of projected legislation by the South African government, and to understand how and why this happened, one needs to know something of South African labor laws without necessarily going into their ramified complexities.

Two laws are of particular importance, for they represent the intentions of the government and highlight the difficulties African trade union organizers faced. They are the Bantu Labour (Settlement of Disputes) Act of 1953, (to be referred to as the Bantu Labour Act), and the Industrial Conciliation Act of 1956. These two have to be seen together for their full import.

African workers were denied almost all rights of organized labor. Originally spelled out in various laws, they were consolidated in the Bantu Labour Act. The term *employee* was defined to exclude African males, so denying Africans the rights of employees under other laws. As Africans were "servants" instead of employees, African trade unions could not be registered and African men could not be members of registered trade unions. An amendment to the Act prohibited strikes, and another of 1959 forbade African participation in the boards set up under the

Industrial Conciliation Act. Separate machinery for conciliation of labor disputes was to be provided for Africans.

The Industrial Conciliation Act affected Africans less directly than did the Bantu Labour Act. The Conciliation Act had a threefold aim: (1) to reduce industrial conflict by providing the machinery for settling disputes; (2) to force the separation of racially mixed unions into racially segregated unions; and (3) to reserve certain jobs to workers of the different races.[5] Of specific concern to Africans was the provision, effective until 1959, that the Industrial Conciliation Boards, which consisted of representatives of employers organizations and of registered trade unions, had sweeping powers to determine the wages of their industry, including African wages.

An anomaly in the law made it applicable only to African men and *not* to women. Trade unions of African women could be and were formed. Unions of coloureds and Indians could also be legally registered. Many of these unions were affiliated to the South African Trades and Labour Council.

The Trades and Labour Council, which had survived much dissension and splintering since its foundation in 1931, emerged as a large and powerful labor organization in 1945, with 115 affiliated unions and a membership of over 168,000 workers. A split resulting from Afrikaaner nationalist influence reduced the number of affiliated unions in 1947, as did the disaffiliation of a group of artisan unions in 1950. The list of affiliated unions and their memberships is evidence of the downward slide:

Year	Unions	Members
1947	111	184,041
1950	80	126,018
1954	45	80,000

This, then, was the situation of the Trades and Labour Council when the Industrial Conciliation Bill was placed before the South African Parliament in 1954.[6]

The chief stumbling block to trade union unity in the face of the Industrial Conciliation Bill, which the unions feared would undermine collective bargaining, was their attitude to the non-white unions. Put in technical terms, the argument was whether registered unions alone should be affiliated to a center or whether the unregistered [African] unions were to be included. After attempts to have the terms of the Conciliation Bill altered by the Minister of Labour failed, the representatives of sixty-one unions met in Durban in October 1954 and reached a compromise. Briefly, the compromise was to form a coordinating center to be called the South African Trade Union Council (SATUC) and to form another ، parallel coordinating body, acting in liaison with the SATUC, for the unregistered unions. Because of the compromise, SATUC emerged with some forty affiliated unions having about 147,000 members.

The question of African unions was not, however, by any means settled. Some ten African unions had been affiliated to the Trades and Labour Council at one time, but their numbers had declined steadily. There were many reasons for this: racialists in the trade union movement had done all they could to make Africans feel unwelcome; anti-African speeches were made at meetings and personal attacks on African union leaders; and many African unions were dissatisfied for other reasons. Many disaffiliated and either remained unaffiliated or joined with the Transvaal Council of non-European Trade Unions, an African coordinating body. By the time the Trades and Labour Council was dissolved, some five African unions, two of which were virtually defunct, had remained with the Trades and Labour Council. The quarrel, ostensibly about this handful of unions, actually rested on deeper issues.

Just as some unions would not remain in a body that had African unions affiliated to it, so were there others that would not continue their affiliation with one that discriminated against African unions in any way. These were some fourteen smaller, left-wing unions, which decided that they could not conscientiously join SATUC, many were later involved in the founding of SACTU. [SATUC must, of course, be carefully distinguished from SACTU. Later to avoid confusion SATUC changed its name to Trade Union Council of South Africa (TUCSA)].

The first meeting of the dissenting unions took place in Durban on October 7, 1954, one day after the Trades and Labour Council had been dissolved. Pieter Beyleveld (a clandestine member of the Communist Party) was elected to the chair and argued that, with the dissolution of the Trades and Labour Council, no trade union coordinating body now represented the workers of all races. Unions desiring the true unity of all workers of all races should combine to establish a new coordinating body. A resolution setting out the aims of such a center was introduced and passed unanimously:

> In pursuance of our desire to retain the principles embodied in the constitution of the Trades and Labour Council (1949), we delegates who attended the recent conference and voted against the resolution to dissolve the S.A. Trades and Labour Council, agree on the establishment of a Committee whose object it shall be:
>
> (a) to coordinate the future plans of the dissenting unions and
> (b) to seek to organize a conference with the object of establishing a trade union center as soon as possible but not later than April 1955, based on the principle of non-discrimination on the grounds of race, color, or creed.

The meeting then elected an Interim Committe to be headquartered in Johannesburg to decide on implementation. The chairman pointed out to those assembled that no individual union was bound by the decisions of this committee.[7]

The Interim Committee on October 19 took a number of substantive decisions. It renamed itself the Trade Union Coordination Committee, and resolved to be governed by the constitution of the now defunct Trades and Labour Council. As procrastination would be the thief of time, interested unions might lose interest if action were not taken, therefore, the Coordination Committee felt that the new center should be quickly established. Another reason for haste was that the Industrial Conciliation Bill was due to be considered by parliament. SATUC was unlikely to offer much opposition, and the new center, once established, would be in a better position to fight the measure. The Coordination Committee therefore pressed the unions to agree to form the new body and convene a conference for this purpose before the end of 1954.

At this point Pieter Beyleveld introduced an idea that was to be decisive in shaping the new organization. Although approving of the desire for speed, he said, he did not want to sacrifice the cooperation of African unions. He urged that the Council of Non-European Trade Unions be invited to meet with the Committee in two weeks time to investigate the possibility of their cosponsoring the conference as they might also be interested in participating in the new body.[8]

As the Council of Non-European Trade Unions (known as CNETU) is of such importance, something needs be said briefly of it.

The CNETU was formed in 1942 to bring the various (unregistered) African trade unions together and to press for recognition of Africans as "employees." Other unions of Africans were added in 1944 and the full style Transvaal Council of Non-European Trade Unions was adopted. The African trade union movement had by this time reached impressive proportions. According to figures furnished by the South African Institute of Race Relations memberships, in September 1945, there were:[9]

City	No. of Unions	Membership
Johannesburg	50	80,000
Pretoria	15	15,000
Bloemfontein	10	5,000
Kimberley	5	3,000
East London	10	15,000
Port Elizabeth	19	30,000
Cape Town	10	10,000
	119	158,000

It is evident from the way these figures are rounded off, both as to numbers of unions and as to memberships, that they need to be accepted with caution. However that may be, a split in 1946 and a new federation, the Council of African Trade Unions, was formed. They opposed CNETU because they claimed CNETU to be under Communist influence.

The split in CNETU was as much a leadership struggle as an ideological one. The leader of CNETU, Gana Makabeni, was challenged by J.B. Marks, General Secretary of the Mine Workers'

Union, and was ousted by him. Marks, in addition to his rank
in the Mine Workers' Union was also General Secretary of the
Communist Party. Apparently at the behest of the party, but
also to make good the poor pay and working conditions of the
miners, Marks initiated a strike of African mine workers in 1946
which failed. After this the CNETU, already weakened by the
Makabeni split, was further emasculated. It had only some
fifteen unions affiliated in 1950, and one of these died during
that year. Their combined membership was some 8,500. In
addition, the affairs of many of the unions had fallen into dis-
order. Meetings were not held regularly, minutes of meetings
were often incomplete and unsigned, funds were in disarray,
and there was a tendency to treat members' money as that of the
union.[10] The CNETU was little more than a small group
of African unions believed to be largely under Communist
control at the time the Coordination Committee came to them.

The executive of CNETU seems to have been happy to accept
the invitation of the Coordination Committee, and with the
decision to establish a new multiracial trade union coordinating
center. SACTU was, thus, to consist of the dissenting unions from
the Trades and Labour Council and CNETU. The importance of
the link was not lost on the founders of SACTU, who in the
Secretarial Report of June 27, 1955, praised the merger as adding
to the prestige and strength of SACTU. The very coming into
existence of SACTU would have been impossible, the report
claimed, but for the support of CNETU.

Once the decision to found a new trade union center had been
taken, it had to be publicized both to correct the bad publicity
the Coordination Committee had received and to catch the attention of possible affiliates. A subcommittee was therefore appointed
to prepare press releases explaining the purposes of the new
organization and to circularize the individual unions calling for
their support. Plans were also made for a pamphlet that would
explain the purposes of the center and expand on its merits in
greater detail.

The publicity of the Coordination Committee was to serve
additional purposes. It was, first of all, to be used to seek the
cooperation of SATUC. For although separated by differences
of principle, there was also common interest. Publicity could be

used to forge a link between them if, when appropriate, each supported the other's campaigns. The publicity campaigns, once initiated, would also link the scattered members of the Committee. Ties to international trade union bodies, the ILO, ICFTU, and WFTU, were also to be established.[11]

Publicity was also to be a means of protest about the banning of trade union leaders under the Suppression of Communism Act, which denied them the right to participate in any organization or any kind of political activity by law.

The publicity lines laid down at this early stage were to be those of SACTU to the end. There was an unending flow of pamphlets, press releases, letters to national and international trade union bodies, and to the general press. Anyone who might possibly listen or read was approached. The general press printed the releases from time to time, but SACTU could always count on publicity in *New Age*, a largely Communist-run paper, which usually gave much play to the affairs of the Congress Alliance.

The material issued varied from soberly written reports on wages and working conditions in different industries to the far from sober newsletter, *Worker's Unity*, which appeared shortly after the formation of SACTU. Much of the *Worker's Unity* was a rehash of *New Age* articles, and the rest was sensationalized reports of the activities of different SACTU unions. Exaggerated and usually premature claims of successes were followed by silence or by reluctant admissions of failure where this was unavoidable. *Worker's Unity* was usually full of fervent praise of the Soviet Union and later of Communist China and consistently hostile to the United States, Britain, France, and Germany. In the international sphere the World Federation of Trade Unions, a body supported and financed by the Soviet Bloc, was generally hailed as right and good, and the ICFTU, supported by the West, as uniformly inept or malevolent. About the only praise meted out the United States was in the first issue of *Workers' Unity* for instituting May Day as a symbol of working class unity.[12]

The Organization of SACTU

Publicity could not long be carried on without the actual establishment of SACTU, and as long as it was not organized, efforts to publicize different unions were hindered. It took four weeks to draw up a plan of organization. The delay was due to arguments on matters of principle, such as a constitution for the new body, and to practical questions of organizing it in different parts of the country.

One of the first questions to be considered was the name the new trade union body was to have. The intention at first seems to have been to profit by the symbolic appeal of the Trades and Labour Council, and to call the new organization, "South African Trades and Labour Council (1955)." For some reason this idea was dropped, and the name South African Congress of Trade Unions adopted. Perhaps it was because all other organizations in the Congress Alliance had the word "Congress" as part of their names, and it was felt that the name of the trade union body should be uniform with them. The name chosen, South African Congress of Trade Unions, with its initials SACTU, did have more "swing," and this no doubt entered into consideration.

The basic constitution adopted for SACTU was that of the Trades and Labour Council. Before its adoption, questions arose as to the role the new coordinating center was to play in the affairs of the individual unions affiliated to it. A subcommittee appointed to consider constitutional amendments wrestled with this and other questions. The Trades and Labor Council constitution provided that the center's role was to be coordinating and consultative only. Elias Kunene, a member of the Coordination Committee, believed that this would be too restricting. The constitution should provide for closer control, he maintained, as such control could prevent individual unions taking action harmful to the movement as a whole. "It might, at times, be necessary to advise the unions at the Council's own volition [sic] where their actions might affect other sections of the movement," he maintained.[13] The acting secretary opposed this, believing this to be contrary to the democratic spirit in which the new organization was founded. In addition, he argued, the opposition to the Industrial Conciliation Bill rested on the government's efforts to undermine trade union autonomy, and so how could the Coordination Committee itself propose similar conduct without defeating its own purposes? This argument carried the day. The new amendment was unequivocal on the independence of the unions. It read:

The Council [the name SACTU had not yet been adopted] shall
not usurp any of the functions of any of its affiliated unions, nor
interfere with the domestic affairs of any such unions, but shall
confine itself to work of a consultative, organizing, and coordinating nature, provided that it shall enjoy such powers in respect of any affiliated union as may be specially delegated to
and conferred upon it by any such union.[14]

Other questions considered at the time were the qualifications for
membership, the qualifications of delegates to meetings, and the
qualifications of executive officers. The conditions for acceptance
of union records were also discussed.

Membership of the coordinating body was to consist only of *bona
fide* trade unions. Membership of the National Executive Committee was to be based on one member for every three thousand union
members or part thereof and one representative for every 500 at
national conferences, a provision negated in part by another which
read:

An annual return submitted by an affiliated union to the General Secretary at the time of application for affiliation and there-
after as at the 31st December of each year shall be deemed evidence of that union's membership, provided that, if an objection be raised, the NEC shall have the right to inspect the
books of the union concerned. Affiliation fees for any one calendar year shall be based on such returns.[15]

This provision opened the floodgates of abuse. A union with, say,
100 members would calculate the affiliation fee of 1,000 members,
and divide this sum among its members. It would then claim 1,000
members and demand representation accordingly. Shrewd union
secretaries often calculated the maximum their members were likely
to be willing to pay and then adjusted their "membership" to this
figure. For this reason the memberships of SACTU unions were
often expressed in surprisingly well-rounded figures which were
maintained from one year to the next.

The constitution was accepted at a meeting held on March 5-6,
1955. From the record it seems that 33 unions represented by 66
delegates attended this meeting and that they claimed to represent

41,253 workers. These figures must, for reasons already given, be treated with caution. In addition some three "observer unions" sent 43 delegates claiming to represent another 11,350 workers. Also present were "fraternal delegates" apparently from the different organizations of the Congress Alliance. The organization, it would seem, was set for an impressive start.

The first steps in establishing SACTU were taken quickly. An office was rented, an organizer hired, and a typist employed. The organizer was an African, J. Nkadimeng, indicating that the major effort was to be among Africans. Nkadimeng's duties varied: he was to attend to visitors at the office; to assist in the organization of trade unions generally, and specifically in the paper and cardboard industry. A qualified bookkeeper was appointed at this time, and the headquarters was ready for business.

It now remained to begin the work of organizing in earnest. The machinery to create more African unions would have to be set in motion, and attempts would have to be put forth to draw established unions to SACTU. A National Executive Committee (NEC) had been elected, and a Management Committee appointed.[16] The success or failure of the organization rested with organization in the field, and so directives were issued to all members of the National Executive Committee calling on them to convene personally conferences of local trade unions to establish Regional Committees which, once active and working, would report back to the National Executive Committee as a whole.

Regional Committees were established first in the Witwatersrand, the Cape Western Province, and the Cape Eastern Province, with Natal following a few days later. These soon encountered serious difficulties in establishing local committees, the basic units of SACTU. Only in the Western Cape was the Regional Committee able to spark effective local committees, because the old established and well-organized Food and Canning Workers' Union was behind it. By and large the local committees were tardy in informing the Regional Committees of problems affecting workers in their areas, in issuing leaflets, and in either forming new unions or assisting established ones. The Regional Committees, in their turn, displayed no great initiative in forming or guiding the Local Committees.

What were the problems? Some of these emerge in the reports

of local and regional committees. In the case of the Natal Regional Committee, its secretary, Billy Nair, told the NEC that the committee had only recently been established and had remained ineffective "due to a number of difficulties." Activities would be intensified, he assured them, after the NEC meeting. Mayekiso, the delegate from Port Elizabeth, pointed out that the unions in his area were in financial difficulties and could barely afford the affiliation fees to SACTU. No practical work had been undertaken in his area in organizing unorganized workers. On the Witwatersrand the committee had given aid to some striking unions in the toy, textile, and peanut industries. It had established a subcommittee to raise funds, but to little effect. The Western Cape was the one bright spot in a bleak session. The Regional Committee there had made a personal canvass among unaffiliated unions, and had been the only one of the committees to report to the NEC in advance.[17]

The first year saw no great improvement. Although the NEC had, at its first meeting, urged all local committees to set one day aside to popularize the organization and to raise funds for it, there virtually was no money. The local committees thus not only lacked experienced personnel but also the means to hire people with experience. The local committees could make little headway as a result.

The Witwatersrand was one of the most important industrial complexes in South Africa, yet the local committee could afford no organizer. It had to make do with voluntary help from the secretaries of established unions who, believing themselves already fully occupied, could spare little time for SACTU. Although the report of the region contained vague references to having "accomplished some achievements" it is difficult to tell what these achievements were. They seemed to consist of such minimal aid as could be given in the strikes spoken of earlier and celebration of the tenth anniversary of the foundation of the WFTU.

The Western Province, which had made such a good start, had regressed because there too personnel were available only for limited times. All that the committee could claim was to have mimeographed and distributed a leaflet.

The Natal story was equally dismal. The committee had "failed to make an impact on the workers of Natal generally, and besides maintaining contact with affiliated trade unions" had accomplished little.

Port Elizabeth, which had made a slow start, now once more justified its position as a center of African militancy. The committee in that area had met regularly and has closely associated itself with "progressive associations"—presumably the African National Congress which was always strong there. New trade unions had been formed, and shaky unions resuscitated. A number of industries had seen the beginnings of organization: milling; the chemical industry; the hotel and restaurant trades; the candy industry; confectionery; stevedoring; and some branches of the engineering industry. A protest meeting called after a police raid "was attended by 500 workers."

On March 1-4, 1955, when the first SACTU conference was held, affiliation of some 19 unions was claimed and membership was stated as 20,000—even this was probably an overstatement.[18] Most of the unions records were in poor order, memberships were inflated for technical reasons, and it is unlikely that an accurate estimate could be made.[19] The figure seems more soundly based than the earlier one, of the year before, when 33 unions with 41,000 members were claimed. There was, in any case, a good deal of variation among the different unions affiliated to SACTU. Some were well-established unions with the support of a strong membership in their trade. Many were registered and had unregistered African counterparts with whom they maintained close liaison. In addition some locally strong unions were affiliated, but most of the unions listed were small and insignificant.[20] They appeared and disappeared as SACTU's fortunes waxed and waned.

A number of major African unions did not join SACTU and others which did affiliate to SACTU were not its creatures. The African Clothing Workers' Union is an example. It had been organized by the Garment Workers' Union of South Africa as a union for African men. Another union had been organized for African women by the same people. These powerful unions with many thousand members took their time about affiliating. The S.A. Tin Workers' Union, on the other hand, had been set up and organized by SACTU. It had perhaps fifty members. Much the same can be said for ten of the unions affiliated to SACTU at the outset, which had little more to them than their grandiose titles—they were hardly more than empty shells.

Another strong union SACTU tried to enlist was the National

Union of Distributive Workers, which had sent five observers to the founding conference of SACTU. The National Union was not affiliated to SACTU and thus, if it decided to affiliate with SACTU would greatly enhance the power of the latter center. The Distributive Workers discussed the whole question of affiliation at their Eighteenth Annual Conference and decided to remain unaffiliated. They rejected affiliation with SATUC because it had supported the exclusion of unregistered unions, and rejected affiliation with SACTU because it was "too political." The matter was reconsidered six months later and the earlier decision still stood. The objections to SATUC on liberal grounds remained, and SACTU had, in the six months that had passed, done little to justify affiliation.

The Emerging Difficulties of SACTU

The problems that plagued the leadership of SACTU remained unresolved for the life of the organization. Among these the major one was lack of funds. To achieve the grandiose plans the leaders had made, to expand and organize the African unions to the point that they could become politically powerful, meant the harnessing of energies of full-time staffs. There was nothing in the till to pay them with, so SACTU had to limp along barely able to finance even the most modest schemes. The root of the money problem lay in the kinds of workers SACTU was out to organize, who of necessity were among the poorest with lowest wages and least knowledge of union organization. How money was to be raised thus remained a perennial problem.

The acting secretary of the Coordination Committee had called for donations from the unions.[22] The appeal remained largely unanswered. As donations were slow in coming, loans were sought from the individual unions. As donations and loans trickled in, the hopes of the SACTU leadership rose and suggestions to open a bank account were ventured.[23] These hopes proved without foundation. Toward the end of December the secretary said that no account had been opened because the amounts received simply did not warrant it. Donations were generally absorbed as soon as they were received. A donation of the Food and Canning Workers' Union and that of the Railway Workers' Union, for instance, were used to hire the hall for the founding conference. As this still was not enough to meet costs, another additional delegation fee of about $1.40 per delegate was levied. This contributed toward the cost of the conference which the new organization still could barely meet.[24]

The financial state of SACTU in January 1955 is evident from its balance sheet:[25]

Income		Expenditures	
Donations:			
African Chem.	$3.50	Hire for Hall	$16.10
Anonymous	1.40	Telegram	.90
Laundry Union	14.00	Postage	7.46
S.A.R. & H.W.U.	4.20	Bank Charges	.77
Loan: Beyleveld	4.20	Cash at bank	1.33
		Cash on hand	.74
	$27.30		$27.30

SACTU's plight had eased slightly by the end of 1955, though still giving little cause for rejoicing. Three reasons for SACTU's financial difficulties were enumerated by its President, Piet Beyleveld: many of the unions represented at the inaugural conference had not affiliated, so revenues were very low; on the other hand, unions that had affiliated to SACTU needed funds, and appealed to SACTU to make appeals on their behalf; although the Management Committee responded to these appeals immediately and solicited aid from the other unions, the other unions did not respond. The unions affiliated to SACTU found it difficult to maintain themselves, Beyleveld continued, and could hardly be expected to make generous donations so SACTU's position remained, on the whole, "extremely poor."[26]

SACTU's problems were compounded by police raids in which books of account and correspondence were removed. Without records, the tendency was for SACTU officials to resort to guesswork as the only alternative and the handling of financial transactions grew confused. The administration of union trust funds and subscriptions became a sore point. Subscriptions were received from workers where no union existed, and no separate arrangements were made for banking this money which was lumped with other SACTU funds. Consequently, those who paid in the money lost control over it and found difficulty recovering it when needed. Lastly, there was confusion over the "basic fee" of about $1.40 per month which was paid by some (but not all) affiliated unions. The amounts of affiliation fees for unions unable to pay the standard fee was not regularized, there were no minutes of decisions taken in these matters. No one quite knew what was going on, and the difficulties of financing SACTU and of sorting out what was due to unions and what was due to the coordinating body soon became virtually insurmountable.

From the first the problems that were to dog SACTU were clearly manifest. They persisted from 1955 until the organization virtually ceased functioning in 1964. The problems of organizing SACTU were also plain in 1955. If little has been said of them, it is because little was done in the first year of SACTU's existence. The chapters that follow will unravel the patterns and show how the organization developed and what it did from the outset to the end.

Chapter II

Organizing the Unorganized

Political trade unionists, to succeed, must first build mass support for economic ends and then convert this into political coin, for economic considerations are at the heart of union demands. Viewed superficially, this would not seem difficult to achieve in South Africa. African labor certainly had plenty of grounds for grievance, and were largely unorganized. In practice this was harder than it seemed. The prejudices of employers and workers of other races made organizing Africans a formidable task. Laws limited the range and scope of union activity, circumscribing the economic actions possible for Africans to undertake in their own interests. Organization to this end had, therefore, to be rationally planned to move within and around the various laws hedging African workers. Were SACTU'S schemes rationally planned in the interest of their affiliated unions, or were they taken largely for reasons of propaganda? And were they intended to arouse rather than to ameliorate?

Difficulties in assessing SACTU tactics result from the steady flow of exaggerated reports that the organization issued. Each plan and each ploy was aired with triumph, every victory, no matter how petty, was hailed as a great triumph. One may well argue that even small victories were hard won given the intransigeance of the government, but this trumpeting abroad was, if anything, counterproductive. It may have contributed to the determination of the government to make as few concessions as possible, and so to deny SACTU any possibility of exploiting a gain at its expense. Another SACTU technique was to claim any action of the government, which happened to coincide with a SACTU stand, a result of its agitation and pressure. After the State of Emergency (imposed at the time of Sharpeville) was lifted in August 1960, for example, a report of the World Federation of Trade Unions declared: "The State of Emergency officially ended on August 31 after a strenuous campaign by SACTU and other liberation organizations for its abrogation."[1] It needs hardly be said that the ending of the State of Emergency had little to do with the agitation of the "liberation organizations." It was ended because the government felt it no longer had anything to fear by ending it.

Continual exaggeration may have been necessary to maintain the fighting spirit of SACTU and its allies, which is understandable. Claims, however, do have to be sifted carefully from fact.

The Situation as Seen by the SACTU Leadership

As SACTU leaders surveyed the South African scene, they saw some 2,000,000 unorganized workers, of whom 1,800,000 were in the larger centers and in major industries such as manufacturing, mining, and agriculture. Others were in less important industries scattered among small and relatively isolated towns. Mining and agriculture, they believed, could not be organized at that time (1955) both because of the complexity of the industry and because of the funds it would take to do this. SACTU had neither the men nor the money for such a venture. Other fields in which many Africans were engaged, such as domestic service and commerce, would also present insuperable problems, for workers were scattered and less vital to the economy. Building too, as an essentially "local" industry, did not seem to lend itself to unionism. SACTU would have to look elsewhere for workers to organize.[2]

The industries considered most suitable for SACTU endeavor were the metal industries, transportation, and docking. For the metal workers, wages were settled on a country-wide basis, which made it important to organize in all centers. A promising beginning had been made, as SACTU had been invited to send two representatives to a meeting of the Transvaal Metal Workers' Joint Committee, and the metal workers seemed ready to accept SACTU leadership. With transportation, the railway workers were to be the target. Once more the organization would have to be countrywide. The railways were a thornier problem, for the railways ran their own unions, named "Staff Associations," similar to company unions of private industry. SACTU leaders nevertheless believed that the railway workers had seen the futility of the Associations, and "are realizing [sic] the need for genuine trade unions." Dock workers already had a fine tradition of organization. Strikes had been initiated in Cape Town and in three other major ports—Port Elizabeth, East London, and Durban. In the last two instances "scab" labor had had to be brought in from outside to break the strike. These categories of workers were, it seemed to SACTU, most likely to promise successful organization.

Once the target groups of workers had been selected, the means of organization had to be considered. Weak unions were to be urged to affiliate to SACTU and so "strengthen themselves." Unorganized workers would have to be persuaded to organize, and the means and methods of organization provided for them. Workers on strike were to be assisted, and unions were to be built from strikes of unorganized workers. Lastly, workers were to be shown how to recognize and deal with trade union racketeers.

SACTU activity was also to be directed to advising workers of their rights under the existing laws. Africans could, for instance, be shown how to avoid hardships visited on them by the Native Labour (Settlement of Disputes) Act and to warn them of its dangers, of "its pretence to offer an alternative to collective bargaining." SACTU leaders feared that, because of this law, employers would ignore the unions. Once a dispute was under way, the SACTU report complained, officials of the Settlement Board were on the scene, driving off trade union leaders, and driving workers back to work with the promise that their grievances would be investigated through their elected spokesmen. The Act, and the Boards established under its terms, "must constantly be exposed to the workers. Each effort of the Boards to disrupt the workers' unity must be concretely exposed." Even employers were prepared to ignore "these government stooges," the report continued, where the workers themselves stood fast. "Clearly this is an issue on which the bosses too must be educated."[3]

Implementing these objectives was more difficult than stating them. SACTU, it has already been stressed, was short of money and men. Government bans, prohibiting political activity under penalty of law, created an acute shortage of experienced organizers. The problem might be met by freeing organizers from work that could be done by others, but even this done, there still would not be sufficient organizers. The only way of solving the shortage of experienced men was for them to organize not only in their own industries but also others. To overcome shortages of money, organizers should at all times stress economy and the importance of fund raising. Union overheads should be reduced by sharing offices and staffs. SACTU resources were thin and had to be spread over a large area.

In sum, the intended strategy was to urge poorly organized unions to affiliate to strengthen themselves; to organize workers wanting organization; to help workers on strike and to build unions on the basis of strikes by unorganized workers; to show workers how to deal with racketeers; and the main target groups were to be metal, transportation, and dock workers.

The Divergence of Theory and Practice

The broad outlines of SACTU strategy has been set out. How was it to be realized? Guidelines were provided for local committees which were to be at the center of the struggle. Their first responsibility was to ensure that workers knew where the committees were situated. The address of the local committee was to be widely disseminated so that those wanting advice would know to whom to go. In addition, "collective leadership" was to be the rule, policies were to be worked out by the committee as a whole, and then delegated to individuals for execution. The local committees were to seek out individual union members—not leaders—who could be called on for help, and their workplaces and homes were to be recorded by the local committees. This band of active trade unionists was to be constantly expanded and they were to be involved in organizational work as participants—officials of the local committees were not to keep all work in their own hands, "and then not do it because they were too busy." Organizing unions, distributing literature, speaking at meetings, and other tasks were, as far as possible, to be delegated so that many people would be drawn actively into SACTU. Workers were to be rallied by reminders of immediate grievances, such as underpayment, employers who flouted or evaded laws, bad working conditions, and so on. These were to be coupled with concrete demands which should "be drawn up by the workers themselves." How effective was this is practice? How well did these precepts translate into reality? Description is difficult because of the state of SACTU records, and because of the many different bodies involved. However, information is available, fragmentary as it is, which may provide a useful picture.

Everything depended on the local committees. They had to make contact with the workers, to distribute the SACTU newspaper, *Workers' Unity*, and SACTU leaflets. Contacts were to organize factory meetings, discussion circles, and other means of publicizing the organization. Financial aid to the local committees was to be used for propaganda material, expenses of meetings, defense of workers brought to trial, and for other things that would bring SACTU to workers' attention and open channels of communication.

Communication was one of the thorniest problems, not only between local committees and their contacts, but between the local committees and the NEC. It was to become a perennial issue. Local committees told headquarters little, other than to acknowledge the receipt of circulars. Johannesburg was not told how, if at all, any directive had been carried out. The most regular reporters were the Port Elizabeth local committee, which at first was the most active in organization. The Cape Western local committee sent reports from time to time. The Durban local committee did not send reports for months. Many of the defects in communication rested in the dual role of the secretaries who, in addition to the local committees, were often the secretaries of other unions and had more than their share of work. It was obvious that full-time organizers were needed on the local committee level, and local committees were urged to raise funds to pay for them.

The activity of local committees was sporadic rather than nonexistent. Effort might, for instance, flare up and then die down as it did in Port Elizabeth in 1956. There was little continuity or consistency, and so every area had to continuously be built anew. SACTU leaders had correctly identified the cause of the problem, lack of full-time organizers, but the solution could not be furnished. Organizers could not be hired so, in Durban, for instance, of the nine unions affiliated to SACTU, six were organized by one overworked secretary and the full potential of the unions could not be realized.

As far as can be determined, the Durban local committee did little from 1956 to 1958. In 1958, however, a beginning was made in forming new unions, particularly among railway, bakery, dairy, and metalworkers. According to SACTU, "the workers joined steadily and the stream became a torrent after the militant struggles which began in Natal in June, 1959."[4] The events were the largely abortive attempt at a general strike of 1958 initiated by the Congress Alliance to coincide with the South African general election, and the Durban riots of 1959, in which beer halls were attacked and more than $280,000 worth of buildings in the African township of Cato Manor were destroyed.[5] Seizing on the atmosphere of unrest, SACTU had begun pressing for increased wages, and had met with representatives of the Chambers of Commerce and Industries, who supported claims for increased African wages.

Contributing to the growing strength of SACTU in the Natal area was the call by the President-General of the African National Congress, Albert Luthuli, urging every ANC member to join SACTU. A rush of Africans into SACTU followed, of such proportions that a special kind of union, known as the General Workers' Union, was established to accomodate them. These unions were to be depositories for workers until they could be placed in unions of their individual trades, which were still to be organized. Spurred by this expansion, the Natal regional committee established other local committees in Pietermaritzburg, Ladysmith, Estcort, and organized and affiliated more new unions than any other committee in the country.

The General Workers Unions were an interesting development, and much hope was held out for them since the original plans for their establishment had been drawn in 1955. They were intended to act as unions for industries too small to be individually organized, and were to be formed as soon as possible, their formation depending upon their drawing sufficient representatives from the major factories in each industry in the area. After their success in Durban, it seems that steps to establish unions were more vigorously pursued, and leaflets urging their establishment and describing their workings were issued in 1961. According to these the control of each General Workers' Union was to be vested in the local committee of each area, each industry in the union was to have its own subcommittee, and all of these were to be coordinated by the central committee of the union. "If factory committees had already been formed in certain industries, they should become part of the General Workers' Union until such time as they could be established as separate trade unions."[6]

This amounted to an admission of failure of earlier policies advanced in a succession of reports between 1955 and 1960. It had been impossible to establish strong unions in the industries planned for: metal, transport, and docks. For this reason, perhaps, General Workers' Unions seemed to provide an answer. They were to be launched with a maximum of publicity and as part of a campaign to recruit as many members as possible for SACTU.[7] The fee suggested for members of these unions was about 56¢ monthly of which about 42¢ was to be allocated to the account of the union, 13 percent to the local committee, and one cent to SACTU for affiliation fees. This was a complicated system for an organization as rudimentary as SACTU and was little practiced.

Why was the change made to the General Workers' Unions? There were a number of reasons. The first was that after 1960 the African National Congress, the strongest element of the Congress Alliance, had been banned, and the General Workers Unions provided a clandestine base from which it could be continued. Another reason was that General Workers' Unions were a useful format for throwing workers together with little effort. Individual unions could always be organized later, if they were organized at all. The General Workers' Unions appeared attractive because of the failure of factory committees at the time of the "stay-at-home" strike of 1958. Factory committees were ineffective in such strikes, which were not popular among workers. Most of them were unable or unwilling to sacrifice their wages for the three days the strike was planned to last and had to be intimidated into participating. Once at their places of work, the workers could not be controlled so strikes were best organized by keeping workers at home. The more inchoate General Workers' Unions gave more scope to mobilization and intimidation.

It may be added that the success of the Natal Committee in 1961, seems to have continued into 1962, when according to a National Conference report, it was "an example to all local committees in the activities undertaken." Natal had organized unions, led strikes, submitted memoranda to wage boards, and done many other things though the local committee established in Pietermaritzburg had ceased functioning.[8]

How were things going in the other areas? The local committees had varying success. Port Elizabeth had been the star committee in 1956 having organized the following unions:

Union	Members
African Sweet Workers	72
African Milling Workers	198
Stevedoring Workers	113
S . A . R . & H . Workers	612
Biscuit Workers	75
Cement Workers	271
African Hides, Skins, and Mohair Workers	278

Efforts to organize the workers at a synthetic board plant had proved abortive as the workers lived in a township and the township manager would not give SACTU organizers permission to enter it and hold meetings.[9] Other African unions were, however, organized without SACTU aid and these often did better than SACTU unions. The African Clothing Workers' Union and the Engineering Workers' Union are examples of two unions newly organized which did not affiliate to SACTU. SACTU was, thus, not always able to attract the most energetic unions despite its claims.

The very militancy of Port Elizabeth worked against SACTU plans at times. The general restiveness of Africans in Port Elizabeth had led to sterner police measures after the State of Emergency of 1960. Many leaders had been interned then and others had been syphoned off earlier into the Treason Trial which had begun in 1956 and was to drag on for some four years. With the declaration of the Emergency it was difficult to keep the SACTU office open; nonetheless, the local committee seems to have been able to keep some of the affiliated unions going in those hard times. The greatest success SACTU scored in Port Elizabeth was a strike in May 1961, which picked up momentum after its first day and did slow production without actually bringing it to a complete halt. Port Elizabeth also had an active General Workers' Union.[10]

The Western Cape had made a promising start in 1956 by

organizing three small unions among bag workers, timber workers, and metal workers. Various campaigns and publicity efforts were mounted and local committees were established in Cape Town, Paarl, and Worcester.[11] The unions organized were soon striking their factories and the prospects looked good.

There was slippage in the following years for reasons due both to bad leadership and external circumstances. Meetings of the local committee were well attended and were held regularly. There was no trouble in that quarter. What was at fault was contact between the local committee and the public. Members of the committee did not appear at the mass meetings they were scheduled to address, either because they feared being banned, or because they considered themselves too busy. In Worcester, for instance, the members of the local committee were afraid of banning and were, therefore, in the words of a SACTU report, "weak and ineffectual."[12] The conduct of speakers was excusable for there were cases in which members of the NEC itself, living in Johannesburg, failed to attend meetings and made no excuse for their absence. This was even done by A. Mphahlele, the then vice-president who did not attend the second session of the SACTU conference.

The Western Cape was involved in the Emergency of 1960 in much the same way as was Port Elizabeth. The events of that year in the Western Cape were not sparked by the Congress Alliance but by the Pan-Africanist Congress, a breakaway body, which organized a nonviolent campaign against "passes." Violence erupted and the townships of Langa and Nyanga were in turmoil with concommitant strikes, police cordons, and deaths. As in Port Elizabeth the best leaders had been arrested in connection with the Treason Trial and those at liberty were pulled into the net on the declaration of the State of Emergency. The threat of a strike was effective in at least one instance, for it secured the release of Liz Abrahams, the general secretary of the Food and Canning Workers' Union.

Violence was double-edged. A white vigilante group that adopted the name and some of the tactics of the Ku Klux Klan made its appearance and attacked the offices of the Food and Canning Workers' Union, destroying their records, burning their typewriter and mimeograph machine, and writing obscene slogans on the walls. This did SACTU and its affiliate no harm, for a fund was launched to replace the destroyed equipment, and the whole incident used for publicity in South Africa and abroad. Contributions came from many individuals and bodies, the Food Preservers' Union of Australia donating $140. In spite of this, the local SACTU committee was seriously set back by the troubled times.[13]

To indicate the difficulties in the Western Cape one must remember that the region did not have large numbers of African workers. What is more, if African workers gave trouble they could be deported to the rural areas of the Eastern Cape from which they mainly had come. Africans were, therefore, uneager to invite prosecution. The effect on unions, given the laws, was obvious enough. It was unendingly difficult to maintain those that already existed, let alone form new ones. Nevertheless, efforts were made at organizing small unions among mineral water workers, hospital workers, and cement and quarry workers. African elevator operators, whose jobs were threatened by new laws reserving this occupation for whites, were approached and attempts were made to set up a union in their defense.

The greater part of the labor force in the Western Cape were Coloured, and as their unions could be registered, a number had been formed. These, however, were mainly conservative craft unions and were cold to SACTU. Being dissatisfied with the lack of vigor of the established coordinating centers in fighting the Industrial Conciliation Bill, which greatly affected Coloured workers, they had thought of forming a coordinating center of their own. This was to consist only of Coloured unions and was to devote its energies to fighting the clauses of the Bill that reserved certain jobs presently held by Coloured for whites alone. SACTU feared the establishment of such a center, which would cut into its constituency, and therefore sent its national treasurer to the Cape to appeal to the Coloured craft unions. He was successful in at least one thing, the unions agreed not to form a coordinating center, but they would not affiliate with SACTU.

There were few new affiliations to SACTU in the Western Cape. The most powerful SACTU union, the Food and Canning Workers' Union was fully occupied with its own troubles, and could not spare the time for organizational work. As a result the region as a whole was of dubious value as a focus for organization. Efforts were made to establish a General Workers' Union in 1962, but because of tardiness in reporting, it was difficult for headquarters to know what, if any, progress had been made. The Coloured unions, which might have given aid, feared deregistration should they engage in political activity. There was, thus, limited scope for the energies of organizers, even had they been willing to devote themselves to SACTU.

Among the most inactive of the SACTU local committees was the one that should have been the most important—that of the Witwatersrand. On this "ridge of white waters"—the translation of "Witwatersrand"—was concentrated the greatest industrial and mining complex in South Africa. Radiating to the east and west of Johannesburg was much of South Africa's light and heavy industry and most of her mines. It was the hub of her transport system. The Witwatersrand contributed much to making South Africa the industrial giant of the continent. Failure here, therefore, was tantamount to failure everywhere.

The poor functioning of the local committee on the Witwatersrand was a critical defect in the entire organization of SACTU. And the poor functioning of the committee was attested to in repeated references in SACTU reports. In 1956 this local committee had organized no new unions though some individuals, acting on their own, had formed a Transport Workers' Union and a Typewriter and Allied Workers' Union. There was somewhat more activity in the following year, though the report still describes it as functioning poorly. Two more local committees were formed, one in Pretoria and one on the Western Witwatersrand, and a new local committee to serve the Eastern Witwatersrand was also being considered. However, the 1957 report points out that the Witwatersrand local committee had not worked from July to December of that year, and that representatives of the unions did not attend meetings, with the registered unions as the worst defaulters.

The fault was not entirely with the local committee. It overlapped with the national body, which had its headquarters in the same city—Johannesburg. As a result the local committee was overshadowed by the Management Committee. The State of Emergency of 1960, in which most of the higher officials were detained, solved the problem in part. The lower men were now able to organize their unions without the overwhelming weight of the national body pressing on them.

In the years after 1957, some of the local committees on the Witwatersrand took root, and others such as that in Pretoria died out. The Eastern Transvaal local committee, for instance, met every week and "did a tremendous amount of work." The advantage enjoyed by members of this committee, it was said, was that everyone knew everyone else, whereas the rest of the region was perhaps one of the most linguistically and racially diverse in the entire country.

Progress was slow before the Emergency of 1960. Once the Emergency ended an organizational subcommittee was appointed to approach groups of workers, and a national organizer on a full-time basis was appointed to establish factory committees in Johannesburg, the Eastern and Western Witwatersrand. A number of relatively minor unions were organized in the glass, tin, and biscuit industries, and the moribund toy workers' union was re-organized. An effort was also made to revive the Pretoria local committee. Officials of established unions were urged to take factory committees under their wing and to give them moral and organizational assistance. These moves were sharply interrupted by the State of Emergency of 1960. The arrests on the Witwatersrand were particularly heavy, two-thirds of the local committee and shop stewards, among them the national organizer, being detained.

The disruption of the Congress Alliance and of SACTU was so complete that, according to the 1960 report, "no protests or demonstrations took place in Johannesburg or on the Reef [the Witwatersrand is also referred to as the "Reef" because of the reef of gold rock that underlays it] in the weeks following the Emergency." The workers of Vereeniging and Van der Bijl Park, major industrial centers on the Witwatersrand, struck for a week. Yet, despite the ravages of the police raids, the 1960 report claims that the local committees were quickly reconstituted, and in "replacing members who were detained it has found new workers who are developing into true Trade Unionists." The Emergency had undoubtedly shaken the Congress Alliance to its foundation, and in so doing had inspired some of the members of the lower ranks to renewed action. The fact that so many were now new men revitalized the organization, and broadened its efforts.

A General Workers' Union several hundred strong was established in 1962. The local committee engaged in a number of campaigns against rent arrests and provided volunteers to distribute leaflets among mine workers. An attempt was made to organize farm workers as volunteers visited farms on weekends. In addition an effort was made to organize workers in some major undertakings in the chemical industry without much success. Otherwise activity followed the usual lines being concentrated mainly among workers in smaller industries such as mineral waters, stonecrushing and quarrying, university janitors, and timber workers.

The Actual Effects of SACTU Activities

The success of SACTU is very difficult to assess. The reason is that although the reports issued before 1959 were critical and evaluative this is not true of later reports which are full of inflated claims. These have to be carefully read and judgments made of what is contained between the lines. If the effects of SACTU activites are to be evaluated, the scattered reports of the Management Committee have to be considered alongside those of the conferences, newssheets, leaflets, and press handouts. These throw a strong light on a number of major organizational problems.

One recurring question was representation at conferences. The inflated membership claims, mentioned before, were worrying to the Management Committee. More particularly was the issuance by the local committees and the unions of membership cards whether a union existed or not. Thus, a worker was made a member of a nonexistent "industrial union" simply because he worked in a certain industry. The "organizer" of such a nonexistent union would then claim representation at the conference on the basis of membership cards issued and keep the members dues. The Management Committee asked the local committees to recall these cards but to no apparent effect.[14] The statement from the Management Committee on this theme explains the predicament: "According to local committee bye-laws, each union was entitled to 1 delegate per 200 members, with 8 as a maximum. It was agreed to make sure that the Local Committee was aware of this; *that they would have an up to date list of affiliated unions in the Transvaal showing the affiliated strength."* (Author's italics). It was agreed, in addition, that a high SACTU official would speak to them on the functions of a local committee.

Another problem was that of organizing the unions and implementing policy decisions. As a member from the Furniture, Mattress, and Bedding Workers' Union put it: "We decided last year that mineworkers and farmworkers should be organized, but we have done nothing about it. My suggestion is that not everyone is capable of organizing a trade union."[15]

The nub of the difficulties was that organizers capable of organizing unions would have to be paid and that there were no funds. As a result, as a representative of the textile workers explained, many workers joined a union when it was organized, were disappointed, and then disappeared.[16] In the Transvaal, for instance, groups of workers from the timber, jewellery, tobacco, plastics, and other light industries had been organized into a General Workers' Union. Once organized, however, their complaints had been handled by any person who happened to be available. There was, therefore, no continuity in the management of complaints. A special organizer was obviously needed, but as usual, funds to pay him were lacking. Unions were organized but the General Secretary of SACTU said, it was one of SACTU's defects that little further effort was made to ensure that it "flourished and remained in existence." Indeed, when called on for assistance, SACTU officials tended to hide behind the noninterference clause in its constitution, in order to spare themselves effort.[17]

The working of the local committees was not, it would therefore seem, all that could be desired. An analysis of the working of the individual unions helps further clarify SACTU's workings and is taken up in the following chapters. It is impossible, given the number of SACTU unions, their appearances, disappearances, and reappearances, to describe them all. Those discussed are, in many senses, typical. A description of their working will allow for inferences to be made about the others.

Chapter III

SACTU and Industrial Unions

Although the local committees which were to coordinate trade union activities in an area have already been discussed, little has been said of the unions themselves. The indications were that existing unions were neglected in an eagerness to establish others. What did the neglect amount to and how did it harm the workers in the Unions? Where did SACTU succeed? These are the questions this chapter seeks to answer, drawing the answers from cases cited, not because they necessarily are the most important, but because they are among the few that are relatively well documented. Clearly, SACTU's failures are among those more debated and more spectacular. Failure should not blind one to the fact that SACTU unions did, from time to time, win small concessions from individual employers, even if they were not very effective on the whole. In part this was because experienced personnel could not be hired, and because the laws of South Africa and their implementation militated against success. In addition, the energies of many SACTU people were divided among the unions and the other components of the Congress Alliance. Their limited strength and time was severely taxed. Nevertheless, the effort to organize and coordinate the work of unions was made, which is important for an understanding of the workings of political unionism.

The Transvaal Broom and Brush Workers Union

The Transvaal Broom and Brush Workers' Union was originally organized in two sections, one registered and one unregistered. The union had been organized by a local committee of the Trades and Labour Council and when the Council was dissolved, the union, under pressure from SACTU supporters in its ranks, decided to affiliate to SACTU.

In mid-1957 the chairman and members of the executive of the registered union came to TUCSA (the later acronym of SATUC) and asked for aid to disaffiliate from SACTU, asserting that SACTU had not held regular meetings with committee and had made no attempt to take up the complaints of workers. SACTU officials had not approached employers to improve conditions, and the union's finances had been handled in an unsatisfactory manner.

The TUCSA officials then approached SACTU who would give them neither records nor details of financial or any other transactions of the union. The SACTU people said that the person given the books for auditing—a person unknown to the union executive, who it turned out was neither an accountant nor a qualified bookkeeper—had had the books stolen from his car together with property of his own. All that was available was a receipt book, which TUCSA officials maintained should have been in the hands of anyone auditing the books anyway. This, together with a number of out-of-date books, letterheads, and membership cards, were only obtained through the intercession of TUCSA's legal counsellor.

Revelations followed quickly. Despite the legal prohibition on African membership of a registered union, a number of African workers had been included as members, their subscriptions apparently being paid into the account of the union. As proper records had not been kept, it was impossible to say how much of the money in the accounts of the registered union properly belonged to the unregistered African unions.

Once the registered union was set on disaffiliation, the question was what would the African union do? SACTU tried hard to prevent it from disaffiliating. Two workers loyal to SACTU at first condemned the TUCSA effort. Yet, once these same men had spoken to the general secretary of the Trade Union Council, the secretary of the registered union also agreed to disaffiliate.

TUCSA reorganized the registered and unregistered unions and began negotiations for improved conditions in which two Africans participated with the consent of the employers. Individual complaints of workers were taken up and apparently settled.[1]

The SACTU version of the dispute, which appeared in *New Age,* claimed that a small group of workers at a general meeting proposed disaffiliation from SACTU, giving no reason. Their motion was overwhelmingly defeated, after which this group removed the union's check book from the offices and refused to return it, and as a result the union's organizer could not be paid. Next, the voluntary unpaid secretary of "this small union" received a registered letter from its chairman, levelling accusations against her and terminating her services. The chairman demanded that she hand the union's books and documents over to the general secretary of TUCSA. The secretary of the union believed the chairman did not have the authority to ask for the books, and refused to give them to him. She felt that outside influences were working to split the union. The report goes no further, and ends with an implied accusation of TUCSA.[2]

There are obviously a number of thin spots in the SACTU story. If the accounts of the union were in order, there should have been no difficulty in getting another checkbook. Why then could they not pay the organizer? And why were the accusations not aired at the meeting? How could disaffiliation be demanded without reasons being given? These arguments seem barely credible. The TUCSA story, on the other hand, seems to hold together far better. At any rate, the Broom and Brush Workers' Union apparently vanished from the pages of *New Age* after this point.

The Textile Workers' Strike

Another interesting SACTU venture was the textile workers' strike of June 1957 which, once again, gives insight into SACTU's workings.

The unions at the Consolidated Textile Mills in Durban had obtained better conditions from this firm than those obtained in the industry as a whole. Consolidated cooperated with the unions, registered and unregistered, even deducting union dues from the workers wages for the unregistered union, although not obliged to do this by law. The unions—the Textile Workers' Industrial Union and the African Textile Workers' Industrial Union—instead of attempting to bring all other factories into line with Consolidated, continually pressed it for further concessions, eventually striking the plant in 1957, with the result that Consolidated refused to have further dealings with the unions, and no longer helped them by making wage deductions.[3] Not only did the strike lead to increased difficulties for the unions, but to internal dissension that induced a split in their own organizations. As usual, it is difficult to tell exactly what happened. There is a thicket of conflicting claims. The aim is to present whatever is possible of what happened.[3]

Once the strike had begun, *Workers' Unity* claimed, a body of "right-wingers" in the union assisted by certain "ex-labor leaders" and with the "blatant support of the bosses," formed the Spinners, Weavers, and Allied Workers' Union as a rival to the Textile Workers' Industrial Union. The new union was, according to *Workers' Unity*, formed for the express purposes of smashing the strike, destroying the national union, and replacing it with "an anti-working class 'Company' union." Through the influence of the "right-wingers" the leaders of the African union were dismissed, and "the disrupters and right-wingers became such a menace during the third week of the strike that the union was compelled to call in the help of its fraternal organizations and Congresses." In response to this call the African National Congress threatened Consolidated with a boycott of its products, which were mainly blankets of a type bought largely by Africans. As *Workers' Unity* puts it, the "Bosses capitulated when they were on the point of victory." The SACTU union's success was only partial, however, for though the "bosses" agreed to recognize the registered union, the Textile Workers' Industrial Union, as the only representative of the workers, the level of wages remained unchanged.

The *Workers' Unity* report continues to describe the further activity of the "right-wingers" who, "knowing the bosses would never dismiss them" began a "vicious campaign of lies and disruption." They would, the paper states, conspire before Industrial Council meetings to ensure that the union would gain nothing for the workers, and then afterwards "scream from the rooftops" that the union leaders had betrayed the workers. *Workers' Unity* continues to claim that it became dangerous for workers to oppose this group for fear of dismissal.

Because the union failed to win any advantage for spinners, the "right-wing group" early in 1961 argued that the executive of the Durban branch consisted mostly of weavers who were not concerned with the welfare of spinners. Many spinners voted for the "right-wingers" in the union election, unseating the chairman and secretary, and winning a "slight majority" on its executive committee. On taking office, the new executive came to the union's office with a lawyer and demanded that the books and assets of the union be handed over to them. The secretary refused to hand these materials to them on the grounds that this would require the permission of the executive committee, and insisted that the union had its own lawyer, who had denied strangers the right to peruse the books already audited and approved by the union. The officers then tried to dismiss the secretary, who refused dismissal and appealed to the rank-and-file for support. The members of the union, according to *Workers' Unity*, rallied to the secretary's support and passed a vote of no confidence in the executive. The executive apparently refused to resign, and the members went to court. It was finally agreed that a new election with independent scrutineers be held, and the "right-wingers" were defeated.[4]

Troubles continued in the Textile Workers' Industrial Union, but information becomes even more biased and scantier. Eventually the union seems to have ended its association with SACTU for, by 1964, it seemingly could no longer carry out its functions. There is no indication in the documents when this disaffiliation took place nor is it to be found in either of the Horrell studies.[5]

The General Workers Unions

These unions have been considered mainly in relation to the local councils and not on their own. They are of great interest as entities and were later used as substitutes for other organizations, particularly the banned African National Congress. The major intent in forming the unions appears to have been to create a mass base for the Congress Alliance. The conception of General Workers' Unions (also referred to here by their initials GWU) was endorsed at the SACTU annual conference of 1960. As envisioned, these unions were to have a total membership of some 20,000 Africans who, because their work forces were too small to allow individual unions to be formed, or because they worked in small industries in isolated places, could not be at once organized into regular unions. The recruitment of these workers was not to be where they worked but where they lived, and was to be combined with campaigning for "£1-a-Day." (See chapter V following). The General Workers Unions were to be completely under SACTU's control. They were not to elect their own executive committees, but were to come directly under the local committees. The reason given for this somewhat unusual arrangement was that the GWU was only to accommodate workers temporarily until individual unions could be formed.

Yet, even within SACTU some were worried about the General Workers' Unions. They feared that workers would be drawn from the established unions and would join GWUs where they would stay indefinitely. They were reassured when told that workers of different trades would retain their identity and would be organized into separate sections. Durban and Kimberley were pointed out as examples, their membership cards had different symbols for the different trades, and where recruitment was by trade.[6]

Kimberley is a very interesting case in the workings of the General Workers' Unions. There were no specific trade unions organized by or affiliated to SACTU in Kimberley. The only SACTU affiliate was a General Workers' Union made up of the following groups of workers:[7]

Railways	250
Kimberley City Council	170
Garage workers	50
Shops (i.e. stores)	25
T. B. hospital workers	35
Domestic workers	25
Engineering	16

Building	15
Butchery workers	10
Total	530

Support for this union was readily forthcoming, as wages were low even according to the Wage Board appointed by the government. The union wrote to Mr. Harry Oppenheimer, the chairman of de Beers Diamond Mines known for his liberal views, that his workers received only about $5.40 every two weeks. They claimed that, because of this letter, a survey was made and negotiations took place between employers and the union resulting in increased wages and benefits.[8]

Later the union again interceded with Mr. Oppenheimer on behalf of a worker who had been with de Beers since 1917, and who had been given "five minutes" to either resign from the General Workers' Union or to resign his job. Shortly afterwards the threats and action against the man concerned were dropped.

The directorate of de Beers, and especially Mr. Oppenheimer, were known for their concern for their workers, and appeals to them were bound to be investigated and matters righted where a genuine case was made. This was not true with the local authorities or the police. Not only did they refuse to have dealings with the GWU, they did all they could to hinder the work of the union. At a meeting of the domestic workers section, for instance, the police cancelled the meeting on the pretext that the lights were out of order and that they feared a riot. Union leaders were often arbitrarily arrested for addressing meetings in the townships, which made organizing on a larger scale hazardous. Altogether the authorities did all they could to make life difficult for those engaged in establishing the GWU there.

Much of the success of the General Workers' Unions thus depended on the goodwill of those with whom they negotiated. When dealing with liberal employers, they could expect to obtain some of their demands, but when employers were unsympathetic, there was little prospect of success. A complaint to the principal of the University of the Witwatersrand is an instance of negotiation with an employer of inherent goodwill. SACTU presented a lengthy and well argued report on the university wage structure in which they drew attention to the underpayment of Africans employed there. After both sides had argued their cases to each other by letter, the university increased wages by some fifteen percent and gave bonuses to some workers. Like other English-medium universities in South Africa, Wits (as the University of the Witwatersrand, in Johannesburg, is often affectionately called) saw itself as a liberal bastion in a reactionary land. Refusal to yield to reasoned demands would doubtless be personally repugnant to the men involved. This was not necessarily true of those in higher civil service or corporate executive positions, who were much harder in their dealings with African unions. Generally, they conceded as little as they could, and this was very little indeed. The stick was more often resorted to than the carrot.

One of the tasks SACTU had set itself was the creation of unions out of strikes, and this was attempted at the Klipfontein Organic Products Company, a large chemical works owned by the South African government. Learning from the press that some 600 Klipfontein workers had been arrested for striking illegally, a member of the Witwaterstrand local committee and a member of the Management Committee went to Klipfontein to ascertain the position. There they learned, according to the SACTU report, that the main cause of the strike was the living conditions of workers at the plant. The workers had to live in compounds, that is in single-men's quarters, as on the goldmines. If any man slept out at night, he was fined on his return. Understandably, African workers resented this, and it was the major cause of friction between labor and management.[9]

Although the large number mentioned had been arrested, no more than two were actually detained and charged with organizing an illegal strike. These two, SACTU officials said, had been imprisoned for several weeks before the SACTU officials arranged for bail and for defense.[10] A letter setting out the workers' grievances was sent to the Minister of Bantu Affairs ending with the following statement:[11]

> These workers are entirely without protection and their complaints extend back many years. We submit that these were the cause of the alleged strike when the workers were arrested. They appear to have no way of getting their complaints discussed and their grievances redressed.

The minister sent the stock reply to this complaint, namely that "the matter was receiving attention" and then no more was heard. The Department of Bantu Affairs was seemingly not prepared to discuss matters with SACTU.

Although illegal, strikes took place fairly frequently, the ends of the strikers sometimes being attained. Only a few of the strikes were initiated by SACTU. The following table indicates the scale and outcome of the different strikes, showing the number of strikes; the number of workers involved in each, and the outcome.[12]

	No. of Strikes	No. African Workers Involved	Outcome Prosecu-tions	Convic-tions	Unknown
1955	82	9,479	340	314	—
1956	92	6,428	—	524	—
1957	113	6,158	539	274	—
1958	64	7,128	588	453	—
1959	36	3,462	822	221	1
1960	33	2,199	364	294	1
1962	11	400			
1963	17	1,100			
1966	14	1,374			
1967	20	1,302			

This does not, of course, show the labor disputes which did not end in strikes but were settled by the Labour Officers of the government authorized Boards. Nonetheless, considering the legal situation in South Africa, the number of strikes is impressive. Strikes, as such, were forbidden and the maximum prescribed penalties were severe: a fine of about $1,400 or three years imprisonment or both. These were, of course, the maxima and the full severity of the law was seldom invoked. Nevertheless, the fact that African workers *were* prepared to risk such sentences tells much of working conditions in South Africa and of the mettle of the men involved.

The major year of SACTU strikes seems to have been 1961 though strikes were organized in other years.[13] The methods and outcome of these strikes are interesting. Once again, only a few are singled out.

In August 1961 the news spread that eleven African student nurses at the King George V Hospital in Durban had been caned by the sister-tutor.[14] As a protest some 300 African nurses staged an eight-hour walkout and were joined by the rest of the non-white staff including orderlies and laborers. The African nurses also began to boycott the hospital meals, and the local committee of SACTU supplied them with food. SACTU then broadened the issue adding demands for higher wages and better conditions through the SACTU controlled Hospital Workers' Union. The police were called out during a demonstration by the staff, and when the Chief Bantu Affairs Commissioner for Durban tried to intervene, the nurses, according to SACTU refused to speak to him. The Hospital Workers' Union wrote to the Medical Super-intendent of the hospital demanding that he negotiate with them. There was another work-stoppage the next day and again the po-lice were called in, some even patrolling the wards.

The end results were hardly advantageous to the nurses. During the boycott of meals, which lasted for two weeks, some twenty nurses were dismissed. Then, on August 29, all nurses who did not resign from the Hospital Workers' Union by August 31, were threatened with dismissal. The Durban local committee at once informed the head office and a protest was telegraphed to the Superintendent. SACTU also informed overseas bodies who added their protests in such volume that, according to SACTU, the threatened dismissals did not take place and the nurses were not required to resign from the union. The twenty nurses dismissed, however, were not reinstated, and a number emigrated to Tangan-yika to work in hospitals there.

The report adds that the Department of Health (of the South African Government) issued a statement saying that the eleven nurses had not been caned but "were playfully tapped." "One wonders," the report continued, "what the reaction of the Depart-ment would have been had any instructor 'playfully tapped' European (i.e. white) nurses."[15]

Another strike was that launched at the Lion Match Company in Durban. In March, 1961 some 360 African workers staged a demonstration at the factory. The police and Labour Department officials tried to intervene, but as at the King George V Hospital, the workers refused to speak to them. The employers agreed to wage concessions, granting higher wages than those laid down in the relevant wage determination, set up a noncontributory pension scheme, and made medical services available free. But, in August one of the Trade Union leaders was dismissed, and about half the work force tried to see the manager of the firm to secure his reinstatement. When the manager refused to see them, they staged a demonstration in the lunch break, marching with placards stating: "Recognize our Union," "Demand £1 per Day," "Low Wages Breed Crime," and "Kwashiorkor [a disease caused by malnutrition] is Killing Us." The police were called in. A convoy armed with Sten guns arrived. The workers were called on to halt their demonstration and told that their claims would be considered later. They were not satisfied with this assurance and continued to demonstrate. They were then given five minutes to disperse, and 140 were arrested, 136 of these being fined about $15 each. As the SACTU report points out, leave to appeal was refused, and the union had to find about $2,000 to pay the fines. All the strikers lost their jobs, and attempts by the SACTU head office to negotiate were refused by the company.

More pathetic was the strike of blind African workers at the Constance Caworth Institute for the Blind in Durban. In this strike some eighty sightless African workers demanded an increase in wages from the Natal Bantu Blind Society—a charitable organization—which ran the Institute. The workers made cane furniture and basketry which the Institute sold, using the proceeds to pay the workers, most of whom earned about $28 monthly, and to maintain the Institute. Unable to gain more from the administration of the Society the blind workers struck. As usual, the police were called in and all workers were initially dismissed, and then all but thirteen reemployed. No increase in wages was granted. All that SACTU could do in the end was to give the matter publicity and to appeal to its affiliated unions for funds.

Other SACTU strikes fared in this same fashion. Events seem to have followed each other rather like those of a Greek drama. A strike was initiated, often with strongest encouragement from the SACTU local committee, this was followed by police repression, dismissal of workers, and few actual gains in salary or working conditions—if any gains were made at all. Some of the strikers invariably ended in prison. SACTU was somewhat defensive about this: "Those who are not friendly to SACTU have accused us of 'engineering' these strikes and encouraging the workers to act irresponsibly. The facts tell the truth. The workers who chose to strike did so because they could no longer bear their intolerable condition."[16] There is some truth in SACTU's assertion, but not the entire truth. In some cases SACTU appeared after the workers had taken things into their own hands, and then purported to represent them. At other times SACTU instigated strikes which were often badly judged, and against firms that had been willing to meet some of their employees demands. In these cases strikes were ill-judged and ill-fated.

The Problem of Financing

Financial problems dogged SACTU from the first, setting limits on what it could achieve. The lifeblood of a coordinating center is in its affiliation fees, and these did not come in regularly. A number of unions were, for a variety of reasons, in continual arrear. Others were understandably unable to pay because they had been involved in strikes, and these included the Textile Workers' Industrial Unions—both registered and unregistered, the Broom and Brush Workers' Union, and the Bedding Workers' Union. They all promised to make good on their arrears although this was difficult. The Metal Workers' Union and the Bag Workers' Union had been exempted from affiliation fees which, of course, increased the pressure on other unions. The burden was largely borne by the large and well organized unions such as the Garment Workers' Union of African Women and the Food and Canning Workers' Union, who both paid their affiliation fees scrupulously, as did the smaller Natal unions.

Where unions were regular defaulters, it was often because no information could be obtained as to membership or much else. Thus the Cape Town branch of the Railway union sent little information and so their arrears could not be calculated. This union was, in any case, soon completely defunct.

Money was constantly needed. It was needed not only to maintain SACTU as a going concern but also to maintain *Workers' Unity*. Suggestions were made in 1957 for a *Workers' Unity* day on which money would be collected for the paper, and local committees, with the assistance of the Witwatersrand local committee were to hold this celebration.[17]

Just as the head office was chronically short of funds, so did the local committees complain about their plight. They complained that they could not carry out their work because headquarters failed to provide financial assistance. Whenever TUCSA established local committees, they said, they helped it with funds and saw to it that it could carry out its tasks. If SACTU wished to lead the workers, a delegate said, it should have an active local committee in every center, and this meant that these would have to be properly financed. An African delegate pointed out in turn that the Transvaal local committee had formed itself without the assistance of the head office, and once formed had only called on SACTU for advice and to furnish lecturers. He suggested that it might not be a bad idea for the local committees to follow the example of the Transvaal and function without funds. As this study has shown, little of moment was achieved in the Transvaal, so the argument is not as sound as might appear. The notion, however, appealed to those at the SACTU conference and was allowed to pass.

Another important question raised was the right of the local committees to a portion of the sums collected through levies on member unions as permitted in the bylaws. Who was to have priority of payment? Was it the head office or the local committee? The principle of the head office subsidizing the local committees was considered desirable, but this was only possible in practice if affiliation fees were paid regularly. If all unions paid their affiliation fees, much would be possible, a national organizer might, for instance, be employed, but if few paid it meant that SACTU had no fighting strength. The arrears were, unfortunately, quite substantial:

		(Converted)
Union	*Amounts Due*[18]	Approximate
African Textile Workers	£ 61	$170.00
S. A. Clothing Workers	28	78.00

		(Converted)
Union	*Amounts Due[18]*	Approximate
Furniture, Mattress & Bedding Wkrs	6	
Railway Union (S.A.R. & H.		
Non-Europ.)	2	6.00
Food & Canning Workers	50	140.00
African Food & Canning Workers	60	168.00

These sums, owed in 1957, were not untypical of later years if the frequent references to financial problems are any guide.

The reasons for nonpayment were not necessarily due to wilful omission or strikes. In some instances dishonest officials, the bane of African unions, were the reason. In the Stevedoring Union and the Sweet Workers' Union two of the union's officers had decamped with their union's monies, leaving the local committee to rectify matters. Then there were unions that simply disappeared without anyone hearing of this until much later. This happened with the Municipal Workers' Union in Port Elizabeth and there were a number of others as well. In general, unions broke up easily, their fragile structures lacking cohesion unless a full-time organization could be found to keep them running. This meant that funds were owed by or expected from dead unions, and this expectation led to faulty budgeting. In addition, there were unions that were in the course of breakdown and which had to be re-formed and which therefore had no money to send.[19]

The key to union operation is in efficient organization, and this requires persons who will undertake this task and make it their own. If they are to be effective, they have not only to be honest and capable, but must have the time to devote to organization. This means full-time work, and if the work is to be full-time the organizers have to be paid salaries if they are to live. This was the crux of the money problem in SACTU's case. There was not only insufficient money to pay organizers, there was barely enough to keep the head office running. Money to pay the organizers, and the organization to ensure that these carried out their work were essential.

In fact the head office paid out wages to organizers, the Assistant General Secretary said, but received no information as to how these performed their tasks. They received no statements of sums collected as subscriptions, and so they were in ignorance as to whether these unions were becoming self-supporting or not. In the past, he pointed out, these unions had simply collapsed as soon as headquarters stopped sending funds. This, the Assistant Secretary added, was equivalent to throwing money away for there was nothing to show for it in the end. The secretary of the Railway Union, on the other hand, argued that the root of the evil lay in that salaries were paid by the head office and not by the unions. It would be better to make an outright grant of money to the union, for the organizer, seeing that his salary came to him from the head office did not feel beholden to the union and therefore did nothing. This applied particularly to the raising of subscriptions, for a man would exert more effort if he knew that his work led to the payment of his salary. In all, it seems that the organizers did very little, especially in the all important field of raising funds.[20]

An example of how financing affected organizations is evident with the Metal Workers' Union in 1958. They then had about $55 available for leaflets but not enough to pay an organizer, and as their existing organizer had fallen ill, they could not find a replacement. In Durban two trade unionists were prepared to organize the metal workers if they could be guaranteed about $14 for expenses, but the state of the union was such that the agreement could be made for only one month and for the position then to be reviewed. In Cape Town an organizer had been hired for $28 per month, but no news ever came from him.[21]

Things did not become easier with the passage of time. The problem of collecting affiliation fees remained a continual bugbear. SACTU, on paper, had a surplus of monies equivalent to some $770 but had no cash in the till. The cries of the Treasurer that SACTU could only flourish if priority was given the payment of affiliation fees seems to have fallen on deaf, unwilling, or incapable ears. The Treasurer pointed to what had been resolved at earlier conferences, that one penny per member should be levied against the individual unions and that that sum, together with an affiliation fee of $1.40, be paid over to SACTU.[22] The payment of this sum would be no hardship to the individual member and would be the saving of SACTU. This was the position in 1958 and in 1962 it was no better. The Management Committee

described the plight of SACTU as so desperate that an immediate
start should be made in collecting the penny levy from members
"to avert the financial disaster facing SACTU."[23]

SACTU's plight had been critical since February 1962, and
SACTU had been bailed out temporarily with a check for £10
(about $14) given them by the Textile Workers' Industrial Union.
There had been no improvement in payment of affiliation fees
and the penny levy had not been made effective. The appeal made
to the Annual Conference of 1962 brings the plight of the coordinating center out in striking relief. It is, therefore, quoted in
extenso:

> The financial statements presented to Conference should
> be carefully studied by all delegates. The strength of SACTU,
> its ability to meet its responsibilities, to employ organisers,
> to issue trade union material can only come from the members
> of our affiliated Unions. Our work over the past year in-
> creased twenty-fold, our income not at all. Our major task
> of organising the unorganised workers cannot be carried out
> unless we have the funds to employ organisers. We need thirty
> to fifty in all the major industries—we struggle with one or two.
>
> Head Office has issued appeals to affiliated Unions to make
> a concerted drive to collect the 1 cent per member per month,
> which could bring us in sufficient money not only to run
> Head Office, but to widen the scope of our activities in all
> areas. As it is we struggle to maintain our organisation. Our
> expenditure is cut to the barest minimum and we often can-
> not issue sufficient memoranda, lectures and educational
> material to our affiliated unions because we do not have the
> paper to do so.
>
> Our Local Committees and affiliated Unions constantly
> apply to us for assistance for the employment of organisers
> and we are also constantly asked to assist in collecting vast
> sums nor legal defence and for fines when workers are
> prosecuted for strike action.
>
> The solution lies in the hands of the delegates at Conference.
> We hope that this Conference will debate this matter realis-
> tically and on a constructive basis so that we are never again
> placed in such a precarious economic position as we are at
> present.[24]

Even this appeal failed to elicit much response. Shortly after the conference was over the Management Committee were told that collection boxes had been obtained and distributed to all unions to facilitate the collection of the money so sorely needed by SACTU. The matter of money was again raised and a Fund Raising Committee to consist of three members to be entrusted to raise money was urged.[25] At this point the documents available come to an end.

What happened after 1962? There is a clue in an article in *Contact* of November 1, 1963, published by Mr. Patrick Duncan, a son of a former Governor-General of South Africa, and sympathetic to the Liberal Party. In this article Duncan speaks of the way the 90-Day law which enables the police to hold suspects without trial for that many days, and which is infinitely renewable, was strangling the African unions. Most of the leading SACTU officials fell under the ban, and those left were minor figures incapable of keeping it running. Duncan goes on to say that the remaining SACTU officials were known, and employers cooperated with the police against them. When they appeared at a factory the management would telephone the Special (i.e., political) Branch of the police and have the organizers arrested. Thus, in Cape Town, the affairs of one union which was normally handled by a team of eight trade union leaders was handled by a typist and a messenger.

If these factors are taken into account the astounding thing is not that SACTU functioned badly but that it functioned at all. The industries considered in this chapter have, by and large, been light industries. Heavy industries were to be a major object of SACTU's organizing endeavors.

Chapter IV

SACTU, Heavy Industry,

and Agriculture

One of the major aims of political unions is to organize heavy industry, for heavy industry is vital to the economy and is a powerful pressure point on government. Heavy industry and agriculture are the bases of all else in any industrial society, hence their political potential. In agriculture, the laborers are readily radicalized, as Hadley Cantril has shown for France and Italy.[1] However, it is light industry that is the more readily mobilized, or at least, this was so in South Africa among non-whites. Philip Selznick has pointed out that urban light industry allows for the creation of a mass backing through the Communist unions and a variety of "fronts." Here large crowds can be assembled for publicity-oriented demonstrations which call for massed numbers in halls or streets.[2] Light industrial unions also seem more politically self-conscious and being concentrated in cities have more readily available workers.

Heavy industry, especially in the South African setting, lent itself less readily to trade union organization among Africans. Various legal and residential requirements laid down for the black labor force limited the scope of organizers. The financial problems of organizing heavy industry were more acute than in the light industries. Workers in heavy industry were on the whole worse paid than were those in light industry, and as a result could contribute even less to union treasuries. The building of union funds was thus even harder to realize. The light industrial unions were the mainstay—such as it was—of SACTU.

SACTU was thus in the awkward position of a union coordinating center seeking to organize non-white workers, particularly Africans, and able to function least in those spheres where most Africans were working. Transport (included as a heavy industry here), mining, iron and steel, and heavy engineering engage most of the African labor force, yet SACTU had to concentrate on that sector employing least African workers, light industry. It is hardly surprising, therefore, that SACTU would make repeated efforts to organize heavy industry, despite the odds.

The Metal Industry

The idea of organizing the metal and engineering industries had been part of SACTU's most cherished aims since its formation. The metal industry and transport were seen as particularly important for SACTU had already made some small inroads through the affiliation of a number of small unions in these trades. These unions were to be the nucleus of a larger and growing body of unions. National Committees could be set up to organize these industries, as was done in the metal industry in June, 1958.

The National Committee, like so many SACTU committees, did not do its work particularly well. In 1958 it contacted metal workers' unions in Johannesburg, Durban, Cape Town, and Port Elizabeth, and in that year provided funds for organizers, but the funds soon ran out and the organizers left. It would be an error, however, to think that funds were the only obstacle. The lack of experienced organizers was almost as great a hindrance. After the 1958 experience the General Secretary made it clear that better organizers would have to be found. Nonetheless, even if allowance is made, as it must be, for these drawbacks, the committees did not display particular zeal.

An indication of how a National Committee worked emerges from the documents. A rally was planned for August 29, 1959, and leaflets were prepared and sent to the main branches of the African National Congress in Johannesburg, calling for their support. Lists of the main engineering factories were prepared and organizers were told to visit these factories and to distribute the leaflets. In addition to the effort in Johannesburg, Pretoria was to organize demonstrations of its own and was given some 1,500 copies of the leaflets and a list of ten large factories where the leaflets were to be handed out. Once this was done, the National Committee would meet again and decide on the next steps to be taken.[3]

What happened? The mass rally among the engineering workers foundered because the leaflet distributors visited very few of them. Concern was expressed about the organizer of the Metal Workers' Union who had not done much in the campaign "although it was his union that was being organized."[4] The campaign was seen to have been abortive, and it was obvious to the SACTU leaders that a far greater effort was necessary.[5]

The campaign was a national campaign, and it was not only in Johannesburg that it had proven nugatory. Attempts to organize the metal workers in Port Elizabeth had been unsuccessful, the local committee claimed, because requests for help in performing this task had not been met. The Management Committee, in its turn was concerned that the previous organizer in Port Elizabeth had vanished with, it seems, the union's funds. He was employed on a three-months trial basis, and seems to have used this time to his personal advantage. No report had been sent to the head office from Port Elizabeth in these matters. The local committee then assured the Management Committee that, from then on, monies collected would be devoted to the purpose for which they had been raised, and the Management Committee decided that the Metal Industries Organizing Committee (i.e., the National Committee) raise about $90 for Port Elizabeth to be used to organize metal workers, and subject to regular reports being sent by the local committee.[6]

In addition to the metal workers' union which was organized in Port Elizabeth, SACTU had three other similar unions in other parts of the country.

The largest was the Metal Workers' Union (Transvaal) which had an estimated (and probably inflated) membership of about 1,000 in 1960. This figure seems impressive until it is measured against the 90,000 non-white workers engaged in the industry. The Johannesburg-based union had established branches in

Pretoria and other Reef towns. The National Organizing Committee, in view of this progress, appointed a full-time organizer to assist in organizing the 7,000 steel workers in Pretoria on March 1, 1961. In 1962 the National Committee extended its efforts, attempted to establish an office in Pretoria, in the same place as the National Committee for Transport Workers. A branch office was established in Boksburg on the East Rand, and was kept open every Sunday to be available to metal workers in that area.

The Metal Workers' Union in Natal was smaller, with some 600 reported members, and that in the Eastern Cape had about 500. There are no comparable figures for the Western Cape. Even the National Committee considered these to be tentative figures, for other than from Johannesburg, as usual, no reports had been received. Contact had been established with Port Elizabeth after some trouble there, (see p. 82 above), and the local committee was now encouraged to organize the motor car assembly plants, the most important engineering industry there.[7]

In the hope of uniting the different engineering unions and using them for common purposes, they were invited to meet at the SACTU conference to discuss the possibility of forming a National Union of Metal Workers. A similar move had been posited in 1957 when all the unions affiliated to SACTU in the metal trades had made their names uniform as Metal Workers' Unions and had established a Committee of United Metal Workers' Unions to prepare the ground for the formation of a single union. As so often seemed to happen with SACTU initiatives, this one remained a dead letter until revived in 1961.[8] Once again nothing concrete seems to have come of it. SACTU was, however, not to be so easily discouraged. A fresh initiative activated another move to unite the unions. The underlying purpose was to bring at least 20,000 workers into SACTU, the majority to come from the heavy industries. Metal industries were to figure prominently in the new drive, as the iron and steel industry itself employed upwards of 24,000 African workers.[9] Initial steps to form such a union using the slogan "Organize or Starve" which was publicized in a special issue of *Workers' Unity* and repeated from such limited platforms remaining available to SACTU speakers.

The campaign was soon in trouble. The NEC learned of the unsatisfactory state of the Metal Workers' Unions everywhere.

The National Organizing Committee, intending to organize these unions and sustain their working, rarely met. Yet how could more be done? The secretary of the Committee was, at one and the same time, also secretary of the Witwatersrand local committee. He could, therefore, give little time to organizing metal workers.

In pointing out these defects something must be said about the difficulties under which SACTU labored. Not all failures were due to the incapacity of its people, for it functioned under conditions of greatest difficulty. It faced the open hostility of employers, government agencies, and the police. For instance, the Group Areas Board made it impossible for the unions to remain in any one set of offices for any length of time, and so workers often did not know where the union's offices were. Laws were complex and cumbersome with varied clauses relating to wages and working conditions in different trades. Workers in any one industry might fall under different sections of an agreement each specifying different conditions. The Industrial Council for the Engineering Trade in the Transvaal was particularly unfriendly to the African union and to its members when faced with their complaints. Nimrod Sejake, of the Iron and Steel Workers' Union, for instance, was arrested for trespass at an engineering works when he tried to present the workers' demands. When the workers at the plant protested, all 106 were dismissed, though some 104 were later reinstated. This did little to help garner support for the unions.[10] The National Organizing Committee, according to its own records, tried to assist these unions in their difficulties but could do little. The National Organizing Committee also claimed that it had both trained and paid organizers, and the latter seems truer than the former.

In addition to the hostility of various Boards and Councils, the unions were subject to continual police raids. Experienced leaders were banned, removing them from their unions, and making their continued political or union activity impossible. Those who remained active had far too large a workload and could not discharge their functions with any degree of efficiency. Full-time staff was unreliable and often incapable or dishonest.

Only by concentrating on a few unions and building these, rather than on the scattergun methods applied earlier, could SACTU regain momentum.

This new policy was unveiled at the Seventh National Conference of April 21-22, 1962. The importance of the basic industries was reiterated, but the conference was told that one basic industry should be tackled at a time "and that as soon as we have achieved the position where the workers in that particular industry have achieved considerable organizational success, steps should be taken to repeat the same procedures in respect of the next industry." An appeal was issued to the local committees and to all affiliated unions to assist in this task. The metal industry was a prime target. As the chairman of its Management Committee said in 1962, he wanted "every union and all volunteers to assist, to 'thing, eat, sleep and dream' of the metal industry."[11] More organizers should be employed for the steel and metal industry, there should be regular rallies of the workers, and demands should be made afresh to their employers. The local committees and affiliated unions should learn of the conditions in the metal industries and of the wages paid so that they could act among these workers with the greatest effect. The same day should be set aside each week for organizing the metal industry, and speakers' notes should be assembled and used together with imaginative activities among the workers. "We appeal to the conference to bear in mind that an organizational campaign of this nature depends upon inspiring fieldwork. It is not necessary for Committees to draft one set of blueprints after another and dissipate energy in perpetual discussions but to organize consistent day to day practical activities."[12]

The NEC, in taking this line, had in mind the increases won by the municipal workers, although these had not yet been consolidated. The fatal flaw of the SACTU organization again emerges: that inability to stick to one thing even when the need to do so is clearly manifest. Although SACTU was to concentrate on the metal industry, the General Secretary of SACTU was also to concentrate on the needs of the other basic industries (among them municipal workers) and to prepare a series of campaigns in these industries.[13]

The campaign garnered some small gains. A campaign launched on February 7, 1962—associated with the £1-a-Day campaign (see chapter V)—brought some 350 workers to the union. Otherwise there was little to show.

In its efforts to organize the African metal workers, SACTU had an unexpected ally. SEIFSA (Steel, Engineering and Industrial Federation of South Africa) was an employers organization which, in 1961, had called for the recognition of African trade unions and this had no doubt encouraged SACTU to concentrate on this industry in 1962. Thus heartened, SACTU embarked on a recruiting drive at Iscor (Iron and Steel Corporation of South Africa) and at the steel and engineering complex at Van der Bijl Park. But little seems to have been achieved. Except for Johannesburg, no reports were sent on progress, and this may be because there had been so little progress to report. A conference of metal workers for the country seems to have been considered, but nothing was done to bring it into effect. The attempt to again form a national union (see p. 83 above) seems equally to have come to naught. By the end of 1962 the SACTU leaders who had not been caught up in the government's net were too much involved in other campaigns to give SACTU and its unions much of their time.

The Railway and Harbor Workers

The affair of the Railway and Harbor Workers Unions is much more tangled, because these unions had existed for a time before they became involved with SACTU. There had been difficulties in the different offices of the union which were distributed among a number of centers. The headquarters of the Railway and Harbour Workers' Union was in Cape Town. It had a branch in Johannesburg and a few members scattered in other towns with railway works, such as the important junction at De Aar in the Cape. The Railway Workers' Union, as we will refer to it here, was affiliated to the Trades and Labour Council almost to the time of its dissolution, and the TLC had done all it could to assist the union. For instance, when the Council took over the Johannesburg office of the union, it found that there was practically no money in its coffers and that two of the union's organizers were helping themselves to the members' contributions. So poor was the union that it lacked even the $1.40 a month to pay its affiliation fee to the TLC, which, nonetheless, ensured that the union at least paid the affiliation fee to the Council of Non-European Trade Unions with which it also was affiliated. Yet, for all this, was pressure to disaffiliate from the TLC which returned the books and monies that it had held. The Railway and Harbour Workers' Union then affiliated to SACTU shortly after its formation.

In 1957, two years after affiliation to SACTU, the affairs of the union seemed in particularly bad shape. The members had been persuaded to make two leading SACTU officials the sole trustees of the union. When officers of the union began looking into its affairs, they discovered that a sick-fund scheme they had initiated had some $500 in the bank, whereas the union itself had virtually no money, much less than the sum returned on disaffiliation. They therefore approached TUCSA and asked for their help. The General-Secretary of TUCSA made enquiries at the Railway Union's bank and found no change in the trusteeship could be made without the prior consent of the present trustees. Being an African union, the Railway Workers' Union was not registered, and therefore had no corporate existence. It could not take legal action as a body, so the individual members would have to agree to institute joint action to recover control of their money. The union had insufficient funds to institute such legal action, leaving the members helpless.

Learning of the steps taken by the Railway Workers' officials, SACTU, through its influence over one of the organizers, arranged for the Germiston office to open a separate banking account and paid all union subscriptions for the Transvaal into this account, although no decision of the union executive permitted this, nor was any executive body in Germiston empowered to take such a decision.

The General Secretary of TUCSA then tried to settle the matter with the appropriate officials of SACTU only to be told that the executive committee of the union did not consist of railway workers but of "scoundrels" intent on using the funds of the union to illegally trade in liquor. On being told of this, the Railway Workers' executive was understandably furious, and produced their employment cards showing that they definitely were workers. The concern of the General-Secretary of TUCSA was most unpleasing to SACTU officials, and she was attacked in *New Age* for meddling in the affairs of SACTU unions.[14]

The version of the dispute in *New Age* differs substantially from that cited. According to that report the Railway Workers' Union had held a general meeting to discuss various complaints of the Germiston branch whose organizer, Lawrence Mzanga, was also assistant-secretary to the union. The Germiston branch, which had become the largest in the union, was dissatisfied with the way the secretary had carried out his duties, and especially that he had not called an annual general meeting to allow for the election of new office-holders. The secretary and his faction, on their part, counterclaimed that the Germiston branch was not paying its dues to the Johannesburg head office, and that the trustees (the SACTU officials) had refused to hand over the $500 of the union's sick fund which would have to be diverted to pay wages and the rent of the union headquarters. According to the *New Age* report, the secretary of TUCSA attended the general meeting and used the occasion to launch a violent attack on SACTU and its leaders, urging the workers to hand the administration of its affairs to her as secretary of TUCSA. After a speech by a SACTU official pointing out that the union could not affiliate to TUCSA as it did not accept African unions, the meeting decided to set up a commission of enquiry consisting of its own members to investigate the dispute.

The result was the inevitable one in African organizations. There had clearly been a power struggle between the Johannesburg and Germiston leaderships in which each side tried to line up allies of its own, Johannesburg turning to TUCSA, as Germiston seems to have had the support of SACTU. As a result Johannesburg followed its leaders and Germiston its own.

Difficulties multiplied because the struggle was now centered on who was to control the various small union branches at different junctions and sidings. These had all been organized by the Johannesburg secretary and seemed likely to follow his lead. The government then inadvertently made things easier for Germiston by deporting the Johannesburg leader in 1959. The Germiston union, which supported SACTU, then sent its organizer to all the branches and explained that Johannesburg had split the union. Some of the branches remained faithful to Johannesburg, but others agreed to join with Germiston and their leaders agreed to act as shop stewards. The result was, therefore, indecisive at best. The Sick Benefit Funds, which had been frozen by legal action in 1956 were released and deposited to SACTU trust account, to be used only on specific written instructions from SACTU's lawyers. The Johannesburg group had, therefore, lost control of these funds.

There were similar difficulties at other centers in the late 1950s and an attempt was made to rebuild the railway workers unions in the 1960s, a National Organizing Committee similar to that of the metal industries being established.

There are great inherent difficulties in organizing South African railway workers. There is, first of all, the gigantic spread of the railway network with smaller and larger pockets of workers distributed over a broad geographic area. The workers were, in addition, concentrated in compounds (barrack-type single-men's quarters) which made managerial control easy and access for SACTU organizers difficult. Because of this, and because of the factional conflicts and the problems of organization, the railway unions which had seemed so promising in the early fifties had largely collapsed by 1960 in which year the State of Emergency hastened the decay of their fragile apparatus.

When the Emergency was lifted at the end of 1960, SACTU found itself with a collection of virtually defunct railway unions and had great difficulty in reconstituting the National Organizing Committee for Transport Workers. The problems that had always complicated its affairs continued, such as the unwillingness of unions to communicate with headquarters and the general lack of money. Nevertheless, steps were taken to bring the railway unions back to life.

The state of the unions was pathetic. In Cape Town, once the site of the strongest railway union, the organization had virtually disappeared when its organizer had left for other work. An organizer had been appointed for Port Elizabeth but little could be learned of what he had done, and the funds to pay him soon ran short. Two organizers remained in the Transvaal after the dust had settled over the split, one was in Johannesburg and one in Pretoria, and membership in the former city had risen to an estimated 700 workers. These unions had, in addition, been able to settle some minor grievances of the workers in their jurisdiction.

Natal was the brightest spot on the SACTU canvas. Although

the figures of memberships are, as usual, unreliable, the Railway Workers' Union there claimed some 3,500 members, making it the largest non-white transport workers union in the country, employing some four full-time organizers. Although this is an impressive achievement, it still made only a small dent on the total employment of non-whites on the railways, which had numbered some 116,606 Africans in 1959. Although the Natal union was working well there were other sources of friction between it and the National Organizing Committee. This centered on the demand of the National Committee that an organizer be appointed on a full-time basis for the dockworkers of Durban. This was opposed by the chairman and secretary of the union in Durban who argued that the dockworkers should be organized separately. Discussions between the Management Committee and the Durban executive were deadlocked, for clearly the Durban branch feared that if dockworkers were added, this would weaken the railway union as funds and effort would have to be diverted, even if an organizer was paid by the National Committee. Their response was to maintain silence on what was happening, which was not to the advantage of headquarters.

The difficulties of organizing the railway workers have already been pointed out, and an example also showing the problems of individual organizers may make this more evident. The Johannesburg organizer of the Railway Workers' Union and an assistant visited the compound to collect subscriptions to the union. There they were accosted by police in plain clothes who, according to the organizers, intimidated the workers, threatening them with dismissal if they joined the union, and who, in front of the organizers said that it was the government's intention to smash the union. When the organizer asked if the union was illegal, the police admitted that it was not, but that it was illegal to organize on railway property, the union's activities could only be carried on outside. The assistant organizer, according to the organizer's report to SACTU, was arrested shortly afterwards and charged with using the white entrance at Jeppe railway station and with impersonating a police officer, charges which seemed to be to victimize him for his SACTU work. This had happened on other occasions, the SACTU report continued, and legal aid had been obtained.[15]

The organization of railway workers suffered a further setback in 1962 when the police raided the union offices, confiscated the membership cards and then, according to a SACTU report, threatened the members with dismissal unless they resigned from the union. SACTU, as usual, wrote to the Minister of Transport and asked whether this act of intimidation was carried out with his consent. SACTU's foreign correspondents, among them the various international trade union organizations, were informed and a letter was also sent to the International Labour Organization in Geneva.[16] These bodies were rightly wrathful, but this had little practical effect.

To bolster the Railway Workers' Unions in the face of increased government pressure, an effort was made to link the cause of the black railway workers with that of the white. The new slogan was to be: "Unity with White Workers." A leaflet entitled: "An Open Letter to White Workers" was prepared in the thousands and circulated among white railway workers. *Workers' Unity* expressed the reasoning of the new campaign: "SACTU believes that a new situation has now arisen in South Africa where conditions for workers to act together as a united force is more possible than ever before. The days of racialism in the trade union movement must be a thing of the past and the ground must now be prepared for workers to speak with one voice. . . ." Implementing these ideas, the white railway workers were approached by the Railway Workers' Union and asked for their support, the support of the African workers being pledged in return. After reprimanding white workers for their stand in the past, the union promised to make their demands its own.[17]

These overtures were rejected by the white unions, which answered that, as registered unions, they were bound by the terms of their registration. They did not wish to encroach on the preserves of another union "of whatever creed or colour." Just as they would resent any other union making demands on behalf of their members, they did not want to do this for others. They were, therefore, precluded from making representations on behalf of any other staff group. The white workers, in other words, were unwilling to join their demands with those of Africans for to do so would antagonize the more racially-minded of their members without gaining any advantage for white workers as a group. This avenue was closed to African railway workers before it had opened.

After this rebuff, the Railway Workers Unions in a weak position both with regard to recruiting and in gaining benefits for their members, began again to slide into decline. Even Durban, which had seemed so promising, was compelled to dismiss three of its four organizers. Cape Town and Port Elizabeth still had one each, and two remained active in Johannesburg, but there seemed little to show for their activities.[18] The National Committee also ceased effective functioning, meeting rarely, and making little effort to maintain contact with areas outside the main centers. The whole organization was in steady retreat.

The decline of the Railway Workers' Unions is shown by the failure of later SACTU reports to devote much attention to them after 1962. The SACTU annual report of 1963 contains virtually nothing relevant and *New Age* (renamed *Spark*) had ceased publication in 1963. The unfailing impression conveyed is that, as far as railway workers went, as with metal workers, SACTU leaders were involved in other projects than organizing unions, which was in any event becoming more and more impossible.[19]

The Attempt to Organize Agriculture

Among the more important resolutions passed at the Fifth Annual Conference of SACTU in 1960, was that concerning agriculture:

> . . . Conference recognizes the urgent need to link toilers of the towns and country closely together in their common struggle against oppression. Conference accordingly resolves to render all possible assistance to the people of the countryside in their struggle, and to assist them to form peasants' organizations. Local Committees are also instructed to assist agricultural labourers on farms to form agricultural workers unions. People in the countryside must also be encouraged by means of written and spoken propaganda to join trade unions when they come to work in towns.

The aim, then, was to organize agricultural workers against oppression, a political end, and if possible to combine this with economic objectives so forming the basis for mass support. The problem, as always, remained how to get started? To this end a National Organizing Committee for Agriculture, similar to those already discussed, was established.

In the first year this Committee confined its efforts to the Transvaal, apparently because a peasant's organization previously established had written SACTU and asked for support.[20] The exact nature of this organization is unclear, and nothing much emerges in the documents. It was, however, seen as a possible beginning for a larger scale organization in the Transvaal.

The work in the Transvaal remained limited. Some 100 farm workers paid membership fees, formed themselves into a Farm, Plantation and Allied Workers' Union in October 1961, and forwarded their complaints to SACTU. However real the complaints, it was obvious that this group was no more than a miniscule part of the 1,500,000 African agricultural workers. Nonetheless, it was a start, no matter how small the union was and four regional committees were set up to cover the eastern and western parts of the province with separate committees in the important agricultural districts of Benoni and Delmas.[21]

Once this was done, the National Organizing Committee seems to have engaged in the usually futile correspondence with various white agricultural bodies to whom they supplied the usual long (and often accurate) memoranda to little effect. Resolutions of the newly formed Farm, Plantation and Allied Workers' Union were sent to the Prime Minister, the Minister of Bantu Affairs, and the Minister of Labour who apparently did not acknowledge them. The Transvaal Agricultural Union (of white farmers) did acknowledge receipt, but did nothing to carry matters further. The resolutions were given to the press and to the various overseas bodies with whom SACTU corresponded which may have helped publicize them, but did little else to promote the interests of organized farm labor.

The problems of organizing farm labor in South Africa were overwhelming, far harder indeed than those connected with urban workers. Just to begin with, farm workers, unlike urban workers, were scattered over a large number of sizeable farms. Many were illiterate, and as Heribert Adam points out, many lacked the consciousness of alternatives, their ability to do so impaired by their viewing apartheid as imposed and inevitable.[22] Farm workers had the least rights, less than urban workers, being governed by Masters and Servants Acts that gave "masters" considerable power over "servants." Africans, in terms of the Acts, were subject to criminal prosecution for such things as breach of duty, absence without leave, while whites employing them could be prosecuted for withholding wages or food.[23] As membership of a trade union must make members fall foul of the Masters and Servants Act, the prospects for organization were not propitious.

Nonetheless the farm workers' union seems to have grown to some 300 members in August 1962, for the unions could protect workers from breaches of labor contracts under the relevant Acts. They could act on behalf of farm workers when wrongfully evicted or when labor contracts were unlawfully broken. Farm workers could not have handled these on their own, for they often were barely literate and frequently unaware of their rights in the complicated maze of laws and amendments. Conditions varied not only from one province to another but from one area to another. It would have taken expert knowledge to know what any particular members rights were.

The very success of the union in handling claims under the Master and Servants Acts made effective functioning more difficult. The more cases that were successfully handled, the more the cases came. The union needed legal advice to handle these questions. Lawyers fees were mostly borne by the workers and were a heavy burden the union having no funds to relieve them. The Management Committee of SACTU suggested that a leaflet on the rights of farm workers should be prepared, which by enabling farm workers to know what they could and could not expect under the law, would hopefully reduce legal expenses. The union lacked the money to have the matter researched and the leaflets printed. The Management Committee then suggested that a questionnaire be prepared and circulated to the various local committees, but once more they were told that it cost money to prepare a questionnaire and this could, therefore, not be done.

The organization did not attract more workers for a number of mainly organizational reasons. The union could only employ one organizer and his work had to be supplemented by voluntary visits to farms by members of the National Organizing Committee. The size of the farms and their distance from each other created a difficult transport problem. To this must be added the difficulty in finding anyone to prepare written materials. To a suggestion that a memorandum be drawn up for Native Commissioners, the members of the Committee replied that this had occurred to them but they had found no one who could write such a memorandum.[24] The single organizer concentrated on the Eastern Transvaal and "tried to visit other areas and other provinces." The great size of the Transvaal limited what he could do in the time available.

More of the difficulties of organizing agricultural workers emerged in the annual meeting of the Farm, Plantation and Allied Workers' Union. Nine areas claimed to be represented, with representatives coming from as far afield as the northern Cape and Natal. The meeting affirmed its affiliation to SACTU, and elected a committee of eleven members. The problems of unionizing farm labor were raised and members were given the encouraging news that the Food and Canning Workers' Union would assist in organization. The Sugar Workers' Union was also suggested as a source of assistance.[25] Letters were to be written to all SACTU local committees urging them again to go out and help organize the farm workers bringing them into the national union. They were also to be asked to donate 50¢ monthly (presumably 50¢ per member of each affiliated union) to the National Organizing Committee for Agricultural Workers' to further the creation of unions of farm workers. There is, however, no clear record of any of these things being done. It is, once again, difficult to tell which of these initiatives were undertaken and which, if any, bore fruit. Going by what seems to have happened to SACTU in 1963, the year in which many of its leaders were arrested in connection with the underground resistance movement *Umkonto we Sizwe*, it is unlikely that the Farm, Plantation, and Allied Workers' Union made much progress.

The Mining Industry

Much of what was true of the farm workers was also true of workers on the mines. The mine workers had been unionized long

before SACTU appeared on the scene, indeed before the Nationalist Government came to power in 1948. Organized by members
of the Communist Party, particularly one of its most able leaders,
J. B. Marks, 60,000 African miners struck in Johannesburg in
August 1946. As the mining industry was implacably opposed to
unionization of the black miners, the police were called to repress
the strike, and in an affray, six African miners were killed and
another 600 injured.[26] Although the strike had been forcibly
ended, some improvements in wages and conditions did follow.
There had, however, been little attempt to organize the African
miners since that time.

Because of its importance to the country, the mining industry
was a major SACTU target. The gold mining industry was not
only vital to the South African economy, it was also a major
source of African employment. The mines had a work force of
some 400,000 Africans coming from various parts of the country
and from the then Protectorates of Bechuanaland (Botswana) and
Basutoland (Lesotho). The mining industry was, thus, in SACTU's
eyes the backbone of "the South African Government's immoral
policy of cheap 'native labour.'" The SACTU report on the mining
industry continued:

> It is an established fact that, as long as so large a contingent
> of the South African labour force are paid starvation wages,
> it will be difficult, if not impossible, to bring about fundamen-
> tal changes in the wages earned by workers in secondary in-
> dustry. The African mine labourers are regarded as the pre-
> serve of the Government and mining magnates—'the Goose
> that lays the Golden Egg'—hence all obstacles are placed in
> the way of those wanting to organize them.

Organizing the miners was difficult because of the "compound
system" of housing miners, begun on the Kimberley diamond
mines late in the nineteenth century. Designed to reduce diamond theft, drunkenness, and the other evils to be found among
men removed for prolonged periods from their wives and families,
it sought to minimize contact with the outside world. They were,
as G. V. Doxey describes them, partly a way of controlling labor
and partly a solution to the acute shortage of housing on the diamond fields:

As the vast majority of the Africans arrived at the fields without their families, and as few, in any case, showed any desire
to settle permanently, the easy solution to the housing problem was to provide barrack-room type accommodation,
under conditions similar to that provided for the armed
forces.[27]

Holding meetings or organizing unions was almost impossible in
the compounds themselves. Nevertheless, after making what it
termed a "study" of the situation, the decision was to "make an
all-out attempt to organize the hundreds of thousands of African
miners into a body that will act, make representations, and speak
on their behalf."[28]

The first step was to distribute a leaflet among African miners
pointing to their inadequate wages and intolerable conditions of
work. The response was seen as promising, and the Management Committee turned its eyes to the Natal coal miners, and decided to work with the Natal local committee to organize them.
Soon afterwards a National Organizing Committee for the
Mining Industry was appointed.

In 1961 the National Organizing Committee employed one full-
time official and a full-time national organizer. The organizer
soon fell foul of the law and was arrested and jailed as a prohibited immigrant. As he would only be jailed again if he did not
leave the country, SACTU officials realized they would have to
find a replacement for him. In the meantime the National Organizing Committee embarked on a frenzy of organizational activity.

A mass meeting of mine workers was planned for August 13, and
for several weeks before SACTU went, in their words, into a "perpetual distribution of leaflets, which were taken out to the mines
every week." The meeting was, nonetheless, poorly attended. The
organizers put this down to "intimidation" for, they said, letters
were received from mine workers, and where possible, their complaints had been taken up with authorities. A new leaflet was
meantime being prepared and distributed without much result.
SACTU reported that organization of mine workers had not advanced much. There had been a number of casualties among those
distributing leaflets and many other difficulties. Some 100 mine
workers had joined the union in Kimberley, but the true number

could not be ascertained. Meantime "teams of organizers" were visiting the mines each week end.

The National Organizing Committee was criticized by the NEC. Many of these criticisms seem both obvious and justified, making clear the weaknesses of these Organizing Committees in all industries. The question first of all was whether the "full-time official" was doing a full-time job? The NEC was answered that he directed the work of the organizer, handled complaints, and performed a number of other necessary tasks. When the National Organizing Committee was pressed if this really took all his time, the NEC were told that "the full-time official was extremely helpful" and that he "had very worthwhile contacts." The NEC then raised the question as to correctness of tactics. Were the tactics used those most suitable among mine labor? A survey conducted by the National Institute of Personnel Research (a nongovernmental agency) was brought to the attention of the National Organizing Committee in which it was clear that most of the mine workers still mainly regarded themselves as peasants, in which case, it was put to the Committee, would it not be better to to recruit for the union in the same place as they were recruited for the mines? This, the Organizing Committee said, was worthy of study.[29]

Progress, if this is the right word, was slow. After the abortive meeting of August 13, a trickle of mine workers visited the union offices and paid the membership fee of 14¢ per month. They were issued membership cards. Members had been recruited on a number of mines, the organizers maintained, and these were fully conscious of the importance of trade union organization and willing to assist the union in its work. Although hindered by compound police, mine detectives, and a network of spies, the workers were showing keen interest.[30]

To capture the interest of mine workers, the leaflet on wages and working conditions was run off again. Plans were made to write to interested workers in the Transvaal and later on the new gold fields of the Orange Free State. As the leaflet would soon be completed, volunteers were called for to distribute them on the mines. The National Union of Mineworkers in Great Britain was, at the same time, to petition the parent companies of the South African mines in London, to improve the conditions of their workers.

In spite of these apparently promising moves, matters soon bogged down in the Transvaal and little was done to increase the organization of mine workers. A somewhat more serious effort was made to organize workers in the Orange Free State, and four members of SACTU went down to Kroonstad, which was not a mining area, while two others went to the gold field.s. There they found, as they had expected, a large number of compounds with many dissatisfied mine workers. But there was little progress beyond this point. As with the other unions, the year 1963 was not auspicious. Given the hostility of both the government and the mining industry there was little that SACTU could accomplish.

In all, for all its vast plans, SACTU had little with which to achieve them. SACTU had little money, and few able organizers. How far SACTU's resources fell short of thier needs is evident if the magnitude of their task is assessed. Assuming the figures are correct, then it took four full-time organizers to muster 3,500 union members in Natal. That would mean that it took one full-time organizer to organize 1,000 workers and to maintain their union. This would mean, if SACTU were to have functioned to best effect, some 2,000 organizers would be required. Granted that this figure is probably too high, some 200 organizers for about 1,500,-000 workers is surely not too many. SACTU could not afford to hire anything near this number and it is doubtful even if it had them, that the government would have allowed them to operate. Another point is important: during the time the SACTU leaders were supposed to be engaged in organization, they were engaged in a whole variety of campaigns mounted by their allies. Had SACTU concentrated on creating unions their work might have been better, but then this was not the fundamental purpose for which SACTU had been founded. The aim was the political use of economics, the use of unions as a means toward a mass base to effect political change. Political change might have been in the interest of the African workers, but there were more pressing concerns at hand. SACTU, as a result, did not draw the support from workers it might have had, even with the legal system directed against it and its constituency.

Chapter V

The Search
for a Mass Base

SACTU, from its foundation in 1955 until about 1957 had carried on the more or less regular practise of either building its own unions or of seeking the affiliation of existing unions. A decision of 1957 radically altered this approach. Instead of formulating demands in specific industries and related to direct needs, SACTU was to join in a campaign through a mass movement in the entire country to press for a national minimum wage higher than any existing. The campaign was to have two aims: it was to activate Africans, within and without SACTU, and to induce them to join SACTU and the ANC; and it was to attempt to win a minimum wage from the government which, if done, would open the government to other pressures.[1] The campaign, aimed at a gain of £1-a-day (a pound was about $2.80 at the exchange of the time), and was known, not inappropriately, as the "£1-a-Day Campaign" and is so identified here. It is dealt with in detail because of the importance attached to it, and because of the length of time it was continued— five years—from 1957 to 1963, when SACTU records dwindled to the vanishing point.

As with any campaign of such duration, it went through a series of metamorphoses and was carried out with varying degrees of vigor. The main campaign of the series was a demand for higher wages in a low-wage economy (for Africans), and its appeal would seem irresistible. Indeed, this was what Congress leaders thought. They saw the campaign as a device enabling them to add members to their organizations on a scale surpassing earlier efforts, and making the ANC and SACTU of a size never before witnessed in African organizations. The target was the mobilization of the whole African population.

Officially the campaign opened on February 10, 1957, with a mass conference of workers held in Johannesburg demanding increased wages. *New Age* in its issue of February 14 claimed that 300 delegates attended representing some 24,000 unionists and "many thousands" of unorganized workers from some 150 shops, factories, and compounds. Quite understandably the conference held what it claimed to be the average African wage, some $30 per month, to be inadequate and urged what would have amounted to a threefold increase. They pointed out that "cost-of-living" allowances had been pegged since 1955 and bore no relation to the increase in cost to the African of the essentials of daily life—the prices of food, rent, and clothing. The inspiration for the campaign had come from the National Coordinating Committee of the Congress Alliance, but there is no doubt that the grievances, as framed, were real enough. In addition, African militancy had been raised by outside events such as the bus boycott of 1957 in which thousands of Africans had chosen to walk to work rather than pay the one penny increase in fare demanded by the bus company. SACTU, no doubt, hoped to capitalize on this spirit of militancy before it dissipated after settlement of the dispute. The declared aim thus became one of recruiting at least 20,000 new members for SACTU and to press for the one-pound-a-day.

The campaign was launched with the usual Congress *panache*. Some 100,000 leaflets were distributed to which application forms for union membership were thoughtfully attached. Lapel bades with the vernacular slogan "Asinamali—Sifun'Imali" ("we have no money—we want money") were issued. SACTU was, as usual, to rely on the "enthusiastic support of the ANC and other progressive organizations for the success of the campaign."[2] The whole thing was, as will be made clear, to become very much a show of the Congress Alliance itself, with the ANC in particular playing a key role. The tone was set by Oliver Tambo, then General Secretary of the ANC, who said: "Every [member of the ANC] should appreciate the importance of the campaign. Every African worker should apply to SACTU for trade union membership."[3] The campaign was already claimed to be bearing fruit, for employers were increasingly interested and employers organizations indicated that they would consider the minimum wage. Opposition came mainly from the government and the mines, the latter particularly fearing that higher wages would adversely affect the marginal gold mines and lead to their closure. Selling a commodity at a fixed price, the gold mines saw themselves as incapable of paying higher wages and trapped by rising prices if higher wages forced other prices up.

As plans for the campaign were made, evidence of ANC support became more and more manifest. The executive committee of the ANC on the Witwatersrand pledged support for the campaign in a message from E. P. Moretsele: "The struggle of SACTU is that of [the African National] Congress. Their demands are those of Congress. The campaign for £1-a-day is ours."[4]

Councils were divided in the National Executive of SACTU itself. Although there was great enthusiasm for the campaign in itself, serious questions were raised as to its conduct. Mrs. Phyllis Altman, for instance, pointed out that she did not know where the personnel to organize the campaign was to come from, who was going to do the organizing at the factories when applications for membership came in? Furthermore, what would happen when people in isolated areas began sending in forms? These were practical questions, and intelligent questions at that, but they were airily dismissed by an organization never strong on the practical aspects of organizing. SACTU leaders had the bit in their teeth and were unresponsive to efforts to steer the campaign to practicable paths. One member said that the difficulties were "theoretical," that the problem would not be as great as envisioned when the campaign had actually started. Sufficient workers to organize the campaign would be forthcoming to organize the factories, while people in isolated places would be put into touch with the nearest ANC branch. Another said that although he did not seek to minimize the difficulties foreseen by Mrs. Altman and others, he believed that "when the people realized the necessity of standing together to obtain their demands the campaign would succeed. This had been the experience of the [bus] boycott."[5] There was clearly a difference of view between leaders concerned with more orthodox trade union organization and those who wanted an "organizational weapon," and the weapon wielders had won. The year 1957 was, thus, a crucial one, and marked a turning point in SACTU history. From having concerned itself largely with the organization of unions SACTU after 1957 began to largely concern itself with the goals of the Congress Alliance in the broadest sense. It had, of course, always associated itself with Congress Alliance goals, but now these ruled exclusively. It may be appropriate, therefore, to say something briefly about the Congress Alliance.

The Congress Alliance

The Communist Party had been formally banned by the government in 1950, but dissolved itself ahead of the ban, and was thus able to destroy its records and to maintain certain membership lists secret from the authorities. The party secretly reconstituted itself in 1952 and began penetrating some existing organizations and at the same time forming a number of "fronts" of its own. Some of these "fronts" collapsed because they failed to win any support from liberal non-Communists, but some succeeded and were drawn together. The most notable success the Communists had was in their influence in the ANC, the most significant African political movement, which while heavily infused with non-Communist and indeed anti-Communist members, came increasingly under Communist influence. The Communists had also succeeded in gaining control of the South African Indian Congress, a body ooriginally founded by Mohandas Gandhi, through the dynamism of Drs. Dadoo and Naicker. The remaining pure "fronts" were the Congress of Democrats (for whites) and the Coloured Peoples' Organization (later Congress). SACTU was the other member. Control over the ANC was exerted after they had acceded to the "Freedom Charter" at a "Congress of the People." The "Congress of the People" was a vast mass meeting in 1954 at which the "Charter" was accepted which contained, among the usual human rights principles, demands for the nationalization of industry and agriculture.

Both the ANC and SACTU adopted the "Freedom Charter," which became a policy document for both. Now the aim was to collect signatures and a "Million Signatures Campaign" was launched to gather that number of signatures in support of the "Freedom Charter." As it happened, the campaign flopped, and the number of signatures actually garnered was quite small, but the ANC itself was sorely divided through adoption of the Charter. The reason was the increasing opposition to Communist influence in the ANC among extreme African nationalists. The nationalist Africans opposed Communism as foreign to Africa, and meant, in the end, exchanging one form of domination for another. The question of the Freedom Charter smouldered for a time after its adoption, but participation in the "£1-a-Day" Campaign brought it to burning point. The militant "Africanists"—the extreme nationalists—hived off and formed their own organization, the Pan-Africanist Congress under a university lecturer, Robert Sobukwe, and openly opposed the ANC. They eventually became involved with their own trade union group, or one professing to support them, FOFATUSA, which will be referred to later. (See chapter 7. FOFATUSA stands for Federation of Free African Trade Unions.)

A result of the Congress of the People Campaign was the decision to retain the organizing body, the National Coordinating Council, or as it was known the NCC, on which all bodies of the Congress Alliance, regardless of size, were equally represented. The NCC was not, according to its articles, supposed to be a policy-making body, which did not prevent it from making policy. It was, in effect, a "front of fronts," for the real decisions were taken behind the scenes by the Central Committee of the Communist Party which then manipulated the ANC through the associated Congresses on the NCC. As Africans were members of the Central Committee and of the ANC, this gave the Communists added leverage.[6] Unity was, in this way, to be combined with control, as emerges in the words of Leon Levy, the President of SACTU in 1957: "The alliance of the trade union movement with the forces of liberation has given adequate direction to their struggles and aspirations."[7] The fate of SACTU was that of the Congress Alliance.

The Initiation of the Campaign

The decision to mount the £1-a-Day Campaign was taken at the second SACTU Conference, and the conditions of the campaign were defined. This was to be a national campaign and aimed at all employers as a body. Clearly, if it were to be directed at individual firms, and one or two complied, these firms would be at a competitive disadvantage and the greater part of the work force little aided. SACTU was encouraged by a statement of the Johannesburg Chamber of Commerce agreeing that the wages of unskilled (largely African) labor were too low and offering an "across the board" increase of five shillings (about 70 cents) per week. This offer was rejected by SACTU as totally inadequate.[8] Encouraging as things seemed at that point, the old bugbear, disorganization was beginning to take its effect. Even as negotiations were being carried on with the Chambers of Commerce and of Industries, the Food and Canning Workers' Union launched a strike of its own which clearly contravened the national character of the effort.[9] Partly as a result of this, and partly because of other reasons, the negotiations with the two Chambers proved abortive.

Meantime plans were being put into effect for the big campaign, according to SACTU spokesmen, the Transvaal was being "zoned" by the £1-a-Day Committee—a committee apparently consisting of SACTU representatives and others from the Congress Alliance. The zones, covering convenient areas, would be the responsibility of teams for each zone. Natal had also responded positively and was taking steps to implement the campaign.[10]

Careful reading—always essential with *New Age* reports—shows that things were not advancing in quite the way and at quite the pace indicated. In Natal, for instance, "Congress leaders in Durban *meant* to get together a team of their most capable workers" (author's italics), and no news had reached the Committee about what was being planned or done in the vital Eastern Cape or the Western Cape. Nevertheless, the National Secretary, Leonard Masina, was confident, for "knowing the people in those areas [he] was confident that they [were] getting on with the job." A Conference of Workers was planned to ginger up the organization and consolidate the campaign. Consisting of representatives both of organized and of unorganized workers, the conference would "be fully representative of the whole country," and to this end a flood of leaflets, printed in four African languages, were released. The objective had been broadened, as the leaflets indicated, for not only was the one pound wage a day to be an issue, but also the struggle against the pass laws, deportations, and passes for women. "Job apartheid" by which skilled work was reserved to whites was to be another target.[11] These were serious issues, but their espousal meant that the objectives of the campaign were blurred and effort unfocused.

The means of collecting delegates for the National Workers' Conference, scheduled for both February 15 and 16 were to be by getting the workers together, electing delegates, collecting money for their fares, writing for their admission cards, and sending demands and suggestions to the conference. The same points were to be discussed at a Special Conference of SACTU on December 7-8, 1957. The themes of the conference, as far as the campaign was concerned, were the readiness of SACTU for the campaign and the contributions to it of the local committees.

The work of the local committees, as they emerge from the conference, is particularly interesting. This is the more the case when they are compared with the press reports. In Durban, for instance, the local committee felt that as the demand was principally an economic demand a broad front should be formed, so they had sent invitations to all trade unions asking them to nominate delegates for a meeting to discuss the campaign and to form a "£1-a-Day" Committee. The invitations were also sent to the other Congresses and the Liberal Party. The local committee had, in addition, prepared a leaflet of its own, and invited speakers to address meetings, and to this end had mapped out the whole Durban area to ensure that the entire industrial portion would be covered. Factory committees were to be formed at the same time to form new trade unions where existing trade unions were hostile to SACTU. The new factory committees would work for the "£1-a-Day" campaign. Some eight meetings had already been held, but with the parallel campaign against "job reservation" the campaign for "£1-a-Day" had come to a standstill.[12]

The report from Worcester, in the Western Cape, was to the effect that the campaign was not explained clearly to workers, and many were under the misapprehension that it was the government that was going to give them one pound a day. They could not understand what was causing the delay. Additional organizational work was obviously needed, the local committee reported. The delegate from Port Elizabeth, in the Eastern Cape, said that workers understood its objects, but believed that only African workers were to be involved. There was also feeling that the better paid workers were not concerned, that the campaign "was being divorced from the general struggle of the workers." Another question that called for answer was what happened in industries that were covered by a published agreement or wage determination? These were put out by the government and were binding. The solution suggested was to secure a "gentleman's agreement" that £1-a-day be paid by employers, and then that efforts be directed to get the ruling changed.

Another crucial area, Johannesburg, was backward in its actions. The Johannesburg local committee had done little for the campaign, as affiliated unions did not send representatives to the meeting where this was discussed. Workers in important sectors of industry, iron, steel, and timber were not organized. ("We were not doing much about this.") Leading the struggle were the Amato Textile Mill workers, organized by the textile union, who were militant and ready to engage in the campaign.

Cape Town was more encouraging in the state of its preparations. More had been done, though it is unclear what this "more" amounted to.

All in all, it seems clear from the record that little had actually been done to make this major campaign real, both because SACTU had its fingers in too many pies already, and because the nature of the campaign was not fully understood everywhere.

Indeed there was doubt whether the National Workers' Conference should itself be held as planned. If it were held on February 15-16, it might allow insufficient time for areas outside the principal centers to send delegates. The question arose as always: should the workers first be organized and then harnessed to the campaign, or should the campaign be launched in the hope that organization would arise out of action? The result was a compromise in which it was decided that the local committees first hold conferences all over South Africa on February 16 and that the Workers' Conference itself be postponed to March 15-16. In this way all areas were to be given a chance to organize.

There seems to have been an attempt in the different regions to follow up on this resolution. *New Age* speaks of a rally of some thousand Africans in Uitenhage in the Eastern Cape, with a sprinkling of Coloureds and whites in attendance. The meeting was graced by the Special Branch of the police, as all these meetings usually were, who stood around taking notes. After some seven hours of intensive discussion a resolution passed with thunderous applause.[13] The meeting accepted the campaign. In Johannesburg five rallies took place, which were reported without mentioning participation, while at the Port Elizabeth meeting referred to above 1,500 participated in a rally which directed its attention chiefly at passes for women. In Cape Town 300 people, including 200 delegates from 22 industries and 7 organizations, met to consider the question. In Durban 449 delegates from 74 factories, the ANC, and other organizations met, and "numbers of speakers" called for a national general strike.[14]

Support was soon forthcoming from the President-General of the ANC, Albert Luthuli, who stated that the ANC stood for mass agitation and mass action to achieve a living wage and the repeal of the pass laws. "We are for widespread activity among the voteless peoples at election time so that the voices and opinions of the voteless may be taken into account seriously by the voters before they dare saddle us with another five years of Nationalist rule." The action that Luthuli referred to, in addition to the wage campaign, was a strike being called for to coincide with the general election of 1958—again an example of the way in which the Congress Alliance attenuated its meager strength in several simultaneous campaigns. Luthuli, returning to the former theme, admitted that there was some ambiguity and confusion about the conference proposed: "Because of the name of the [National Workers'] Conference some people in our Congress organizations are treating it as though it is to be a trade union affair, primarily concerning the active trade unionists, and confined exclusively to delegations elected from the factories."[15] Such conceptions were mistaken, he went on to say, and there were important issues in the campaign other than a national minimum wage. Two errors had to be avoided, in Luthuli's view, the first was that they should not think of a workers' conference exclusively in trade union terms, and secondly, that they had to remember that the ANC was not exclusively a workers' organization although many Africans were workers. The ANC thus staged the National Workers' Conference on March 16 and its resolutions were conveyed to SACTU, although many SACTU executive committee members had participated in the meeting. The National Workers' Conference had not been held as a special event on its own, what is more, but was the climax of various other regional conferences, at least five of which had been held in Johannesburg. The conference was attended by some 1,673 delegates, according to the report, and the strike resolution (i.e. to strike during the General Election) was put to the meeting. A resolution calling on workers to burn passes was defeated, and the normal series of resolutions, by now standard at meetings of this sort, on a broad range of issues, passed. A resolution to participate on the "£1-a-Day" campaign was among them.[16] Support was, however, far from solid. Many of the younger ANC members mutinied at the thought of non-African control of the ANC that seemed implied in participation in the campaign, and against a new campaign in the name of "workers." This manifested itself in violent demonstrations, leaving the ANC sorely divided within itself.[17]

SACTU now had to decide what was to follow the Workers' Conference. Obviously the resolutions at that meeting had to be taken into account if the support of the ANC was to be mobilized. This was the more true as Luthuli had made it clear that ANC support depended at least in part on this. SACTU therefore decided to respond to the call for a "stay-at-home" strike during the election. In such a strike the workers quite literally stayed at home and did not go to work. It was a general strike without the formal appurtenances of strikes, such as pickets. The duration of the strike, which had been debated at the National Workers' Conference was decided there. The question was whether to stay away from work from April 1 or from April 14, and whether this strike was to last two days, three days, or be continued indefinitely. The decision was to strike from April 14-16, with the proviso that the strike could be called off at any time, and that workers were to comply were such an order given.[18]

The "stay at home" strike was a failure, as even the usually sanguine *New Age* reluctantly admitted. An effort was made to rescue some vestiges of success, but this was very feeble. Only a minority of workers had responded to the appeal to stay at home, the majority going to work as usual. Yet, at least as far as whites were concerned, the campaign had not been completely pointless. As *New Age* pointed out: "White voters went to the polls on Wednesday after weeks of debate and agitation at all levels over the issue of £1-a-Day."[19] There had indeed been some discussion of this issue in the weeks before, during, and after the campaign. White South Africans may have heaved a sigh of relief when black workers came to work, but the realization that Africans were underpaid stuck and created pressures for improvement.

In a sense the ANC and SACTU stay-at-home campaign revealed the support the ANC enjoyed in different parts of the country, or at least the militancy of the membership. Port Elizabeth, an old ANC stronghold, had a strike that was fifty percent effective, though this tailed off during the day. In Durban the strike was effective to some thirty percent. In Johannesburg it was largely ineffective except that the Indian stores closed. The overall picture was bleak, the strike had to be called off after only one day.

The Congress Alliance, together with SACTU, naturally sought to explain their failure. A reason was the more pressing because a stay-at-home strike the year before, initiated by the ANC, had been highly effective. The failure was attributed in part to measures taken by the government. The police had staged shows of force in the townships. They had brought trucks to the railway stations to take workers to work. They had staged searches for weapons and arrested the unemployed youths, the *tsotsis*, whom the ANC used as strong-arm squads. In addition the leaderships of the Congesses had been reduced by deportations and bans reducing the pool of experienced and respected leaders. Then, perhaps, the postmortem came to the nub of the problem:

> The question of organization is the key to why the demonstration did not catch on. And the answer is organization, more organization, and even better organization. It is significant that the stoppage was most complete wherever organization was best—in Port Elizabeth and Sophiatown, in Reef industries like milling and textiles where militant trade unions are strongest.[20]

The assessment had been made and what was needed now was to draw these lessons for the future.

The £1-a-Day Campaign
and the Drive for 20,000 Members

The stay-at-home strike was one of the campaigns emergent
from the Workers' Conference. It had not, of course, originated
there, for it had been discussed among the Congress leaders before.
Its implementation was, however, one outcome. Another was to
be the £1-a-Day Campaign and a drive for 20,000 new members
and the organization of new unions. The Third National Conference of SACTU had resolved along these lines.[21] The plan of how
these results were to be achieved was set out in a document with
the unwieldy title: "The Campaign for 20,000 New Trade Union
Members, A National Mimimum Wage of £1-a-Day, and Increases
for All Workers Receiving More." This plan merits more study.

The document claims that despite the failure of the stay-at-home
the national minimum wage of £1-a-day remains a real demand of
workers, and that the urgent task is, therefore, "to give effective
leadership to these demands [sic]." Workers failed to respond,
not because of the demand, but because they were "not sufficiently
organized industrially at the point of production." This meant that
they "could not effectively campaign for advances in wages and
conduct industrial action for political objectives." Where they were
organized, the document continues, they responded to the stay-at-
home with considerable enthusiasm. More seriously, from SACTU's
viewpoint, was the failure to turn the enthusiasm to account in
recruiting. "When the £1-a-Day campaign was launched we also set
ourselves the task of recruiting some 20,000 thousand new members
into the trade union movement, but while we succeeded in popu-
larizing the demand for wage increases, we neglected to implement
our decision to recruit new trade union members. This was a great
weakness in the campaign and contributed to the April 14th-16th
setback. It is our view, therefore, that in intensifying the £1-a-Day
Campaign our major emphasis must now be placed on industrial
organization of the workers."[22]

An imaginative plan was advanced. It was a two-stream campaign, the document states, divided into two sections. It was, in
the first place, to consist of an intensive campaign to organize the
workers in certain selected industries, and in the second, the exten-

sive mass organization of workers. The document is particularly
concerned with the second alternative, and was intended to give
every active worker in the Congress *movement* "a simple and
practical task to do in his own place of employment and a brief
education in elementary trade unionism. The second aim was to
make members of the Congress movement and all workers conscious of the need and purpose of trade union organization."

The goals outlined were to be achieved through a number of
steps. All ANC members and members of other Congresses who
were eligible were to be encouraged to join an existing trade union
affiliated to SACTU. Where no trade unions existed, Congress
members were to be encouraged to form them. As a further step
towards "organizing powerful, well-organized trade unions, a
broad network of factory committees or shop or office committees
etc., should be established which can take up immediate grievances with employers and serve to encourage the workers to form
trade unions." All were exhorted to do all in their power to organize
factory committees at their places of employment which would
become centers of militancy, expressing grievances of course,
but also educating the workers politically and stressing the need
for political action to win economic demands. Factory committees
might enable workers to win small concessions, and once they
saw what united action could achieve, they might be encouraged
to embark on bigger things. The factory committees would create
confidence and so strengthen the initiative of the workers. Workers
were to be encouraged to take the initiative in organizing other
workers for the campaign for a national minimum wage, and before the campaign was launched a set of brief lectures explaining
its purposes were to be issued.

The issue underlying the campaign was that employers were
themselves conscious that they were underpaying their workers
and that they would sooner or later have to meet with them and
negotiate for higher pay. The aim, though this was not a part
of the document, was to create a kind of *Angst*-machine which,
while playing on the consciences of employers, would induce the
workers to militancy. The employers would be softened up for
concessions at the same time as the workers organized to push for
these concessions. The main effort for organization was to fall
squarely on the workers themselves. The campaign was to be

based on three principles: (1) Although it was to be the responsibility of SACTU, it was to be undertaken with the assistance of the entire Congress Alliance, who were in turn to consider this campaign as important as any they were engaged in at the time. (2) It was to be undertaken as "a vital task to free the oppressed people of South Africa." Then, the onus for developing the campaign was to be placed "on the initiative of the masses of the workers themselves, starting from the level of individual places of work." And (3), as already indicated, all Congress members were to be encouraged to join a union or form one. All this while SACTU would be publicizing progress, reporting successes, and generally "encouraging more and more workers to take up this method [factory committees] of struggle." If the Congresses could organize and harness a large movement of this kind, it was confidently predicted, the £1-a-Day Campaign would be given a new impetus which "could transform the present situation."

There were two reasons at least for the new initiative. The stay-at-home campaign had failed, and while this failure hurt the divided ANC more, it also greatly damaged SACTU prestige. It served to discredit those who had urged action without organization. It also threw SACTU back on the more orthodox Marxist methods of union building. The "shop unit" was the basis of Communist unionism, and was cited in a party organization manual as the basic difference between Communist and Socialist organization. The Socialists organized on a branch basis and elections to wards and districts, the manual stated, while the Communist Party is built around the place of employment.[23] The method had the advantage of simplicity, for it ensured that party members working in the same factory would know each other and would not work at cross purposes with each other. The method of organizing in this way, a member told the Management Committee of SACTU, was "as simple as reading your ABC." It did not, he said, take a professor to form a factory committee and take grievances to employers; it was within the reach of all. He continued:

There are brave men and cowards. Speak to these workers where you live in the same way that you have spoken to them where you work. They may have the same complaints that you have. I must warn you. Use brains, not blood. Violence may not lead us anywhere . . . You have a trade union now [once the committees are established that is] but no organizer, no secretary, no office. Call the workers together. Tell them we have a wage complaint and to handle it properly we must have an organizer and establish our trade union on a proper basis. Ask the workers to contribute every month or every week. SACTU will help you to get started. Go to your nearest SACTU office. When your trade union is still weak SACTU will help you. . . .[24]

Unions could, according to this argument, be started easily and organization would follow once initial practises had shown some result.

The building up of unions from the ground up was clearly a threat that the government could not take lightly. It was this and the powers the government had that made factory committees seem a more powerful weapon on paper than in practice. Steps were at once initiated to ensure that the nascent movement was effectively strangled from the outset. A circular from the Director of Non-European [ie African] Affairs was sent to all employers of African labor, and was explicit and to the point. It stated that if an African employee was discharged as a result of taking part in strikes, demonstrations, absenteeism from work, etc., he was not to be employed again except with the specific approval of the Regional Commissioner. The Regional Employment Commissioner was, what is more, to be furnished with records of all such cases.[25] This letter, and the regulations behind it, ended effective factory committee action, although efforts to organize factory committees for political and economic action persisted.

To implement the plan for the £1-a-Day campaign and that for enlarged membership, closer cooperation between the ANC and SACTU was aimed at. An example of working in this direction is that of a meeting in Uitenhage, in the Eastern Cape, at which delegates from both organizations met to draw up a common program for the campaign and to form a liaison committee between Port Elizabeth and Uitenhage to consist both of the SACTU local committee and the ANC branches in both centers. The main stress was to be on improving wages and boycotting storekeepers who paid less than a living wage to their employees. Another aim was to recruit 10,000 new members for SACTU.[26] Other meetings were held in Johannesburg although the £1-a-Day Campaign, there as elsewhere, tended to be obscured by the number of other issues raised. The fact that the issue was submerged is apparent from the heading of an article in *New Age:* "What happened to the £1-a-day?" The article's author urged the workers to stop thinking that April 14 was a failure and that further effort was futile. It is clear, he writes, "that nothing will be done about the problem of African poverty unless the African himself takes further action to compel both bosses and government to pay up."[27] "Where," he asks "is the pressure from the workers which is what is needed today to transform the whole situation? . . . The workers must understand that if, through their own inertia they fail to force concessions from the ruling class at this moment, they will have nobody but themselves to blame for the continuation of the state of their poverty."

The question as to what had happened to the campaign was raised at the Fourth Annual Conference in 1959, and an appropriate statement by a member of the Management Committee on organization has already been cited. The question of higher wages was however to be discussed. The speech with which the discussion of this theme was opened is so interesting that it deserves a lengthy citation:

> You have all heard what has been read to you. A man who goes to work every morning still cannot save his children from starving. We must decide how to solve this problem. It is the duty of all delegates to discuss how to feed these children. We must come out of here with a very good decision. SACTU suggested that workers should get at least £1-a-day. This has been preached to you for a very long time: at least two years. Many of you were at the Workers' Conference but afterwards you scabbed on the other workers. You didn't realize that you were scabbing on yourselves.[28]

This speech, with its nuances, gives an insight into the minds of Congress members, as well as the frustrations of Congress activity. Other statements made at the meeting reinforce this impression. A delegate of the Distributive Workers' Union, for instance, said that "workers were definitely robbed by two thieves—the government and the employers." This is not unusual imagery in that context, but another statement is more original: "it should be clear to us that in order to convince the workers on this subject [the £1-a-day Campaign] we must show the workers who is the enemy. It is the employer. *The government is just a tool.* It is our task to convince the workers of this. . . . When we approach the workers we must confine ourselves to the struggle against the employer." (Author's italics). A delegate from the Railway Workers Union, in replying to another delegate who had been refused a wage increase he had asked for, said: "In answer to the Comrade who has just spoken, I say that in order to get £1-a-day we must be like butterflies, infesting every shop, every factory, every mine and every farm, agitating for £1-a-day."

Resolutions were then passed which confirmed the importance of the £1-a-Day Campaign, which was to be carried on by sending deputations to the employers organizations while at the same time the campaign was to be intensified, with demands included for those already earning more that £1-a-day. Part of the campaign was, as usual, to be directed toward organizing the unorganized workers, with factory committees to be the nuclei of future unions.

In the meantime the campaign, and its slogan, were being overtaken by inflation. Wages had risen and many workers were now earning £1 per day. Yet the slogan was difficult to change without loss of "swing." It was, however, increasingly unreal. There was some argument as to whether, say, "thirty bob-a-day" might serve as a substitute, but this had little appeal. (A "bob" is the slang term for a shilling, about 14¢ in American money at the exchange rate of the time. One pound was twenty shillings.) In the end the matter was settled by asking for one pound for every weekday, instead of only on working days, as was originally planned.[29]

Part of the campaign for the winning of a national minimum wage was the organization of factory committees, but even here the old methods seem to have persisted. It was now to be new Workers' Conferences in all provinces, these to be held on February 28, 1960, as part of the second phase of the Anti-Pass Campaign. This and the events of 1960 were to give a new turn to events and the affairs of the Congresses.

The Year of Emergency and Its Aftermath

As part of the second phase of the anti-pass campaign, an ANC campaign, in which SACTU was also involved was to be staged. Congress organizers in Natal, the Management Committee heard, were touring the factories and holding meetings of workers to elect delegates for the conferences. The cooperation of the ANC and SACTU was hailed as a special feature of the campaign, all of whom were engaged in these visits, so pulling their weight together. Durban was the most active center then, and there the conference was to be preceded by a mass rally on February 27 to launch a drive for some 100 new factory committees with 5,000 new members by June 26. No record of this meeting seems to have been made, probably because the government proclaimed a State of Emergency soon after the Sharpeville incident in March 1960.

In the meantime, all who might have authority over wages or working conditions were bombarded with SACTU literature and letters. An indication of the broad spread of SACTU publicity is the list of those sent the revised memorandum for £1-a-Day:

The Secretary for Labour
The Associated Chambers of Commerce
The Federated Chamber of Industries (which requested an additional 275 copies for its affiliates)
The Transvaal and Orange Free State Chamber of Mines
16 Provincial employers associations
92 Industrial Councils
 8 National newspapers
 6 political parties and organizations
10 overseas international and national trade union bodies.[30]

Attempts were essayed, as this mail was being sent out, to arrange personal interviews with the Chamber of Commerce and the Chamber of Industries. The Chamber of Industries seems to have carried on some correspondence with SACTU, but evaded the vital issue because, as it could rightly say, it was not a wage negotiating body. This reply, reasonable in the event, annoyed SACTU whose executive said that they could not and would not accept this and persisted in their request for discussions. As far as the

Chamber of Commerce was concerned there was some effort to enter into discussions on an unofficial basis with SACTU officials. The representatives of employers arranged that "certain business-men" would meet with SACTU executives and, according to SACTU, "an extremely useful exploratory talk was held." SACTU now felt that, with these in hand, it was no longer regarded as frivolous and irresponsible in advocating a wage of one pound a day. It was, they felt, now accepted that their demand was just and of extreme urgency. Further meetings were planned, but could not take place because of the State of Emergency.

The State of Emergency, proclaimed by the government on March 30, 1960, put most of the Congresses out of action. The majority of the leadership was detained, and sweeping powers were given the police. Even the Emergency was put to use by SACTU, which unlike the ANC and PAC was not banned, and which now believed that there was a split in "the South African ruling class" that might lead to benefits through united action. The weaknesses of SACTU organization, however, meant that beyond the distribution of the usual 100,000 leaflets pointing out that SACTU was still legal and that the workers must continue their fight for a national minimum wage, little was done. The Fifth Annual Conference, held with the ending of the State of Emergency, decided to press forward with the £1-a-Day Campaign.

The leadership was, however, in a quandary. The wage patterns of industry had changed and they were more than ever tied to a slogan increasingly obsolete. At a meeting of the National Executive of SACTU in October 1960, many of its members felt that there was no point in continued reiteration. A study ought to be made of those industries where wages of thirty shillings or more were paid and where there were no agreements on wages. A new memorandum discussing these findings and presenting the history of the £1-a-day Campaign should also be prepared, and a subcommittee was appointed to perform this task. In the meantime negotiations were to continue with employers' organizations.

The major stumbling block to effective action was now held to be the inaction of affiliated unions. These were not submitting their demands for £1 per day to their employers' associations. The African Laundryworkers Union, for instance, had asked for £4 per week (about $7.20) which was embarassingly contradictory of

SACTU policy. All unions were again urged to ask for a minimum of one pound per day.[31] Obtaining the compliance of the unions was not to be an easy matter.

Although a variety of social issues were to be pressed at the same time, these were to be linked with union issues rather than to purely political ends. The campaign for "£1-a-day" was to be at the same time for higher wages and for recognition of African trade unions, the latter an issue to which, the Management Committee agreed, the employers were not generally hostile. The representative of the S.A. Clothing Workers' Union, for instance, pointed out that his union was some thirty-two years old, and he had written to the Minister of Labor that it was surely time this union was recognized. Even without legal recognition, however, a delegate pointed out that employers could be brought to the point where they would negotiate with African unions. He cited the example of the Biscuit Workers' Factory Committee in Springs, in the Transvaal, where employers negotiated with the union. This obviously was an avenue worth exploring.

The effect of SACTU pleas on employers was evident in the line taken by organized employers. The President of the Natal Chamber of Industries, Ken Firth, was reported to have said that poverty was the main problem facing South Africa and unless a solution was found in the next five years, it could create unbearable internal and external pressures, creating such instability in the labor force that the successful operation of industries would become impossible. The same report cited the director of the Municipal Bantu Admistration Department as saying that despite increases from some industries in Durban, eighty-five percent of the African males still earned less that £15 per month (about $42) and only sixteen percent earned more than the estimated minimum cost of living.[32] SACTU was heartened to renew its drive for £1-a-Day, particularly in Natal.

The government, now pressed by organized bodies of employers, called for a conference on African wages to be held in Cape Town in November. This was to be sponsored by the Central Native Labour Board which it had formed seven years before in terms of the Native Settlement of Disputes Act. The conference was to discuss all matters relating to employment and its conditions, with an exchange of ideas on procedures in handling matters between the

State and the African workers. Having agitated so long for government initiative on a minimum wage, one may have thought that SACTU would have welcomed this as a step in the right direction, but instead the meeting was condemned as that of a "sinister body" and one that had no meaning for African workers who demanded the same trade union rights as their fellow white workers.[33]

With this the campaign seemed once again bogged down in rhetoric and futility. Other than to approach employers organizations, little was done other than for individual unions to enter wage claims. As a result, the National Coordinating Committee intervened on behalf of the Congress Alliance to put more steam into the drive for "liberation." The Alliance knew, and the SACTU National Executive was told, that there could be no effective "industrial action" (i.e. stay-at-home strikes) without trade unions. The NCC was now planning an industrial action as part of a plan to force the South African government to call a new National Convention that would include all racial groups. Because of this they would assist SACTU in forming new industrial area committees, and would help strengthen SACTU's national organizing committees at the same time. The reason for the offer was that the NCC felt that SACTU was too tardy in putting effective cooperation into the campaigns, the NCC would therefore itself have to ensure that things worked out well.

The main problems were those of organization, and the NCC proposed a number of changes. They believed that the campaign secretary should be a full-time paid official, whose duty it would be to see to it that directives were sent to all areas and leaflets and propaganda material issued. These suggestions were opposed by the SACTU national executive who felt it an insult that SACTU committees should need to be strengthened with outsiders. "What were required were doers, not additional planners," the minutes of the meeting said, and continued that they did not need people to tell them what to do.[34] Various opinions were expressed at the executive meeting: one member wanted only trade unionists appointed to an Action Committee; another said that the Action Committee should be responsible only to the Management Committee of SACTU and not to the NCC, for SACTU's identity could not otherwise be preserved. Significantly, the Chairman and another prominent SACTU officer supported the NCC and assured the NEC of SACTU that there was no danger of SACTU losing its identity. Finally, agreement was reached. SACTU's aim was to see that industrial action was carried out in the best possible way with maximum cooperation of the NCC in the issuance of leaflets and other materials. The leaflets would be issued in SACTU's name and be fully discussed with the Action Committee. As for the £1-a-Day Campaign, the Minister of Labour was to be asked in introduce legislation for a national minimum wage of £1-a-day, and SACTU would draw up a draft Bill to be circulated to selected members of Parliament.

The plan to organize industries and establish area committees was meantime put into work. A special Action Subcommittee was appointed, had met, and was drafting an industrial "blueprint" showing exactly where organizers were needed. A Trade Union Week was to be launched, with placard demonstrations at bus stops and other places where workers congregated, urging them to join their unions. In addition a house-to-house campaign was to enable members to contact unorganized workers and recruit them for SACTU unions. The culmination was to be Workers' Conferences in each province.

The plan implied improvement in the workings of SACTU, but nothing much had changed. Machinery to carry the Action Subcommittee plan into effect was certainly discussed, and an effort was made to show that fears that SACTU would be bypassed were unreal. The campaign would be a SACTU campaign, leaders stressed, SACTU would take the initiative. One day a week would be set aside to organize the campaign and the Acting General-Secretary of SACTU was to be paid a salary so that he could devote himself to this work.[35] Unfortunately for the campaign, men of words far outnumbered men of deeds. When the Management Committee again met in January 1962, the Action Committee had not started to function effectively. All efforts, they decided then, were to be directed toward making this a militant campaign of industrial organization and action, and yet the Action Committee had not even then completed its blueprint.[36] Because of this the campaign had again to be postponed. The Management Committee now recommended the campaign be launched forth on February 7, 1962, which was now to be the "Day of International Solidarity with the Workers and People of South Africa."

Intensive work was needed if this campaign was to be successful, and a National Organizing Conference, or rather a series of such conferences were planned. Clearly February 7 was only to herald the opening shots of the campaign, and so the organizing conferences were to hold their meetings on February 25 in all provinces and the Action Committee was to be responsible for all propaganda materials for the individual areas. These conferences, the Workers' Conferences, were to be tied to the £1-a-Day Campaign once more and with recognition of trade unions, both issues being, by now, old SACTU warhorses. The usual badges were to be offered for sale, the usual leaflets distributed, and the same slogans offered in somewhat different variants. One of the aims of these affairs was to make SACTU better known, for, despite all efforts of the past, SACTU was still obscure and its treasury reflected this obscurity.

The Solidarity Day and the £1-a-Day Campaign were now completely intertwined. This should not, however, be construed as the only campaigns being actively engaged in at that time. The Action Committee were involved in campaigns about rents, passes for women, unemployment, the organization of the unemployed, and other things which, worthy in themselves, would have taxed a stronger organization than SACTU in fact was. Bearing all this in mind, what can be said of the two campaigns under discussion: the campaign for a national convention and that for £1-a-Day?

A bill for a national minimum wage, was duly drafted and read to the Johannesburg Local Committee, and perhaps to the other Local Committees as well. A delegation from the Cape Western Province Local Committee was to present a copy of the bill to the Minister of Labour, while a copy of the bill was to be sent to Mrs. Helen Suzman, the Member of Parliament for the Progressive Party.[37] Earlier a member of the Managment Committee reported having spoken with Mrs. Suzman personally, who had told him that the session was very crowded with legislation pending and that the Progressive Party was moving a bill for the recognition of African trade unions. SACTU, not having been consulted by the Progressive Party—though there was no reason why they should have been—were disappointed and wrote to her to this effect at the same time as the copy of the bill was sent.

Mass agitation was begun with the February 7 campaign which was backed by the World Federation of Trade Unions. It was intended to promote the £1 a day issue and the other issues by linking

South African workers with those in other countries. Meantime discussions were initiated with the Local Committees, such as that of Durban, where a successful discussion was apparently held. Meetings with the Witwatersrand Local Committee also seem to have been promising. Other problems remained unresolved. Unions had been meeting in Cape Town, but because of the distance and lack of funds, no member of the Management Committee could visit them. The local committe would, therefore have to organize things itself, and this left the campaign in doubt. There were funds for a campaign organizer, and even for an assistant organizer, and leaflets could be printed, slogans painted on walls, and the help of the Congress Alliance enlisted.[38]

The Petering Out of the Pound-a-Day Campaign

The campaign had been prepared. It began with meetings in Durban which were, according to *New Age*, attended by from 2,000 to 3,000 persons.[39] Several meetings had been held at factory gates, according to the same source, and addressed by leading Congress luminaries. A spate of telegrams, addressed to the Minister of Labour, were sent off in support of the SACTU Bill. The planned placard demonstration was staged, and slogans chalked on walls in industrial areas. The police were there, and as usual confiscated placards and arrested their carriers. Eight of the volunteers for the campaign were taken to the headquarters of the Special Branch for questioning, but the demonstration continued. A protest of the arrests was staged on the steps of the Johannesburg City Hall, a favorite venue for open meetings, where the aims of the campaign were restated by Leon Levy, the SACTU President: they were "the recruitment into the trade union ranks of hundreds of thousands of workers." *New Age* extended the message: "The Workers' Rights Campaign, which began on Solidarity Day, February 7, must culminate in the total recruitment of all workers into the trade union movement. It must be the vehicle for the organized expression of the working people of this country in close alliance with all oppressed people for a new life. To achieve this every freedom fighter must roll up his sleeves and go into the field to bring the workers into the trade union movement."[40]

What was the outcome of all this heated action? The NCC, as

the coordinating committee of the Congress Alliance wished to
know of results. It approached SACTU for the numbers actually
enrolled as a result of the campaign. The Management Committee
of SACTU did not know.[41] They decided to ask the local committees, who apparently did not know either.

The government, in turn, refused either to recognize SACTU
or to pay the least attention to the bill it had drafted. The reply of
the Minister of Labour (through his Secretary—not directly) was
much to the point: "There are recognized trade union federations
which are representative of and entitled to speak for organized
workers in South Africa. The so-called S.A. Congress of Trade
Unions does not fall within this category and my Minister is not
prepared to discuss such matters with that organization."[42] This
was, as *New Age* pointed out, a departure. The Government had,
in the past, been willing to meet SACTU delegations. Meantime,
they maintained, the application blanks at the back of the leaflets
were pouring in and SACTU offices were kept busy just replying
to them.[43]

There was no follow-up of commensurate proportions, it would
seem, or if there was, it cannot be traced. This may be due to the
organizational problems mounting in SACTU itself. This seems
evidenced in a circular to all local committees, and affiliated unions
which, after commending the committees for their "wonderful
part" in organizing the workers, said that there was need for yet
more organization if the goal, that of organizing all unorganized
workers, was to be achieved. To further this end a conference of
all full-time secretaries and organizers was to meet in September
to exchange experiences and evolve methods for overcoming organizational difficulties in their areas.[44] Later that month another
circular was sent complaining of a "slackening off" in the trade
union movement and demanding a renewed effort under the
slogan: "Organize or Starve." The slackening was apparent from
the minutes of the Management Committee. At a meeting on September 1, 1962, the chairman pointed out that it was unnecessary
to discuss the £1-a-day campaign at length as affiliated unions had
been campaigning on this issue for some time. The only question
was whether it would be a good tactic to again flood employers organizations with minimum wage propaganda. This question was
mulled over, with agreement being reached in the end that this did

not accomplish a great deal. Agreement was also reached on another issue: as some factories were paying the equivalent of £1 a day, although there was no wage determination from the government, this should be publicized as a success of the campaign. In the end a resolution was adopted for issuance of a history of the "R2-a-Day Campaign," for the currency had been changed with the establishment of the South African republic by which the pound, the old currency, was replaced by a new one with Rands and cents replacing pounds and shillings. This change in the monetary unit lost the slogan its swing. The history was to be the work of three people, and while this was initiated the aborted Minimum Wage Bill would be withdrawn. The organization was, however, to produce more propaganda and this was to take the form of education for trade unionism.

What was left of the campaign which now seemed so deflated? Failure was never admitted, but the campaign had nonetheless failed. The Management Committee analyzed its lack of success as best as they could. Insufficient had been done to familiarize workers with the demand for a national minimum wage, and the mistake could be recovered in another series of meetings, which should be held on February 7, 1963. The local committees were to organize mass demonstrations and deputations to employers' organizations.[46] The campaign, on its usual lines, thus dragged on into 1963. Evidence becomes sparse after that, and there is little evidence of deputations having been sent in the way called for by the Management Committee. What is avilable as evidence is a circular from SACTU to the local committees, affiliated unions, and newspaper editors, which simply stated that the latest cost-of-living figures showed that the SACTU campaign had been right, and that the recently granted round of wage increases had proved beneficial as SACTU had predicted.[47] The International Day of Solidarity with the Workers and Peasants of South Africa seems to have been held; in Durban the meeting, according to the successor to *New Age*, *Spark*, being "packed with people crowding the aisles and even the platform" of the Bantu Social Center there. The usual set of demands were set out to be handed to employers.

More may have been done in the national minimum wage campaign, but if there was, there does not seem to be any chronicle of

it. Because of government pressure, and because of the increased
force brought to bear on SACTU by the police, few leaders of skill
and experience remained to mount campaigns, even had they
wished to do so. Each issue of *Spark* carried news of new police
raids on the offices of the newspaper and of SACTU in Durban
and Port Elizabeth.[48] The remaining public activity of SACTU,
subjected as it was to so many pressures, was confined to calls for
international support particularly from overseas labor bodies.
These appeals particularly concerned those SACTU leaders who
had been banned and deported or imprisoned.

Chapter VI

Friends, Rivals, and Foes

Successive South African governments had prided themselves on being "like granite" on matters of color. The Congress Alliance, of which SACTU was so much a part, realized that the rocklike front could not be broken from within South Africa alone. Allies had to be sought overseas, allies whose pressure on the South African government might induce change. For SACTU the forum was evident; it was to seek allies among the international communities of trades unions. They were to be enlisted, singly or collectively, to press the South African government either to slow the *apartheid* policies, or at least to vouchsafe relief from the many attacks that the government initiated against SACTU and its allies. The two ideas were, of course, closely related. If the government could be induced or persuaded to desist from attacks on the Congress Alliance and on SACTU as a member of that alliance, then the Alliance could, perhaps, itself bring sufficient pressure to bear to change the policies of the South African government.

The role of unions in politics was made clear in a press interview by Walter Sisulu, a key officer in the African National Congress.[1] In the interview Sisulu defined the task of the Liberation Movement in South Africa as that of organizing the workers into a trade union movement. This task was not for union officials alone. "Apart from the economic plight of the oppressed people," he said, "which can only be improved by organized labor, the struggle for liberation and against discrimination largely depends on the organization of workers into the trade union movement. The trade union movement has, as its primary task, to educate and lead the workers for their full participation in the struggle for political rights." He linked the struggle he described closely with the liberation movement in Africa: "The first Pan African Conference which met in Africa in 1958 raised the interdependence of the liberation and trade union movements. This finally led to a decision by the same body to form an All African Trade Union Federation to which the South African Congress of Trade Unions is affiliated."

With their connection established with the Pan African Conference an effort was made to enlist African support, and in 1959 letters had been written to over forty trade union bodies on that continent. In addition, the SACTU executive entered into correspondence with Tom Mboya of Kenya and went as far as inviting him to open the fourth annual conference of SACTU, but Mboya was denied a visa by the South African government.

Support in Africa was insufficient if the aims of SACTU were to be met. The question was also one of enlisting the support of such bodies as embraced unions on all continents, and of these there were two: the International Confederation of Free Trade Unions (ICFTU) and the World Federation of Trade Unions (WFTU). Of these the ICFTU was largely a body of the political "West" while the WFTU was largely an instrument of the Communist "East." SACTU was to attempt a difficult balancing act between the two, in which it would not be particularly successful, at least as far as the ICFTU was concerned.

In addition to these bodies SACTU was in touch with organizations abroad such as the Trades Union Congress of Great Britain, the AFL-CIO, and the Australian Trades and Labour Council.[2] The number of contacts were broadened over the years, and contributions were solicited from and given by, trade unions in a variety of countries. These, of course, were always a welcome addition to the perennially depleted Congress coffers. By 1961, for example, SACTU was in correspondence with twenty trade union centers in Africa and fifty unions in Britain, Europe, the United States, Latin America, Asia, Australia, and New Zealand.[3] So extensive indeed did these contacts become that by 1962 SACTU

was thinking of establishing a foreign department.[4] Because of
its extent it would be impossible and indeed unfruitful to follow
this correspondence through. Much of it was to consist of appeals,
covering letters for mailings of propaganda, and general information. As a result this chapter will be largely limited to SACTU's
dealings with ICFTU, WFTU, the International Labour Organization (ILO), and the AATUF (which is believed to be an offshoot
of WFTU).

SACTU, WFTU, and AATUF

Few of the contacts that SACTU established are as interesting
as its connection with WFTU. The mystery of SACTU's affiliation was not cleared up in the time it was most active: was SACTU
affiliated to WFTU or not? The question was important because
affiliation to what was known as a Communist organization would
have affected SACTU's status in dealing with other bodies at a time
of the Cold War. It applied particularly to the ICFTU which
viewed WFTU with unconcealed antagonism.

The matter came to the surface when officials of ICFTU visited
South Africa in 1957. In an interview with the President and the
General-Secretary of SACTU, they were told that SACTU had
applied for affiliation to WFTU.[5] There was additional evidence
to this effect. On a later visit by ICFTU officials they taxed the
SACTU leaders with being a WFTU affiliate and cited a memorandum by the SACTU General-Secretary, Leslie Masina, to this
effect. The SACTU officials, however, asserted that they were *not*
affiliated to WFTU.[6] Despite this denial, there is some evidence
that WFTU either had become an affiliate or was applying for
affiliation. There was a report in the SACTU newssheet, for instance, that Leslie Masina was a member of the WFTU executive.
The repeated slurs on the ICFTU in *Workers' Unity* and *New Age*
coupled with the elaborate praise heaped on WFTU add weight
to the notion. Later, after its formation, the All African Trade
Union Federation (AATUF) was singled out for praise and con-
trasted with the "imperialist" ICFTU.

The question is why did SACTU affiliate with the WFTU? There
was little that the latter could give that was practical, other than

encouragement. There may have been funds transferred to individuals in SACTU or to the clandestine Communist Party but this does not emerge from SACTU's balance sheets. An "International Committee for Solidarity with the Workers and People of South Africa" was set up, which may have had some responsibility in the £1-a-Day Campaign discussed in the last chapter.[7]

The first Pan African Conference was held in Accra, Ghana, in December 1958, and there the idea of an all-African trade union organization was proposed. A period of maneouver followed and out of it came a Pan African Trade Union Conference, held in Casablanca, September 8, 1959. A month later, in October, the Executive Committee of the Conference of African Peoples (the formal name of the Pan African Conference mentioned above) met in Accra and resolved to call for "the immediate convocation of a conference of all *representative* African trade unions, with the aim of creating a united African trade union movement."[8]

At this point the ICFTU seems to have entered the picture in earnest. They decided to hold their second regional conference in Lagos in November 1959, to establish an organization for Africa in their turn. The African nationalists who had met at the Pan African conference saw this (or purported to see it) as an attempt at foreign intervention in African affairs. The Ghana TUC withdrew from the ICFTU and simultaneously announced the coming Pan African Trade Union Conference to be held in Accra in November 1959. This conference was, thus, aimed to take place at the same time as the conference in Lagos. In this way the critical split in African trade unionism was made public.[9] In broadest terms, things shaped so that the pro-Western unions found themselves in Lagos and the pro-Eastern in Accra.

SACTU was to play a significant part at Accra because of its status as representative of oppressed African workers who had the sympathy of all delegates. It was, thus, one of the bodies elected to the standing committee of representatives of nineteen unions charged with preparing the constituent conference of what was to be AATUF, to be held in Casablanca in 1960.

Before moving ahead with the story one thing needs be made clear, and that is that the hidden hand of the WFTU was manifest at least in part. The conference in Accra decided that AATUF, when founded, would be independent of the various rival coordinating bodies, but, a *New Age* report has it, "the delegates were unanimous in the opinion that non-alignment on the part of the proposed federation did not mean isolation from the general labor movement. On the contrary the Federation will cooperate with all trade union centers friendly to it."[10] But in scheduling the conference to found AATUF at the same time as the ICFTU Lagos conference, it had already declared itself hostile to the latter, and the way was open for WFTU. In addition, the ICFTU was sharply attacked in Accra by delegations from Gambia, Nigeria, Uganda, *and South Africa*—the last being, of course, none other than SACTU. Some unions, despite this atmosphere, managed to steer between the poles. Kenya serves as an illustration, for Tom Mboya went to Lagos and the left-winger, Odinga Oginga, went to Accra. The major resolutions were the usual ones: to intensify the struggle against "colonialism" especially in Algeria, the Congo, Central Africa, and South Africa.

SACTU seems to have had great hopes for the effectiveness of AATUF judging from its public utterances. It obviously hoped for a strong stand on a world boycott of South Africa, to be brought about by African pressure and which might spread to other countries eager to do business with the "new Africa."[11]

The attempt to focus international pressure was continued in a later conference in Ghana intended to give life to the International Trade Union Committee for Solidarity with the South African Workers and People, held in Accra at the end of July 1961.[12] This conference was attended by representatives of a galaxy of "democratic" trade unions, China, the German Democratic Republic (East Germany), Cuba, Brazil, the French Communist trade unions, and the WFTU. The attendance of East Germany is interesting, for this is the country which had been entrusted in the Soviet bloc with South African affairs. The meeting was addressed by Moses Mabhida, Vice-President of SACTU and former acting President of the ANC in Natal, who had gone abroad to denounce the South African government's *apartheid* policies which, in his words, "had the blessing of the United States and Britain." According to *New Age*, the committee made a "stirring call to workers" to force an end to *apartheid*, and that this should be done by isolating South Africa and maximum pressure to topple the regime should be brought by other countries.[13]

The Solidarity Committee did not go smoothly, and SACTU soon found that coordinating the activities of its overseas representatives and the organization at home was very difficult. This resulted, in part, from the absence of proper channels of communication. Some national centers and individual unions wrote to South Africa directly, others wrote to the overseas representatives of SACTU. Complications increased because overseas representatives did not always inform SACTU regularly, and as a result SACTU headquarters did not at any particular time know the location of their foreign representatives.[14] These difficulties notwithstanding, the Solidarity Committee was behind the February 7 campaigns which have been discussed, and this did give the Solidarity Committee a purpose.[15] It was at least more useful to SACTU than the AATUF.[16]

AATUF was launched in May, 1961, in the fever of excitement generated by the prospective independence of the entire African continent and the emergence of a number of African states. Few could tell then that so many hopes would wither, and AATUF is one of these hopes. As a result of the confidence it felt in AATUF then, SACTU initiated the idea of a Conference of Agricultural Workers to be held in Bechuanaland. The main purpose seems to have been to give members of the AATUF an opportunity to meet members of SACTU. This suggestion fell flat, and the Secretary of AATUF, John Tettegah, instead invited SACTU to send delegates to the Ghana Agricultural Workers' Conference in March 1962, but the time was too short to permit this. Consequently the overseas representative of SACTU was to be sent to Ghana and discuss things with Tettegah, but nothing seems to have come of this either. SACTU soon came to recognize that there was little to be gained from AATUF. The General-Secretary of SACTU reported in 1961 that AATUF had "not yet managed to function properly and it was possible that the office bearers were not highly experienced."[17] Nevertheless SACTU persisted in its efforts to establish a regional office of AATUF in Johannesburg. In spite of these drawbacks, SACTU tried AATUF again, this time with the suggestion that a conference be held on migrant mine workers, the conference to be attended by workers and heads of states. By November 1961, no progress had been made, although contact had been established with the Mine Workers' Union of Tanganyika. Research into the feasibility of holding a conference of mine workers in Johannesburg or in another suitable place was mooted. This, of course, was even less likely to be permitted, and in the event was never held.

Neither the contacts established with AATUF nor those with WFTU seem to have established anything of apparent value. Of course secret arrangements may have been made either with the latter or through the latter with other Eastern Bloc organizations. Otherwise support seems to have been scanty. Some funds did come from individual unions and from WFTU itself but most support seems to have been ideological. SACTU found itself largely in agreement with WFTU and its objectives. Its relationship with ICFTU was different. Not only were ideological questions at issue, but so also was the question of which coordinating center in South Africa was to control the African trade unions. Being fought on so many levels, SACTU's conflict with the ICFTU is extremely involved.

SACTU, the ICFTU, and the ILO

The World Federation of Trade Unions was originally intended to embrace all trade unions, but Soviet dominance over that body was established early and most of the trade unions in Western countries left it to form ICFTU, and developments in ICFTU led in turn to great American influence over that body. As Ioan Davies puts it: "between 1953 and 1957 the Americans worked behind the scenes to erode the influence of Britain in African affairs by increasing their own independent activity throughout Africa."[18] This was owing, in part, to traditional American anticolonialism, and also to the fear that the emerging nations would come under Soviet influence unless the "imperialist" powers were displaced. This, indeed, is not the only occasion that the crusading zeal of the Americans ran parallel to that of the Soviets. American influence in the ICFTU and Soviet control of WFTU ensured that both hoped to influence African unions by demonstrative sympathy for African claims and an equally demonstrative hostility to "imperialism." The Soviet Union sought to exorcise the same devils and to enshrine the same pantheon of saints, although from different perspectives.

From the American viewpoint, espousing African claims and

championing anti-imperalism ensured that African unions could affiliate with ICFTU without automatically earning the sobriquets of "pimps," "sellouts," or "stooges of imperialism"—terms freely bandied by African nationalists at that time. ICFTU, in its turn, made substantial concessions to African nationalism and made African causes its own.[19] This was, of course, not a bad thing in itself, but it did involve ICFTU deeply in questions of southern Africa.

The policies of the South African government seemed an unbearable affront to an Africa rapidly moving to independence and to new dignity and status. It was, in a sense, a continuous and living denial of all the Africans had won for themselves. The ICFTU had, therefore, to take a definite stand on this issue, and the stand it was to take was predictable. The men of ICFTU were of liberal mind, and it would be unfair to present this decision as one of pure pragmatism and self-interest. They had, after all, passed a resolution condemning South Africa's policies in 1952, before African pressures mounted, and had lodged complaints about South Africa at the ILO in 1954 and 1956 at a time when they were a great deal more cautious about British policies in Kenya.[20] Nonetheless, the directors of ICFTU could with justification claim that South Africa had always been of serious concern to them. At this time these gestures gained much political capital for the ICFTU, for African politicians had at the outset an almost touching faith in the abilities of international organizations to get the South African government to change its course. Time was to change that, but the readiness with which the ICFTU grasped the South African nettle no doubt impressed many of the doubting.

Although they had shown deep interest in the country, South Africa had not been visited by officials of the ICFTU before the year 1957. Then its president, M. Becu, visited Johannesburg and met, *inter alia*, with the TUCSA executive. Through this initiative, an ICFTU team of two men, Sir Tom O'Brien and P. H. de Jonge, visited South Africa from June 8 to June 17, 1957. Contacts with TUCSA had, however, been extended and cemented before these men left Europe. They were briefed by R. Bennett of TUCSA who at the time was attending an ILO conference in Geneva, and they were met on arrival in Johannesburg by members of the TUCSA executive. They, therefore, came to South Africa well-disposed toward TUCSA, and what they saw on their visit confirmed them in that view.

During their brief stay they visited and spoke with most of the leaders of significant trade unions and important political figures. Having come to learn about the general situation in the country as it affected the labor movement, they made good use of their time.

After interviewing and discussing problems with all trade union coordinating bodies, including SACTU, they concluded that TUCSA was the most powerful, progressive, and potentially most likely to produce results. They felt it should be supported in its efforts to organize African unions. African unions could not affiliate to TUCSA as matters stood, but they were able to obtain assistance through a TUCSA liaison office which, ICFTU felt, could provide a channel for the moral, material, and organizational assistance African trade unions needed. TUCSA would do little on its own, the ICFTU representatives felt, unless there was a permanent ICFTU representative on the spot. He would contribute to the primary task of assisting African unions while at the same time urging TUCSA to greater militancy. Lastly, they believed that ICFTU could do much to educate world opinion on South Africa as no coherent picture emerged from the sporadic press reports on South Africa overseas.[21]

When their turn came to interview the ICFTU team, SACTU did its utmost to inject drama into the event. Some of this was more than showmanship, for both Leon Levy and Leslie Masina were involved in the Treason Trial and were forbidden attendance at political meetings. The two ICFTU officials were met at their hotel, whisked in a car to a house on the outskirts of Johannesburg, and informed that as the executives of SACTU had been forbidden political intercourse, this was a "social gathering." The "gathering" lasted well into the night, and in the end the Africans who had attended expressed fear of returning to their homes in the townships because they had contravened the pass laws. "One by one they slipped off, some living far away having to take a taxi, which we [the ICU representatives] paid for as they had not sufficient money for such an extravagance."

The ICFTU team seems to have had high hopes of SACTU at first, as SACTU was the only trade union center admitting unions

of all races to affiliation as equals. These hopes were soon dashed.
The discussion revealed deep differences between the ICFTU
representatives and the SACTU executive. For instance, they
reported that though Leon Levy was the only white man present
from SACTU he dominated all others. He took the lead in all
discussion, restating African disabilities and their difficulties in
organizing unions, and gave this as the reason that SACTU was
so intensely political. The ICFTU delegates, in their report, stated
that this would not have mattered had SACTU "a strong trade
union position" and if it knew its own mind. They believed, however, that other forces aimed at making SACTU their tool. They
did not identify these "forces," but given ICFTU's orientation, this
is hardly a serious omission. They feared that SACTU, if it had not
already fallen victim to Communist blandishments, would soon
do so. They pointed out to their executive that SACTU had admitted affiliation to WFTU and had appealed for funds to them
as well as to ICFTU. They seemed strangely incapable of grasping
the difference between the two international bodies, the ICFTU
team said, and kept appealing for "fraternal ties" between these
bodies in "the interest of world peace"—something that struck
ICFTU as ignorant or bizarre. They were indifferent when attitudes
to the Hungarian revolt were cited as an instance, and the ICFTU
delegates came away with the impression that SACTU was led
by a few people well aware of their direction and that the others
followed more or less meekly. However, hope was not entirely to
be abandoned for SACTU, and the delegates thought that should
an ICFTU delegate be on the spot he could investigate whether
SACTU could be weaned away from "undesirable influences"
or whether this was impossible.

The lines hardened in time. SACTU was unwise enough to
invite the second team from the ICFTU, to come in 1959 to their
conference, and the invitation mentioned that WFTU had also
been invited. The ICFTU reply was certainly to the point: "We
do not know how extensive your contacts with WFTU have been
in the past, nor what reply you have received from them to your
present invitation. . . . It would . . . be totally inconsistent and
quite impossible for us to be represented on the same platform
with a WFTU delegation."

The ICFTU representatives, once in South Africa, attended
the TUCSA conference where they were pleased to find a new

determination to organize workers of all races, a resolution to this effect having been adopted at the conference. The decision was to set up an independent Interracial Organizing Committee under the auspices of TUCSA and with their financial backing. The pitfall of having this become just another TUCSA committee was avoided by having the committee independent, for now cooperation could not be withheld by other unions on the grounds of TUCSA domination. However, once again the ICFTU delegation felt that it would be insufficient to let matters rest with TUCSA, and that the ICFTU had to lend its prestige to the venture and to act as a unifying influence. They again urged the appointment of an ICFTU representative in South Africa, and indicated that Miss Dulcie Hartwell would be an excellent choice. She was the General Secretary of TUCSA and was resigning her post for personal reasons. Her ability and experience could well be put to use by ICFTU in a year that might well mark a turning point in South African trade union history. The time when the greatest possible number of established trade unions were prepared to help the less privileged workers seemed at hand.

Clearly much of this has to be carefully evaluated, for unless the ICFTU team were remarkably naive, and there are no grounds for assuming this to be so, they could hardly have expected that a committee organized, staffed, and financed by TUCSA could be considered an independent one. Control would obviously continue to rest with TUCSA with ICFTU backing. SACTU, which looked on organizing Africans as its special sphere, could hardly remain without affront. Their complaint that the independent committee was directed against them would, then, seem to have some foundation.

The differences between the views of the ICFTU delegation and the SACTU executive emerged in the later meeting between them. This meeting, arranged in the same melodramatic manner as the first, in which the ICFTU delegation were furtively secreted to another "social gathering" in a private house, exposed these differences. Having left the TUCSA conference early in order to hold discussions with the SACTU Management Committee, they found that SACTU officials considered themselves "cold shouldered" by the ICFTU delegation because they attended the TUCSA conference and not that of SACTU.

Indeed, both sides seemed strained. The ICFTU team found

it "difficult to get a straight answer to a straight question" from Leon Levy who, with Leslie Masina, dominated the meeting on the SACTU side. On its side, ICFTU delegates were concerned with SACTU's relationship with the Congress Alliance and WFTU. SACTU, on the other hand, was incensed at TUCSA's intrusion into what they saw as its bailiwick. When the ICFTU representatives raised the question of WFTU, Levy told them that SACTU wanted to cooperate with anyone who was willing to aid them, and that it followed a neutralist line between the two great international trade union bodies. Levy contended that despite all the evidence to the contrary, SACTU was not affiliated to WFTU. He also stressed that SACTU had taken up the organization of unorganized workers long before TUCSA, and had faced government persecution when the white unions had been indifferent or hostile. Now that they had established a number of unions, TUCSA was trying to induce them to break their ties with SACTU.

There was an ideological as well as a practical component to their hostility. The question was who was to control the African trade unions and for what political purposes were they to be employed. Clearly, if TUCSA gained control, the African unions would be diverted to pure union activity and would not be a weapon in the hands of the Congress Alliance. The unions were, therefore, specially important to SACTU. As the ICFTU team saw it, SACTU did not enjoy any special prerogative in organizing Africans, and its claim was just a pretext for noncooperation. The SACTU members also wanted all assistance for African unions channeled through their organization, a demand that the ICFTU delegates regarded as completely unrealistic. SACTU could not be allowed a monopoly in organizing African unions, the more so because of the power of TUCSA and the many non-white unions that already were affiliated to it. The Independent Committee, when formed, would dilute SACTU's influence while harnessing their experience. SACTU officers would be permitted to join the committee but only as individuals.

SACTU officials saw through the scheme and complained to the General Secretary of ICFTU in a letter sent to all African affiliates of ICFTU, to other African organizations, and to the press.[22] The sense of their letter was that the ICFTU team which had visited South Africa had connived with TUCSA to set up an independent committee to organize workers. The ICFTU delegation had, the letter stated, made it clear to SACTU that they had not come to consult them in a matter in which they [SACTU] had had some experience but to tell them of the plan details of which had already been settled. "They brusquely brushed aside our comments," the letter says, "and we gained the impression that 'we could take it or leave it.' " It seemed that although the unions affiliated to SACTU were to be invited to the formation of the Independent Committee, SACTU as a coordinating body was not to be invited. SACTU, they said, had been prejudged on the basis of biased information, and they believed that the ICFTU team had been influenced by TUCSA.

The problem was aggravated by the appearance of FOFATUSA in 1959, shortly after the departure of the ICFTU delegation, as an African trade union coordinating center. SACTU naturally concluded that this was cause and effect. They saw it as an attempt by TUCSA, with the blessing of ICFTU, to gain control of the African unions, and contended "this unfortunate and divisive move has been taken after consultation with, and with the blessing of, your representatives, acting in your [ICFTU's] name." They adduced as evidence that the ICFTU representatives had demanded that SACTU sever its connection with the ANC, and felt this to be based on a misconception of the connection between the two organizations. The organizations were independent, they insisted, and the two were not affiliated in any way. They had only joined in affirming a common program, the "Freedom Charter." They pointed to the fact that though no conditions for membership existed in any SACTU affiliate, the ANC had urged its members to join unions. They drew attention to a statement by Chief Luthuli, the ANC President-General, who had said: "No worker is a good member [of the ANC] unless he also is a trade unionist." The ANC was therefore a source of strength to SACTU and of great value in recruiting African workers.

Although SACTU felt aggrieved, there was much that was spurious in its contentions. SACTU blamed the ICFTU delegation for having encouraged the establishment of FOFATUSA. The delegation in a confidential report to their headquarters stressed that they had advised the independent African unions [those outside of SACTU] against forming a trade union center of their own. While

it seems most likely that TUCSA officials had played a role in in-
fluencing ICFTU people against SACTU this was not decisive.
What was decisive was, probably, the political affiliations of
SACTU and the increasing Communist influence both there and in
the ANC. The separation of the organizations was also more apparent than real as the NCC and memberships of SACTU officers in the
other Congresses made claims to autonomy seem somewhat thin.
The case of Solomon Mbanjwa, to be treated in more detail later,
can serve as an illustration. Mbanjwa was, according to his testimony, at the same time an active ANC branch organizer and a full-
time union organizer for SACTU. He resigned from the ANC in
1960, when it was declared an illegal organization, but rejoined it
when it was reestablished underground. He was appointed to the
Regional Command of the sabotage organization, Umkonto we
Sizwe, when this was set up by the ANC and the Communist Party,
of which he also was a member. At this time he was also a member
of SACTU and still acting as a trade union organizer.[23] The individual members of the different organizations in the Congress Alliance often held overlapping appointments which made closer organizational ties needless.[24]

A number of influential people were enlisted in aid of SACTU in
its argument with the ICFTU headquarters. Among these the most
prominent was undoubtedly the Bishop of Johannesburg, Ambrose
Reeves. Bishop Reeves was a man of very liberal views who found
the policies of the South African government repugnant. He was
sympathetic to the Congress Alliance, and because of this wrote to a
member of the ICFTU delegation, now back in Brussels, urging
him to use his influence in favor of SACTU, saying that the establishment of the Independent Organizing Committee might "however
inadverdently . . . aggravate an already difficult situation." Having
been aware of the need for organizing African workers for years, he
(the Bishop) was saddened that TUCSA had done nothing for so
long. "One can only rejoice that this body is concerning themselves
with this matter at this late hour, even though I would hope that
ICFTU would still realise that the best contribution that both
TUC[SA] and themselves could make is through the existing organization of SACTU."[25] Although never afraid of supporting unpop-
ular causes, for he was a man of courage and conviction, the Bishop
was a man of little political sophistication. Politics is, unhappily,

seldom a happy place for the saintly. The Bishop was ready to accept the thesis that because the South African government tarred all its opponents with the Communist brush it meant few of its opponents actually *were* Communists. ICFTU, rightly from its standpoint, held differently.

As a result the correspondence that followed between SACTU and the ICFTU was marked by estrangement and exasperation on both sides. ICFTU claimed that the exclusion of SACTU was not the purpose of any organizing drive and that the precise form of aid to be given had not been decided. SACTU, on the other hand, maintained that the "establishment under the S.A. Trade Union Council inspiration of an anti-SACTU Federation of African Trade Unions immediately after the departure of Messrs. Millard and de Jonge [the ICFTU representatives] had naturally given rise to quite different impressions. . . . If you have been misunderstood, it would appear that TUC also misunderstood you, and it is to them that you must make your position clear." Their original fears, SACTU went on, had been confirmed by events, such as a speech by Miss Dulcie Hartwell on October 3, 1959, when FOFATUSA was formally established. It was to organize the same industries in which SACTU was active, and to work not only among unorganized workers but among those already organized as well. This could only be interpreted as a move against SACTU and against the ANC. The President of FOFATUSA, Mr. Nyaose, and the other FOFATU-SA officials, were members of the Pan African Congress which had split off from the ANC and was now its rival. There was a strong impression extant that FOFATUSA had ICFTU backing, the more so as Mrs. Lucy Mvubelo, a vice-president of FOFATUSA, was ICFTU representative of working women at the ILO in Geneva.

There are some arguments to be made on both sides. If the ICFTU had insisted on SACTU breaking its ties to the Congress Alliance and the ANC, it did seem strange that they were willing to countenance the obvious ties between FOFATUSA and the PAC. There are some grounds for believing that as SACTU was obviously bound closely to WFTU, the ICFTU wanted a trade union federation of Africans bound to it in as important an area as South Africa. SACTU, on the other hand, chose to see the formation of FOFATU-SA as a plot hatched between TUCSA and ICFTU to gain control of the African unions. SACTU, as a "transmission belt" of the Communists in South Africa was important to them, and they resented the threat that FOFATUSA represented. Of course, there is yet another explanation, both ANC and PAC needed a base among the African masses. PAC had evidence, before it was banned along with the ANC in 1960, that there was considerable support for its free-wheeling African nationalism among African workers. They may, in turn, have envisioned the possibility of a "transmission belt," but one linking the African workers to PAC. It is, of course, quite impossible to say which of these theories, if any of them, are the true ones.

SACTU grew even more annoyed as they perceived evidence that ICFTU was financing the new organization sponsored by TUCSA. *New Age* reported a two-day conference of the Africa Bureau held in London at which Millard, one of the ICFTU team, spoke, and told the audience that the ICFTU planned to spend £30,000 in South Africa to assist in the organization of African unions. A condition was that they organize through the independent committee to be established through TUCSA. He made it plain, the report states, that unions working through SACTU were not to receive assistance.[26] Again, this shows the ICFTU's perception of the South African scene.

SACTU now sought an opportunity to "expose" the ICFTU and felt that the best venue would be the African Regional Conference of ICFTU to be held in October, 1960. They had been invited to attend on the initiative of Jack Purvis who had visited South Africa as regional officer of ICFTU. As neither the SACTU Vice-President nor the two deputies selected to attend could get passports from the government, they could not appear in person. After consulting with the Secretary of the AATUF preparatory committe, Tettegah, the SACTU executive sent a letter to the organizers of the conference, all ICFTU affiliates in Africa, and to the preparatory committee of the AATUF.[27] The circular letter contained much of the argument already discussed above and does not need further discussion. It does not seem to have changed any minds.

After this incident the relationship between SACTU and ICFTU became one in which SACTU included the ICFTU in the pleas it sent to various bodies for international pressure for the banned leaders of SACTU. Other than this, understandably, the relationship of the organizations remained distant.

As the ILO was relatively free of ideological bias, both the Communist-bloc and Western nations being represented, SACTU established a considerably warmer relationship with it.

Among the issues concerning SACTU and on which they wanted ILO action was the inclusion of SACTU in the South African delegation or the entire exclusion of South Africa from the ILO. It began, apparently, with the second annual conference of SACTU in which it was resolved to press for inclusion in 1957. A letter protesting SACTU exclusion from the fortieth session of the ILO was, therefore, forwarded to the permanent representative of WFTU at the ILO headquarters in Geneva.[28] This remained without effect for the time being. Nonetheless, protest over this matter was an annual affair with SACTU. Thus, for instance, an objection to their exclusion from the forty-second ILO conference was lodged with the latter organization but was overruled. The result was that SACTU determined to lodge still stronger protests at exclusion in years following, and this issue became a hardy perennial.[29] The emphasis was changed in 1959 when Viola Hashe of the African Clothing Workers' Union and Moses Mabhida were to go to Switzerland to argue against the seating of the official South African delegation to ILO.[30] Now the years of protest seem to have had an effect, for ILO decided to insist on the South African government consulting SACTU before appointing the workers' delegate and adviser. SACTU decided to give this decision the broadest publicity abroad and awaited the result.[31] However, when the credentials of the South African delegation came up at the ILO conference in 1960, they were accepted. The effort thus seems to have been no more than a *success d'estime*.

More significant was the ILO decision to hold its first African Regional Conference in Lagos on December 1, 1960. The Management Committee of SACTU selected three delegates to this conference but they were, as usual, refused passports. Instead a telegram was sent to the chairman of the conference deploring this act of the government. There seemed little else that they could do, but events turned out differently. The Management Committee met a K. Descan of the Printing Workers' Union of Mauritius, who was workers' delegate to the ILO Conference in Lagos. After a discussion with him, in which they set out their case, he agreed to raise the matter of SACTU participation. The South African government having refused to send any delegates of its own, the nonparticipation of the country in the conference was also to be raised. This apparently must have had an effect for ILO notified SACTU of the date of their 45th session of June, 1961, and the Management Committee of SACTU at once wrote the Secretary of Labour asking that they be consulted in the choice of the workers' delegate, and a copy of this letter was forwarded to ILO.[32] The government, as expected, refused to consult SACTU and sent two delegates, one for the government and one for the workers to Geneva in the usual way. This time the ILO Credentials Committee again declined to recommend the invalidation of their credentials, merely reiterating the plea to the South African government to consult with SACTU in future in the matter of delegates.[33] Things were not to remain unchalleged, for in 1961 the Nigerian delegation moved the expulsion of South Africa from the ILO, but this was ruled unconstitutional. It was, thus, not until 1964 that effective action was made possible when the ILO constitution was amended by a majority vote. The amendment specified the suspension of countries from membership that were found by the United Nations to be consistently pursuing a policy of racial discrimination. After this the South African government withdrew from ILO.

There were many, however, who whatever their views on apartheid, regretted this step on the part of the ILO. TUCSA continued to send observers to ILO conferences and reported encountering increasing goodwill. Indeed it was their view, in 1967, that relatively minor concessions by the South African government, particularly with regard to labor legislation, might well ensure a sympathetic reception to an application for readmission. The South African government has not, to this time, granted these concessions.[34]

In addition to pressure for the admission of SACTU delegates and the expulsion of South Africa, SACTU sent a mass of memoranda, press statements, newspaper clippings, and articles to the ILO through the WFTU representative. However, as with ICFTU, the government struck harder and harder at SACTU, and the main correspondence became pleas for pressure on behalf of banned or banished leaders. Indeed, except for the spread of publicity abroad, it seems that SACTU had largely ceased functioning by 1963. Its long sustained efforts had, however, not been entirely without result.

Chapter VII

SACTU and TUCSA
The Continuing Conflict

Great as was the concern of SACTU with international influence, its main concerns were domestic, and its conflict with the ICFTU centered on the domestic issue of which coordinating center was to organize African unions. The matter was academic in a sense, for there were a number of African unions outside of SACTU and always had been. But if SACTU could have won international recognition as the organizer of African unions, this would have meant much in prestige at home and abroad. The international influence of TUCSA, in turn, meant that the continuing differences between the two union centers had both a national and an international dimension.

At home, therefore, SACTU sought to establish a network of factory committees and a mass following among African workers in particular, although its emphasis was multiracial, and it viewed anything that came between it and this objective as suspicious and hostile. As a result the principal conflict with other unions was not between SACTU and, say, the conservative Co-Ordinating Council of South African Trade Unions but with the most liberal, TUCSA. TUCSA, which had a long record of interest in African workers was to be both a target for attack and at different times a prospective partner for united action.

One of the major problems of South Africa in the 1950s and the 1960s—a problem that remains today—was the growing numbers of non-whites working in industry. White workers were leaving the ranks of the "blue collars" and moving to white collar work and even to executive and supervisory positions. Given the limited numbers of whites available, their places had to be taken by Coloureds, Indians, and Africans. The influx of large numbers of men of different races into the work force raised the question of the future of trade unions. The TUCSA constitution was such that membership was limited to registered trade unions, and this meant essentially white, Coloured, and Indian unions. But the growing African labor force could not be ignored. African preponderance in certain industries was already such that the bargaining power of white unions could be adversely affected. In addition, the advent of increasingly sophisticated machinery meant that unskilled or semiskilled African "machine-minders" could be substituted for skilled whites. It was thus of interest for whites to have Africans included in the trade union movement and under the guidance of experienced white leaders rather than have them left to "irresponsible elements" from the outside. This meant, in the last resort, that African unions could not long be denied recognition.

In speaking of TUCSA as a "white" union coordinating center, considerable care must be employed, for TUCSA was "white" only in the sense that the absolute majority of its membership was white. It had, in fact, more mixed, Coloured, or Indian unions affiliated to it than it had white unions. Although one might have expected dissatisfaction with the government's policies to have driven the non-white unions into SACTU's arms, this did not happen in fact. As figures collated by Muriel Horrell of the South African Institute for Race Relations show, the proportions by percentages of members of different ethnic groups in registered unions was as follows:[1]

	Indian	Coloured
S.A. Federation of Trade Unions	—	0.2
TUCSA	67.4	58.6
SACTU	9.1	15.9
Unaffiliated unions	23.5	25.2

Thus it seems that the majority of Coloureds and Indians followed a middle path, a path which led them either to TUCSA or to unions affiliated to neither TUCSA nor SACTU. As far as Africans are concerned, matters are harder to judge for all African unions inflate their memberships. However, according to Horrell's figures, FOFATUSA had some 18,385 African members and SACTU had 38,791.[2] Thus very shortly after it was formed, FOFATUSA already had almost half as many members as SACTU. Be that as it may, the main point has hopefully been established: TUCSA was far from a lily-white bastion.

The reason why African unions had not been included when TUCSA was formed is complicated. It was formed at a time when trade union unity in the face of government pressure was of greater concern than any other issue. To allow unity to be realized, only registered trade unions were admitted to membership and the African unions were thus excluded. While this was unsatisfactory to many of liberal mind, the realities of the situation must be remembered. Had affiliation of African unions been made the sticking point, the moderate unions would have lost a center and many unions then wavering would have tied themselves to the right wing of the trade union movement. TUCSA had, in addition, gone out of its way to assist African unions from the outset, but had they sought to make them members laws, actual and prospective, would have crippled its operations. With TUCSA less effective, differences of opinion among the various unions could well have broken the organization. The result would have been that, in the end, only those who advocated the colour bar inside and outside the unions would have benefited.

TUCSA's constitution did, however, permit the creation of a liaison committee with African unions, and although this committee continued to work for a number of years, it could achieve little. African unions found it of little help because what they needed most was assistance in all trade union matters, training in organizational methods, financing, and aid in the establishment of unions. The TUCSA unions did not offer such aid for a number of reasons. They believed that the law precluded them from using their funds to assist African unions though in the 1950s there was no legal impediment to their so doing. Another fear was that the Minister of Justice or the Minister of Labour would act against registered unions that assisted unregistered unions, and this was not a ground-less fear. This is the background to the later decision—in 1962—to amend the TUCSA Constitution to allow the affiliation of African unions, and it is, at the same time, the basis for the most serious conflict between SACTU and TUCSA.

The Basis for Conflict

The conflict between SACTU and TUCSA involved more than ideology, though this was unquestionably one component. In addition personalities, individual rivalries, and other factors entered. However, it can be said in general that in the 1950s and early 1960s SACTU, although attacking TUCSA on different issues, spent much time seeking a common front, provided that this was on the basis of equality. This clearly was an impractical demand, for the differences in the strengths of the respective organizations made nonsense of such a proposal.

An example of the kind of conflict that had agitated both organizations in the fifties is that over the Industrial Conciliation Act which had become law in 1956. SACTU proposed a conference to be held opposing this law, and to this end approached not only TUCSA but also the Federation of Trade Unions which largely supported the government. The Federation did not even reply to this overture, but TUCSA refused cooperation in a letter. The question for SACTU was what should now be done? Should the conference be cancelled or should it be held anyhow? Some of the SACTU executive suggested that the individual unions affiliated to TUCSA be approached, but this was abandoned as it might lead TUCSA to retaliate in kind. There was also some argument as to whether SACTU should go "cap in hand to the S.A. Trade Union Council and other coordinating bodies as our aim was unity." Others argued against such a course. TUCSA, one said, "had always ignored us and sacrificed the principle of trade union unity, and we would waste time appealing to them." On the other hand, there was a suggestion that an approach should be made "for the record for it was important to know that we approached them." It was felt best, however, to convene the conference only with SACTU unions and such unaffiliated unions as would cooperate.[3]

Of greater importance to SACTU was the Liaison Committee that TUCSA had set up. The matter was urgent because the construction SACTU placed on the disaffiliation of the Garment Workers' Union of African Women was that TUCSA had exercised undue influence, although the union's officials denied this and had stated that SACTU was "too political." What action could SACTU take? This was a topic that agitated the leaders of SACTU. One suggested that a leaflet "exposing" the liaison committee be made public. The leaflet would make it clear that the Garment Workers' Union had sacrificed equal status in SACTU for inferior status in TUCSA. The liaison committee should be shown to seek to cash in on SACTU's successes in organizing African workers in part, and in part a response to the attack on the credentials of the South African delegates to ILO in 1956. TUCSA was to be condemned for forming the committee and "selling out to the policies of apartheid."[4]

The second conference, at which these matters were raised, sheds interesting light on the working methods of SACTU. Had TUCSA agreed to accord SACTU equality, this would have provided SACTU with an excellent base from which to penetrate the African unions affiliated to the former body and to win them over. If, as was more likely, TUCSA refused they could be "unmasked." Zinoviev's words seem particularly apposite:

> We did not say to the social democratic worker: we are against a coalition with other "workers' parties," because their leaders are counter-revolutionary. We rather told him: We are ready to enter a coalition, if your social democratic leaders accept these elementary conditions (which, as is well known, are not acceptable to these gentlemen).[5]

The aim in these unity moves is often to neutralize an opposing organization and to gain access to their rank-and-file. As TUCSA was led by intelligent people who were, in any case, suspicious of SACTU, and as the far stronger organization in no need to enter an arrangement with them, TUCSA could afford to snub SACTU.

Nevertheless, SACTU persisted in its efforts to secure a common front with TUCSA. For instance, in 1960, the National Executive of SACTU sought to encourage greater contact with TUCSA in the national minimum wage campaign, which they felt constituted a basis for cooperation, the more so as TUCSA was itself carrying on a campaign for higher wages at the time. Another reason why cooperation was still sought was the effect of bans on SACTU as an organization, which put it in need of allies more than ever. These, again, are largely matters for speculation. The real gage of battle was the formation of FOFATUSA which posed a greater threat to SACTU.

SACTU and FOFATUSA.

Although something has been said of the formation of FOFA-TUSA, the background needs be filled out in greater detail if the conflict of the organizations is to be understood.

When the Trades and Labour Council broke up, after which both TUCSA and SACTU came into being, five African unions decided to remain in loose relationship with TUCSA rather than to affiliate to SACTU or remain unaffiliated. These unions were in the bakery, chemical, leather, motor, and tobacco industries, and were later joined by women garment workers. By 1959 these unions, with the exception of the chemical workers, met with other, smaller African unions, and decided to form a new coordinating body, which they called the Federation of Free African Trade Unions, hence the acronym FOFATUSA. Two factors are closely linked with the formation of FOFATUSA: the first is the split in the ANC and the emergence of PAC, and the second the appearance of the ICFTU representatives.

The founder of FOFATUSA, Jacob Nyoase, a man who longed to be a leader, had had considerable trade union experience, mainly in the bakery union. With the split from the ANC, PAC needed a direct link with African workers. Nyoase, as a Pan Africanist, called together the unions cited earlier and formed FOFATUSA with them. The part played by the ICFTU is less clear. Nyoase claimed that FOFATUSA was affiliated to the ICFTU and that they received monies from them. The ICFTU spokesman, in a speech in London, had said that funds would be channeled through TUCSA. ICFTU did apparently want a non-Communist African trade union center, and may well have inspired the formation of FOFATUSA, either deliberately or inadverdently. However that may be, despite the Pan Africanist stress on African self-help, the FOFATUSA unions seem to have relied a great deal on the TUCSA unions. There were a number of reasons for this: the maze of laws surrounding the African worker could only be solved by expert knowledge, and this the FOFATUSA organizers lacked. In addition many small services were needed which African unions were incapable of supplying. These included bookkeeping and records, membership lists, and other clerical-managerial functions. Another thing that has remained a mystery is the amount of organizing FOFATUSA actually did. With the funds made available by ICFTU, directly or indirectly, they had apparently been able to employ organizers, but did they organize anything? They claimed to have twenty affiliated unions with some 36,000 members in 1962. Yet others have claimed that FOFATUSA was little more than a shell, that it had little more to it than its leaders.

One reason why FOFATUSA may not have come to much is that Nyoase was arrested and imprisoned soon after FOFATUSA was established. This was a blow, but others were left to carry on. FOFATUSA was more seriously affected by the TUCSA decision of 1962 to permit properly constituted African unions to affiliate. FOFATUSA offered to affiliate as a body, but the constitution of TUCSA made no provision for this. In addition, the affiliation of FOFATUSA would discourage their affiliates from joining TUC-SA, for this would involve double affiliation. Nonetheless, in refusing to allow FOFATUSA to affiliate as such, TUCSA made it clear that cooperation at the executive level was welcome. However, the TUCSA decision spelled the end for FOFATUSA, for in the five years following thirteen of the largest African unions decided to affiliate to TUCSA while the weaker unions passed out of existence, so that by the end of 1965 FOFATUSA was left with a strength of twelve unions with 13,000 members, and few of these were much interested in the Federation. The organization then decided that it was best to disband, and advised such of their unions as had not yet affiliated to TUCSA to do so.

The story of FOFATUSA has been briefly set out, but the relationship of this trade union center to SACTU has hardly been touched on. SACTU was hostile to FOFATUSA from the beginning and this hostility was repaid in kind. This emerges from the first pages of *New Age* that took cognizance of the new body. *New*

Age describes FOFATUSA as "under the thumb" of TUCSA and claimed that the meeting called to establish FOFATUSA broke down without a decision because "there was such strong opposition from the body of workers in the hall."[6] What this meant in fact was that the strong-arm squad of the ANC had prevented any decision from being reached. It would be wrong, in describing events, to make out that the PAC was, on its side, completely innocent of attempts to intimidate. It sent its *bravos* to ANC meetings as readily. This means of preventing opposition meetings was just the way things were conducted in the African townships.

Indeed, the ANC was not outdone in rhetoric either, for Nyoase, writing to *Contact*, attacked the ANC for its affiliation to the Congress Alliance which "is known to be hostile to African nationalist and Pan Africanism which is the accepted ideology of the African continent. The Alliance has never adopted the positively neutral stand in international affairs, but has always acted as the distant spokesman of the totaliterian East."[7]

SACTU reacted in two ways: first it played up the present weakness of FOFATUSA, holding it up to ridicule; then, and often at the same time, it looked to its potential with fear. An example of the first attitude is expressed in *New Age*, in an article warning members of FOFATUSA that their actions would not be tolerated and describing their (FOFATUSA's) conference as a flop, claiming that it was attended by only ten people, three of whom were SACTU observers. Nonetheless, from the remarks quoted fully the schizophrenic attitude of SACTU to FOFATUSA is evident:

> Some persons who are members of this organization [i.e. FOFATUSA], together with certain members of the Liberal Party have been white-anting our union during recent weeks," he said. "They have been endeavoring with little success, to divide our members by getting them to join a separate union," he said.
>
> Stating that he could not understand their motive for this disruptive tactic, Mr. Ndhlovu (the speaker cited) said: "I want to take this opportunity of warning both FOFATUSA and the Liberal Party that they are playing with fire . . . we will not tolerate any action, by any group, which is aimed at disrupting and disuniting the workers.

"With thousands upon thousands of unorganized workers crying out for trade union organization I can't understand why these people want to cause trouble in a union that has been long established," he said. "But if it is necessary we shall fight them too, and in this fight we shall rally the entire mass support of SACTU unions," he concluded.[8]

The statement raised obvious questions. If FOFATUSA was ineffective, why was its activity of such concern to SACTU? How could it cause trouble for SACTU if SACTU was doing its work well? The answer seems to be that SACTU was already losing ground.

Events were moving quickly. South Africa was on the verge of a critical decision: was the country to become a republic? The decision was to be put to white South Africans only, and Nelson Mandela, the ANC leader, had instigated a move for a three day strike of Africans to coincide with the referendum. During this time an All-In Conference was to meet and to demand that the government call a national convention to reshape South African society.[9] The occasion inspired the resistance of both SACTU and FOFATUSA, who were both prepared to participate in the All-In Conference and to protest the method by which the decision for or against a republic was being decided. The coming of the All-In Conference sparked some differences between the two trade union bodies. FOFATUSA suggested that a new body be created to organize the support of all African workers, both organized and unorganized. SACTU, however, disagreed. Members of the Management Committee of SACTU believed it best if SACTU were represented in its own name, and that any statement issued should reflect this. The final decision arrived at was that SACTU would be represented directly, but that any statement should be issued jointly with FOFATUSA as "the United Trade Union Committee." The statement should not go beyond asking Africans to support the All-In Conference. It should contain no demands. The committee should, what is more, be dissolved as soon as the meeting was over.[10] Cooperation was, in other words, to be limited to the Conference itself, the task of recruiting was to be continued in competition with FOFATUSA. In any event, FOFATUSA was soon to be eclipsed as a rival, for changes in the TUCSA constitution in 1962 moved FOFATUSA to the wings. TUCSA now held center stage as the most dangerous rival.

SACTU and TUCSA after 1962

The change in TUCSA's constitution permitting it to organize and affiliate unregistered unions presented a real danger to SACTU, which saw itself as the victim of its own success. As the chairman said at the National Executive meeting of 1961:

> . . . our dynamic activity in all provinces has exposed the TUC and placed them in a very awkward position. SACTU was very vociferous both nationally and internationally, In fact, SACTU was the best known trade union coordinating body here and overseas. SACTU was the dominant body because it took up issues vitally affecting the workers, such as trade union rights, skilled jobs, equal opportunities and so on.

TUCSA, he went on to say, was having a difficult time overseas, especially at the ILO, and had therefore to take stock of its position. The question was, if TUCSA dropped its racial bias, what was to be SACTU's stand? SACTU had always campaigned for a united trade union front, but in discussing this with TUCSA it would have to talk from strength, for TUCSA remained strongly opposed to SACTU and thought it could win over the African unions. The National Executive had, therefore, to carefully consider the effects of TUCSA's action. Discussion at the National Executive Committee opened with the notion that TUCSA "hoped to draw the teeth of the workers' movement and to remove [sic] their militancy." It would "pollute the trade union movement and workers would not be as militant as they were. It was not for SACTU to wait for the TUC to disintegrate, but for SACTU to go all out on an organizing campaign." These sentences indicate the general level of the discussion, and it is not surprising that little more than rhetoric emerged. The chairman pointed out, toward the end of the meeting, that TUCSA was not wasting its time—it had already sent SACTU some thirty letters on its letterheadings, a matter unprecedented, and asked that these be circulated to SACTU unions. "They wanted their letterheads and their suggestions to become familiar to our affiliated unions," the chairman continued, and instead demanded that SACTU reply that the demands on the government be coordinated and that it would circulate their unions accordingly.

The official SACTU view seems expressed in a *New Age* article of February 15, 1962. The article was more restrained than articles of this nature had been in the past. It praised the more progressive policy now evident in TUCSA and the signs that some of its affiliates "were beginning to emerge from their 'no politics' cocoon." Ther was still dissension over the proposed change in TUCSA, *New Age* pointed out, and several unions were to attend the conference with a mandate not to press too strongly for the constitutional change if this was resolutely opposed by the more conservative elements. The resolution begins with the handicap that, as one of TUCSA's leading members had said, it was intended to put SACTU "out of business." The danger to TUCSA was, however, greater, for in an interview with *New Age* the TUCSA president of the body, Mr. L. C. Scheepers, admitted that the Electrical Union, an important TUCSA affiliate with over 8,000 members had disaffiliated because it felt that TUCSA was too closely bound to several African unions. Nevertheless, he went on, TUCSA was resolved to amend its constitution and to admit African unions as affiliates.

Faced with this prospect, the Management Committee made its views public in a statement in March, 1962.[11] The statement sought to solve the dilemma SACTU found itself in, for on the one hand it had outspokenly sought unity in the past, and yet now it had to make the achievement of unity impossible without being saddled with the blame. The public statement, which appeared in *New Age* of April 5, 1962, shows how this was done. SACTU would initiate talks, its leaders said, now that TUCSA policy had approached their own, although there was still no common policy, and therefore there was no present basis for unity. Before the question of unity arose certain common trade union goals would have to be agreed to and some common political objectives:

> SACTU believes that the successful struggle for economic demands is inextricably bound up with the struggle to remove

the political disabilities which impede economic improvements. *A mere struggle for the economic rights of the workers without participation in the general struggle for political emancipation would condemn the trade union movement to uselessness and to a betrayal of the interests of the workers.*

In other words, unity will be possible only when . . . one also fights . . . all repressive legislation which affects all non-white workers generally, and the African workers specifically. [Italics in original]

Despite the irresistible urge for unity, the statement continues, African unions would have to pay a heavy price were they to form a union with TUCSA. TUCSA was committed to nonpolitical trade unionism, and so could not, even if it found unity with SACTU desirable, accept SACTU's terms. As result the quest for unity, if indeed this was a serious quest, was stillborn.

Many SACTU members were, however, confused by the statement. They said that the reason for not joining with TUCSA in 1954 was that TUCSA did not admit African unions to affiliation. Now that TUCSA had agreed to admit them, they did not know what differences remained. The answer they were given was that the liberation struggle made the difference. The foundation of SACTU was not only to maintain the old status quo, as was the defunct TLC, but to win political rights. This was elaborated further. The white workers were calling for "no politics in the labor movement," but in their time they had not hesitated to use political means. When political rights had been denied them, they had organized themselves into a political party, the [South African] Labour Party, and they could do this because, as whites, they could vote. But where were the non-whites to get relief?

The next question was whether to meet with TUCSA or not? In the discussion of this issue the argument was made that the President-General of the ANC, Luthuli, had said that he would meet with Dr. Verwoerd (then South African prime minister) if asked and if he could do so without abandoning his principles, and therefore SACTU could approach TUCSA in the same spirit. "If their (sic) was a deadlock over our request to meet them, the world should know of this deadlock." Finally it was decided that the National Executive of SACTU should offer to meet the secretariat of TUCSA subject to a confirmation by the annual meeting of the former. The chairman of the Management Committee ended by saying that SACTU had always opposed discrimination in industry and hoped that the "atmosphere at the Conference would be emphatically in favor of a determined stand against discrimination."[12]

The result was not entirely what the chairman had hoped it would be, for the resolution actually adopted at the Annual Conference differed from the recommendation of the Management Committee. The resolution was to the effect that the Conference did not want TUCSA approached in specific matters such as minimum wages, but wanted it to cooperate in a campaign to drop the color bar in industry. A member of the Management Committee pointed out that the reason for the resolution was that confusion persisted, and that some of the delegates at the Annual Conference had thought that the motion was to affiliate to the TUCSA. As the resolution foreclosed all other approaches, it was suggested in the Management Committee that an administrative measure be employed, and that they write to TUCSA suggesting a meeting of representatives from their respective secretariats so that the new policy could be explained. Such a meeting did indeed take place, the Management Committee meeting with Mr. O'Donoghue of TUCSA, but nothing substantive seems to have come out of this meeting.[13]

The failure to establish effective contact with TUCSA even in specific campaigns, and the fact that TUCSA supported the government in passage of the Sabotage Act of 1962 widened the rift. The Sabotage Act was particularly repugnant to SACTU as it extended the range of banning orders and provided for very heavy penalties for sabotage.[14] To them, as they expressed it:

> The TUC deputation has forever stained the workers' cause by its wilful acceptance and support for the Sabotage Bill. We call on all workers and genuine trade unionists inside and outside the TUC to express their firmest disapproval of those who have betrayed them. We call on them to unite to fight apartheid and fascism.[15]

The failure to make contact with TUCSA and the support that organization had given the Sabotage Bill decided SACTU to fish in TUCSA's waters. It aimed to bring white and non-white workers together, though less well equipped to fight TUCSA than the latter was to fight SACTU. Be that as it may, a circular was sent to all local committees and affiliated unions asking them to seek the cooperation of registered trade unions, and to do so telling them that SACTU "was not on the Black side of the trade union coin as some people seemed to think, but the representative of workers of all races in South Africa." SACTU favored concerted efforts to eliminate racialism in the trade union movement through direct approaches to white workers. All were to work, as parts of the organization of SACTU, to this end, issuing leaflets of a character to educate white workers on SACTU's attitude and goals. The leaflet duly appeared but was issued in English only and not in Afrikaans—the language of most of the workers.

The program also called on unregistered unions to associate themselves in a working relationship with registered unions. An example of this is the relationship between the Shop and Office Workers' Union, a SACTU affiliate, and the National Union of Distributive Workers, a TUCSA affiliate. The unregistered Furniture, Bedding and Mattress Workers' Union had established good relations with its registered counterpart, each advising the other of vacancies and performing similar services for each other. The attempts of unregistered unions to make themselves known to their registered counterparts were not always an instant success, and often met with initial suspicion and hostility. The initial meeting of the SACTU affiliate, the Printing and Allied Workers' Union, with the Typographical Union for discussions of proposals submitted by the latter to the Wage Board was markedly unfriendly, but further meetings were arranged and the atmosphere seems to have softened somewhat. Some other unions, however, refused to as much as respond to the SACTU unions' overtures. The Amalgamated Engineering Union, for instance, apparently refused to reply to letters from the Metal Workers' Union, and there was talk of members of the Management Committee of SACTU visiting officials there.[16] In fairness to the Amalgamated Engineering Union mention must be made of the pressure being applied to that union by an Afrikaans union that had entered the field, and that most of the white workers in the industry were Afrikaans.[17] As *Spark* (the new name of *New Age*) pointed out, the Amalgamated

Engineering Union had already lost over 800 workers to the new union between 1962 and 1963.

Indeed what was happening in the Amalgamated Engineering Union was not dissimilar to what was happening in TUCSA in general. The white unions were increasingly dissatisfied with the constitutional changes allowing the admission of African unions, and this dissatisfaction was exploited by Afrikaans organizers to drag TUCSA's name in the mud. African workers, on the other hand, unsure of their welcome, hesitated to join TUCSA. Another problem, according to SACTU's lights, was that of TUCSA's international orientation. With the color bar no longer an obstacle, TUCSA was free to join ICFTU and thus break its isolation from the international community. But as the ICFTU had to be "choosy" about its affiliates, and this required a lengthy period of consultation with existing affiliates, it could well end with the African unions finding even TUCSA too much to stomach. It was doubtful to SACTU's leaders whether TUCSA was, in any event, ready to take the plunge. The ICFTU supported worldwide sanctions against South Africa; TUCSA, though without an official position, opposed sanctions. These, as *Spark* was by no means unhappy to report, were certainly ticklish problems.[18]

Yet despite these problems, TUCSA was making inroads into SACTU's memberships.[19] The matter of African affiliation was brought back into debate. In 1969 the matter of affiliation of African unions was again a serious issue, and there was fresh pressure for affiliation to be limited to registered unions. The decision to exclude African unions, subject to certain limiting clauses, was again taken.[20]

By 1969 SACTU had virtually disappeared from the scene. The Criminal Laws Amendment Act, refered to earlier as the "Sabotage Act," had severely cramped SACTU's lawful lines of action. In addition the Suppression of Communism Act was ever more severely applied. Heavy inroads were made on SACTU leaderships, while the experienced and able leadership of TUCSA continued to operate. Many unions ended their connection with SACTU, some with reluctance, because it could no longer carry out its policies or fill its role as a trade union center. Many of the smaller unions that SACTU had brought into being faded out. Nonetheless, even in its twilight, SACTU was involved in the sabotage organization

set up to overthrow the South African government and to revolu-
tionize the social system.

Chapter VIII

SACTU

and the Underground

Before 1960 the African resistance movements had operated in a shadowy legality. This ended with the State of Emergency of 1960 in which both the ANC and the PAC were banned and their continuance in any form was prohibited. SACTU was not banned though the leadership was weakened by bannings. This prohibition of the ANC changed Communist tactics once again. After 1950 the illegal Communist Party—reconstituted in 1952—had sought to convey the impression that it was not connected with the ANC or with the Congress Alliance. The party even tried to conceal its existence. All this fell away with the banning of the ANC. The illegal Communist Party now announced its existence and in partnership with the illegal ANC formed a sabotage organization which it named *Umkonto we Sizwe* (the Spear of the Nation).[1] *Umkonto* was officially a separate organization, though individual members of either the Communist Party or the ANC were "permitted" to join it. This was often a formality, for there was considerable overlapping of memberships among the three organizations.

Umkonto was, in a sense, an unwanted child. The ANC had set itself against violence in the 1950s and many leaders remained doubtful about it. Yet the ANC and the Communist Party were losing supporters to the violent arm of the PAC, named POQO. If they were to retain their influence, they would have to espouse

violence in turn. They decided in June 1961 to permit their
members to enter on acts of sabotage was to be against phys-
ical property only, and that to be mainly property of the government.

Intermittent acts of sabotage took place between August and
November of 1961 which were, it seems, tryouts for *Umkonto*.
Satisfied that damage could be done without loss of life, a more
ambitious series of acts was initiated on December 16, 1961, to
coincide with the white commemoration of victory over Dingane
in the nineteenth century. These attacks announced the formation
of *Umkonto*, which was to undertake more than 300 acts of sabotage
before being effectively crushed in 1964. SACTU played its part
in the underground operations of the ANC and of *Umkonto*.

SACTU and the ANC

SACTU was not prohibited as an organization, and this enabled
it to substitute for the other organizations. It was, therefore, a
convenient platform which remained open to ANC leaders. They
could be billed as Mr. so and so "formerly of the now banned
African National Congress." Everyone, of course, knew what that
meant. In addition to this, SACTU could form the basis of
recruitment into the African opposition, the underground ANC,
and later *Umkonto we Sizwe*.

A mass campaign to build up SACTU membership was proposed
in 1961. This can be interpreted either as an attempt to expand
organized union activity or to maintain a mass base for the African
opposition. Though both purposes were obviously intended, the
latter seems to have outweighed the former. Two things give
weight to this suggestion. The first is that formal trade union
activity had been largely foreclosed by 1961. The second is the
role of the Congress Alliance.

The Congress Alliance, although stripped officially of its strongest member, the ANC, continued to function after 1960. The Indian
Congress, the Congress of Democrats, and the Coloured Peoples'
Congress remained in addition to SACTU. They kept in touch
through the NCC as well as through the membership of many
leaders in the Central Committee of the illegal Communist Party.[2]
The Management Committee of SACTU and the NCC had agreed

that SACTU was to be responsible for steering the recruiting campaign through factory committees, the campaign to be on a national level. A national subcommittee, presumably from SACTU and the NCC, was to be set up with powers of cooption, and to be responsible to SACTU.[3] The Congress Alliance would then "throw its full weight" into the campaign for industrial organization, giving "positive assistance to SACTU to organize the unorganized workers and to strengthen existing trade unions."[4] The recruiting campaign was to be effected through area committees. The SACTU organs thus corresponded to those of the now illegal ANC and resembled the structure to be later set up for *Umkonto*. SACTU was thus to be a "front" for the illegal organizations, and a training ground from which the more promising could be selected for further training and drawn into the Communist Party. SACTU had, of course, fulfilled some of these functions before, but now such functions grew in importance.

The methods of recruitment were also discussed at length. A resolution was taken at the national conference of SACTU in 1961 to make recruitment a major SACTU objective. The intent was to "embark on a large scale organizing campaign on a factory to factory, office to office, shop to shop, house to house basis." Report on the progress of this campaign was to be given to the local committees every three months.[5] Recruitment was also to be attempted at places where Africans congregated in numbers such as at social gatherings and sports meetings, special attention being given to the latter.

The importance of organizing in ways to "keep up with the times" was stressed for "the people [being] ready for organization" increased the importance of the trade unions not "lagging" behind the people. One such thing was for members of SACTU to infiltrate sports clubs so that they could influence sportsmen. "The chairman [of SACTU's Management Committee] said that sports committees were not political but that members of sports clubs would become interested in going to trade union meetings" and where SACTU members were also members of sports clubs they could influence others by leaflets, discussions, and readings.[6]

Because the ANC, the Communist Party, and SACTU worked so closely together, and because their memberships tended to overlap, the three cannot be divorced from each other. Their interrelationships can best be illustrated with a case, and one of the best documented is that of Bruno Mtolo, both as a witness in the Rivonia Trial and in his book.[7] As Mtolo betrayed the organizations with which he was connected, and turned State's evidence against his former associates, his testimony may well raise many misgivings. However, his evidence was exhaustively tested in several trials and broadly withstood cross-examination by skilled legal counsel, and his reliability seems to stand up to critical examination. There is also some negative evidence in support of Mtolo's published statements. An article in *African Communist* by J. J. Jabulani (pseudonym?) was to have examined Mtolo's book, along with some others, "under a microscope."[8] The article draws attention to relatively minor errors of fact along with major ones in several books, but fails to refute anything of substance written by Mtolo. Discrediting Mtolo would have been much in the interest of the Communists, and as they certainly would have done so were this possible, one must adduce this as evidence in corroboration of Mtolo. It is, therefore, used here to illustrate the working together of the ANC, the Communist Party, and SACTU.

The Individual and SACTU

Those interested in insurgency and the insurgent should look at Mtolo's autobiography. Much emerges of the psychology of the revolutionary recruit from his frankness and evasiveness, sophistication and naivete, self-confidence and self-pity. To briefly recall Mtolo's life, he felt little antagonism to white men in youth, and became politically conscious only in prison, where he was introduced to ANC ideas by a fellow inmate in 1950. Mtolo, an intelligent pupil, was interested but did little to implement this interest until 1957 when, after attending a number of ANC meetings, he decided to become a member. He remained a member until the ANC was banned in 1960, when it seems he dropped out, until he learned from a girl friend—Mtolo boasts of his many amorous exploits—that the ANC was being carried on underground. He was introduced to Stephen Dhlamini, an officer of the illegal ANC, who induced him to join SACTU because it had, for years, been ANC policy that its members had also to be SACTU members.

Mtolo, who was working in the McCord Hospital in Durban at the time, joined the Hospital Workers' Union—a SACTU affiliate.

As a member of the union, and as an old ANC hand, Mtolo was introduced into political classes, especially political economy which he learnt "is a basis for socialism, which is the road to communism." Marxism, he was taught, "is the basis of trade unionism, which is a preparation for communism. [The pupils] were told that it was important for a trade union member to take a leading part in political matters as the workers' goal should be to overthrow the capitalistic system and replace it with socialism, which is the foundation of communism."[9] This is, of course, typical of the formulations of the Communist Party in South Africa and elsewhere. One day Dhlamini asked Mtolo if he (Mtolo) liked the trade union movement, and on answering in the affirmative Mtolo was asked how he felt about the Communist Party. Mtolo's feelings were, it seems, positive, for he decided to join it though it was illegal. Mtolo was warned not to discuss his joining the party with anyone, not even his girl friends. He was enrolled in a cell of five members and now became active in the Party. He organized a branch of the Hospital Workers' Union in his spare time, and became chairman of this branch. This was his vantage point and center of activities for a time.

The strike to be staged on proclamation of the Republic of South Africa has been discussed earlier (see p. 000). Before May 29, 1961, Mtolo was warned to hold himself in readiness, and he decided, therefore, to claim the leave due him from the hospital and to take an additional unauthorized month as well. During this time he would assist at Pinetown, a town near Durban, where a new SACTU branch had been formed by members of Mtolo's party cell. They had visited Pinetown, distributed leaflets, and generally tried to raise the political consciousness of the African workers, but in vain. The strike effort failed completely. A survey of sorts was conducted to investigate the failure, and failure was blamed on instructions to pickets not to use violence against those going to work. For Mtolo, according to his account, the strike was a lesson gained. He was, he says, able to use his theoretical training to organize two factories in two weeks. Whatever the outcome, Mtolo returned to his work at the hospital and attended cell meetings, the cell receiving directives either from the Central Committee or the District Committee of the Communist Party in this time.[10]

In 1961, as *Umkonto* was in the course of formation, a debate on its role and functions seems to have split the leadership of the Communist Party, while friction between the ANC leaders on the local level and *Umkonto* also corroded both organizations.

The split in the Communist Party was occasioned by differences over the use of violence, and over whether to toe the Moscow or the Peking line. The quarrel led to the usual round of expulsions, some being expelled as "revisionists" because they argued that the country was not yet ripe for sabotage or because they said that guerrilla war would fail.[11] Mtolo and his cellmates had already been incorporated into *Umkonto* and had begun their work of sabotage. They were aware of the split but were warned never to speak of it in public nor to give any sign of sympathizing with either side. The cells were to remain neutral at this point.

Of greater consequence to Mtolo was the quarrel with the Natal ANC leadership, whom he saw as a "stumbling block [in that they] only wanted to sit tight and do nothing." SACTU therefore seized the opportunity and began organizing people on its own, in response not only to pressures in its own organization but also to pressures from the (now banned) ANC Youth League and the Women's Federation of the ANC.[12]

SACTU, according to Mtolo, unlike the ANC, was preparing its members for "whatever might happen," and made the change from non-violence to violence as policy plain in secret meetings. There the members were told of the formation of *Umkonto* and of its nexus to the ANC, the information being given in such a way as not to expose those who gave information as members of that organization (*Umkonto*) but only that they supported the work of the underground. SACTU members were told that when the time came they would know who there real leaders were, and that those leaders who opposed *Umkonto* could lead them nowhere.[13]

Because of the conflict with the ANC, the members of the *Umkonto* Regional Command, in Durban, decided to use their positions as SACTU union secretaries as cover. Most of the Regional Command was made up of union secretaries who, at the same time, were Communist Party members. Mtolo writes:

At this time I was secretary of the Municipal Workers' Union and a member of the Regional Command of the Umkonto we Sizwe. I was also a member of a Communist cell together with Curnick Ndhlovu, Billy Nair, George Poon and Eric Mtshali. All the trade unions in Durban, Pinetown, and Hammarsdale were affiliated to SACTU.[14]

The Regional Committee was, it seems, working out of the SACTU head offices in Lakhani Chambers in Durban. This, together with their trade union roles, enabled the Regional Command to function.

Another indication of the interweaving of organizations is Bruno Mtolo's being sent to Johannesburg to be trained as a saboteur. The Durban group was preparing for the SACTU annual conference, to be held in Johannesburg. Since Mtolo was then chairman of the Hospital Workers' Union, steps were taken to ensure his appointment as a delegate to the conference. On Mtolo's arrival, during April 1962, he was to be met and taken to the place where he was to be trained, but this did not work out. Mtolo attended the SACTU conference, but no one came for him in Johannesburg. Once back in Durban, Mtolo was told that the man from the high command of *Umkonto* had looked for him in Johannesburg but had been unable to find him, and Mtolo then returned once more to Johannesburg. He contacted his link to the high command on this occasion and after some delay was given the necessary training, a training completed by mid-1962. Now fully trained, Mtolo left his job at the hospital and began to work for SACTU as full-time secretary to the Municipal Workers' Union in Durban.

At this time, mid-1962, the campaign to organize *Umkonto* gained momentum through support obtained in the African states by Nelson Mandela, one of the members of the *Umkonto* High Command. Mandela visited the Durban group and encouraged a step up in their campaign of sabotage. Mtolo and his group extended their activities, but the tide was turning against them in 1963. In January of that year Mtolo was detained for a day because of an attack on one of the workers at McCord Hospital. The worker was attacked because he was not a SACTU member, and though the police could pin nothing on Mtolo, he was a marked man after that. On being released Mtolo went to Billy Nair, then secretary of the Textile Workers' Union—a SACTU affiliate—and Nair arranged

Mtolo's legal defense. The suggestion that he go abroad for military training was made to Mtolo, who declined because he had a family to support.

The needs of his family, Mtolo maintains, led to his eventual disenchantment with SACTU and *Umkonto*. Mtolo had left his job on the promise of being paid by SACTU, but pay had not come. Mtolo was hard pressed to provide for them. Now, with the suggestion that he go overseas for military training, came the suggestion, made by Nair, that they could find R10.00 (about $14.00) per month for Mtolo's family if he became a soldier. Mtolo knew this was nonsense, for a friend of his had been sent overseas on a similar promise which had never been fulfilled. Mtolo rightly deduced that if SACTU (and *Umkonto*) did not pay him while he was in the country, they were less likely to do so once he was abroad.[15]

Although he had refused overseas service, Mtolo agreed to go for further training in Johannesburg, and his experiences illuminate the workings of *Umkonto* and SACTU. Told he would be met at the railroad station on his arrival at 9:00 *A.M.*, he found no one to meet him on his arrival. This, it may be added, was not unusual, the failure of couriers to appear on time or to appear at all being customary in *Umkonto*. Mtolo, however, knew where SACTU headquarters were and whom to visit, but even so it was only after much trouble that he was put in touch with the high command. Even so, it was only after he had been identified because his photograph had appeared in *New Age* that the lead was established. After all this, having met the training team, Mtolo found there was little they could teach him, and he was soon sent back to the SACTU office in Durban where he reported to the Regional Command.[16] Mtolo seems to have put his training to some use, but the problem of supporting his family, already referred to, handicapped his efforts.

Although supposedly a full-time worker for SACTU on a salary, Mtolo was not paid much of the time. The trade union he used as a cover was weak and had few members. When Mtolo asked headquarters for more money, or at least to be paid what was due to him, he was told that they were still awaiting money from the high command. Mtolo was advised to reactivate the Municipal Workers' Union, largely defunct, and raise funds for himself through that. This was impossible. There was trouble already among the officers and members of the moribund union because the secretary and some committee members had been taking the monthly subscriptions for themselves. The former secretary had fled the country, decamping with most of the union's meagre funds. This hardly made the union good picking for Mtolo.

Among the worst errors a revolutionary organization can make is not to look after its "soldiers." Mtolo soon began to regret his decision to join the Communist Party:[17]

> I was penniless and the world became too small for me when I thought of my two sons who were going to be orphaned while I rotted away on Robben Island [a maximum security prison]. I was beginning to regard my decision to join the Communist Party as a grave mistake. These people obviously did not care about the welfare of others, but looked after themselves only. . . . They travelled in posh cars despite the fact that they knew less and did less for the movement than I had done. I felt bitter. . . . God knows how my wife and family survived.

Anger at the thought that his leaders were doing well for themselves while the rank-and-file suffered was not confined to Mtolo. Bartholomew Hlapane, a former member of the Central Committee who also turned witness for the State, gave similar reasons for his changed attitude. The difference between the outlooks of Hlapane and Mtolo is that the former thought that only the white Communists were taking all the money. He felt that white Communists had betrayed the movement for African liberation and took funds intended for the dependents of members of *Umkonto* on trial or in prison:[18]

> The money collected through the Defense and Aid Fund falls into the hands of "White Communists" and they are not prepared to part with a cent. While children starve and their fathers rot on Robben Island, "white Communists" are living in the best hotels overseas.

It was hatred generated by this conduct that led to his defection. Hlapane, unlike Mtolo, did not blame the black leaders. Both were alienated from *Umkonto* and Communism.

SACTU and Recruitment

Before leaving Mtolo and his part in the interwoven affairs of the Communist Party, *Umkonto*, and SACTU, the part SACTU played in recruiting volunteers for training overseas warrants attention.

The National High Command of *Umkonto* had urged that SACTU be a funnel for recruits. This the Regional Command carried out, transporting a series of groups, most of which were arrested on the Rhodesian frontier, despite assurances each time that the system of transporting recruits had been perfected. As Mtolo wrote: "It soon became clear, not only to me but to everyone, that recruiting was a waste of time."[19] Why it proved so abortive so often emerges from Mtolo's narrative.

On one occasion thirty recruits had been collected in Natal and Mtolo was to escort them to Johannesburg from where they would be sent abroad. These thirty youths were to be divided into two groups: one would leave Durban in the morning with Mtolo, the other would follow that afternoon to avoid suspicion. Govan Mbeki, who organized the transport with Mtolo, assured the latter that they would be met at Germiston station, near Johannesburg, by someone sent by the High Command, and that this person would also have money for the recruits to continue their journey.[20] These youths were mostly pickpockets at the Durban Municipal Market, and were very keen to receive military training. Mtolo said that "most of these boys had led a hard life and they would form a tough core of guerrilla fighters, even though they would need a lot of discipline. As for Marxism, they would grasp it very quickly, because they had personal knowledge of starvation."[21] The courier was to take them over in Germiston and Mtolo was to return to Durban the same night.

Because a group of boys had been arrested on another occasion on the train, Mtolo asked that he meet only one of the boys so that if the group were arrested Mtolo could escape since only one of the boys could identify him. This was done and every arrangement seemed set.

"Seemed set" is operative, for on arrival in Germiston Mtolo found that no one was there to meet him and his charges. To make matters worse, if this was possible, the boys clustered together attracting attention. After an hour Mtolo advised the youths to scatter while he went to SACTU headquarters for advice. There he was assured all would be well and on returning to the station Mtolo found the boys still waiting and hungry. They had arrived in the morning. It was now 7:00 p.m. It was getting dark and the crowds on the platform were thinning out, exposing the little band. At 8:00 P.M. the courier finally appeared. They had been standing around a whole day in danger of arrest. What more can be said of the way SACTU did these things?

The political career of Curnick Ndhlovu, a companion of Mtolo's, is also interesting. Ndhlovu, according to his testimony, joined *Umkonto* because of the Sharpeville riot, and became leader of the Regional High Command in Natal soon after it was formed in 1961. Ndhlovu was well educated for an African, having gone on to Standard IX (which is about tenth grade in the United States), a level few Africans could afford to reach. A member of the ANC from 1953 to 1960, Ndhlovu had been a member of the executive of the Youth League of the ANC. He had joined the unregistered Railway Workers' Union while working as a porter and became its full-time secretary. He became Assistant-Secretary of SACTU in 1960 and remained active in it until he was banned in 1963. He continued clandestine work for *Umkonto* after that and was among the last to be arrested. Ndhlovu was obviously a man who knew the ANC and SACTU well.

From Ndhlovu's evidence, as that of Mtolo, it seems that SACTU was at the tip of the legal-illegal machinery of the Congress Alliance. It was the visible part of an organization; the greater part was banned and carried on in concealment. It could thus carry out those tasks impossible for a body that was completely clandestine. The argument advanced for Ndhlovu and other SACTU leaders was that they were members of SACTU as "workers."[22] The evidence of Ndhlovu contradicts this, for he maintained, as did Mtolo, that SACTU was the organizational base for *Umkonto*.

SACTU officials continued to be active after the government had largely broken the back of the resistance movement by arresting most of its leaders in the raid of the farm "Lilliesleaf" in Rivonia, a township near Johannesburg. Among those not in the police net was another prominent SACTU man, Wilton Mkwayi. Mkwayi, together with a group of Communist associates, had tried to carry on with *Umkonto* despite its disruption after Rivonia. The reasons

Mkwayi gave could well stand for many who joined in the armed resistance: the years of futile nonviolent protest, and the reluctant conviction that only violence would induce the ruling whites to yield. He insisted, as other *Umkonto* leaders had, that this violence was to be against property and not against people. He, as they, reasoned that responsible violence might make the government change course. Again, like many others, Mkwayi had begun as a trade unionist, and turned into a saboteur, ending in prison.

Communism and African Unions

The political struggle between the South African government and SACTU intensified after 1948, with the government using its massive legal powers and repressive apparatus to ban the older ANC leaders. This removal of the older leaders served to increase the influence of the younger leaders, and these were more often either themselves Communists or profoundly under Communist influence. Few of the higher ANC leaders, according to Bartholomew Hlapane, were not at the same time on the Central or District Committees of the Communist Party.[23] The organizations were theoretically separate but memberships overlapped. The same held for *Umkonto we Sizwe*, the sabotage organization formed jointly by the Communist Party and the ANC. It is questionable whether the organizations were only parallel or whether they were merged in all but name.

The Communist role is not surprising. Until the formation of the Liberal Party after the Defiance Campaign of 1952 and the later formation of the Progressive Party, few white parties have seriously concerned themselves with African politics. This lack of human concern drove Africans with political ambitions or political sensitivity irresistibly towards the Communists, and Communist influence waxed. Naturally other African leaders remained outside the Communist party or opposed it on personal or ideological grounds, as we have seen in the case of the ICU and other African unions. However, after the big split with the Africanists in 1958, what remained of the ANC and the Congress Alliance, along with SACTU, was a largely Communist and fellow-traveller leadership.

Few non-Communists remained in any position where they could seriously affect policy.

The coincidence of leaderships was most evident on the higher rungs of the leadership ladder. There was suspicion of Communists among some on the lower rungs on the grounds of their support of a non-African creed. This was not, however, the only reason. Some leaders were afraid that they would be saddled with *Umkonto's* crimes, although they had themselves been unable to influence that organization's policies. One outcome was that after *Umkonto* began effective functioning many of the Communists of both races left the ANC or the other components of the Congress Alliance and devoted themselves to *Umkonto*. The strength of the underground ANC declined as a consequence. SACTU, though crippled by various government measures continued to function chiefly in support of *Umkonto* which prosecuted the "violent struggle" that had replaced the previous "nonviolent struggle" of the ANC and the others in the Congress Alliance.

As Selznick indicates, Communist trade unions are intended to function as "transmission belts" to the working class and the party has to learn to set up and work through a series of mass organizations and "to systematically utilize mass organizations as transmission belts to the broad masses of non-party workers." The trade union is, in other words, the means by which the Communist "motor" "drives" the workers.[24] It is readily evident that, in a growing industrial economy such as that of South Africa, with a poor and growing proletariat, Communist-directed trade unions could well have become a significant political factor. Aware that such unions could grow into a manifest challenge to their authority, the government did all in its power to impede their growth without actually making African unions illegal. The Industrial Conciliation Boards and Wage Boards were used to make African unions respectively ineffective and redundant. The aim was, as the then Minister of Labour stated, "to bleed the African unions to death." The impossibility of employing traditional trade union negotiation and the intense pressure the government exerted against them doomed any action the Congress Alliance took. Given the government's commitment then to the status quo, it is difficult to see how it could have given African trade unions wider latitude. The Labour Minister put it this way: "the stronger the [African] trade union movement becomes, the more dangerous it would be to the [whites] in South Africa. . . . We[the whites] would be committing race suicide if we give [the Africans] that incentive."[25]

The Communists, given their grasp on the trade unions, might have compensated for their small numbers through the growth of the unions with a controllable if not always ideologically committed membership. If they had, they might have achieved a measure of ascendancy over important segments of the economy. Party headquarters in Johannesburg might have been a significant marshalling point for large-scale activism instead of being, as it was, a center of a small ideological grouping.[26] It might have split non-Communist unions, called crippling strikes in essential industries, merged unions, and even broken strikes of opposing unions to undermine ideological competitors. Few other instruments could have placed such power in Communist hands. Powerful political influences are always to be found in trade unions, but it was principally to the Communist Party that unions were a way of harnessing workers to an ideological chariot driven towards political goals. This was, partly, the cause of the Communists' undoing for many of the members of their unions realized that such unions were not out to achieve advantages on bread-and-butter issues but sought a distant and not presently pertinent goal.

The traditional discipline of Communist parties can effectively increase their strength beyond mere numbers, and so the question that comes to mind is: why did the government not ban SACTU despite its relatively small membership? The government, as it had demonstrated so often before, certainly had the power both to ban SACTU and to make the ban stick. It had the information from the Special Branch of the police to justify its actions according to its own lights. Whey then was SACTU allowed to continue working when the ANC and SACOD (South African Congress of Democrats, an element of Congress Alliance for whites) were banned?

The reasons cannot, of course, be known with any degree of certainty, but some surmises can be ventured. One reason may be concern with international reaction to an overt attack on a trade union body. Trade unions are to be found in most countries and on both sides of the "iron curtain," though their real autonomy and the degree to which members are represented varies greatly. Trade unions, as corporate bodies, are inclined to be most sensitive to threats to other unions and can to some extent concert actions through international bodies such as ICFTU, WFTU, and the ILO. Thus, labor sentiment unsympathetic to Communism under other circumstances could have been amassed in support of SACTU were it to be banned altogether. Pressure for economic sanctions, or refusal by labor unions to handle South African orders, might have conceivably grown in volume. Trade union pressure might, in its turn, have induced governments to officially boycott South African trade, potentially a thornier problem than the unofficial and largely ineffective boycotts of well-meaning groups mounted from time to time. The repercussions in governments sensitive to the pressure of organized labor, particularly Great Britain with Labour in power, would have been unpredictable and dangerous. The need to undergo the risk was reduced by the inefficiency and ineffectiveness of SACTU itself, and even more by the other methods open to the government which achieved largely the same end.

Instead of an absolute ban the organization was rendered impotent by bans of officers, harassment of members, and the provision of alternative methods of settling disputes such as the Native Labour (Settlement of Disputes) Act of 1953 and the Industrial Conciliation Acts which followed in 1956, 1959, and 1966, together with other legislation which, however unsatisfactory from an African viewpoint, did provide some access to wage decision-making. Creating the conditions under which African unions could not properly function and with full command of the internal situation, the government was not obliged to change a course it considered right. This course has come under increasing pressure recently, but in the mid to end sixties the government had many means by which it could break SACTU, and it did so without meeting any serious national or international challenges.

African Trade Unions—
The Way Ahead

This book is concerned mainly with one trade union coordinating center—SACTU, and the complex question of the future of African trade unions cannot be given the full and complete treatment the subject deserves. Prognostication would have been much simpler as little as two years ago. Then analysts did not see much hope for the effective functioning of any African unions and the disappearance of the few still existing seemed likely. The reemergence of a militant African labor force in 1972 and 1973 together with the growing shortage of skilled white labor, has led to some heart-searching and reevaluation of the black man's role in South African society. The new opportunities for African labor and the increasing vulnerability of white workers to employer pressure to give up formerly privileged positions have led to a revaluation of the role of the white unions vis-à-vis their black fellows and black workers in general.

The Strike Wave of 1972-1973

Strikes among African workers are illegal and strikers are subject to criminal prosecution, dismissal, and deportation to a rural area. Nevertheless, sporadic strikes among Africans are by no means infrequent, though till 1972 they involved limited numbers of workers on the whole. SACTU and other African unions were particularly active in the 1950s, but this activity seems to have died down in the early sixties and to have revived somewhat in the late sixties. The numbers of African workers involved were small, the time lost minimal, and the disputes fairly quickly settled. A few figures may help make the matter clear. In the six years from 1955 to 1960 there were some 70 strikes a year with a maximum of 113 in 1957 and a minimum of 33 in 1960—the year of Sharpeville. As that year, with a declared State of Emergency, may be considered atypical, it is worth noting that only three more strikes, or thirty-six, occurred in the year before.[1] A hiatus set in after 1960, there being only some sixteen strikes in 1962 and seventeen in 1963.[2] The number of strikes grew from 1965 to 1971, although their number remained fairly constant from year to year. The average for this period was 62, and the number of workers striking, on the average, was 3074. The maximum number of strikes took place in 1965 and in 1969, in both years there were sixty-nine incidents, the least number of strikes having taken place in 1968 with fifty strikes. Strikes, were, therefore, by no means an unusual phenomenon by 1972 though the average duration of any strike was less than one day.[3]

The situation seemed to change radically in 1972 itself and is still changing in 1974 as these paragraphs are being written. According to the government's figures for Natal, the principal area of strikes, there had been 222 work stoppages between June 1972 and June 1974 with some 78,216 Africans involved.[4] This was obviously of a completely different order to previous strikes by Africans. The astonishing thing is that the strikes did not lead to violence and have led to a revaluation of many white attitudes and to some pay increases for Africans, although their wages remain miserable on the whole. Several reasons have been adduced for the relatively low level of turbulence. The first and perhaps most important circumstance was that the police acted calmly and did not act as strikebreakers. Unlike the pattern of the past, they did not resort to violence in halting or dispersing the strikers but handled any threat to peace firmly and efficiently. The second reason was, perhaps, that employers responded fairly quickly to demands for higher wages, though it took the dramatic strikes to force their hands. The third reason might be the overall sympathy that whites demonstrated towards black objectives. Whatever the merits of this argument, the strikes were peaceably settled with some African gains.

Despite the settlement of the strikes, shock-waves spread through the white communities. The Prime Minister, John Vorster, pointed out that the strikes had lessons for all.[5] "They contain a lesson for the hon. members on the opposite side of the House; they also contain a lesson for me and this side of the House. They contain a lesson for the Wage Board, a lesson for the workers and a lesson for the employers. We would be foolish if we did not all benefit from the lessons to be learned from that situation. . . . Now I am looking past all party affiliations and past employers, and experience tells me this, that employers . . . should not only see their workers as a unit producing for them so many hours of service a day; they should also see them as human beings with souls." The lesson had certainly sunk in to an extent and many meetings were held among employers, white worker, and academic groups to explore the means by which Africans could gain greater recognition of their interests. In the main the argument was for African trade unions.

The plea to permit African unions was heard on all sides. The Natal Employers' Association, for instance, wished to see "house" unions established in all industries, these to be united in regional unions for each industry.[6] TUCSA, on the other hand, began to organize African unions "parallel" to the corresponding white unions. In these parallel unions, their constitutions would be modelled on that of the corresponding white union; the unions were to be bona fide unions and not "fronts" for anything else; the initial organization was to be done by the parent union; and the "parallel" union should be under the overall supervision of the registered union.[7] Initial steps were taken to organize the 20,000 African printers along union lines by the Typographical Union which had, in addition, the approval of employers to work along these lines even before the plan had been made public.[8] Added to pressures from both employers and the more liberal unions was that of public opinion among whites, which indicated that some eighty-four percent of respondents were willing to have black trade union rights manifest in all parts of the country—a result the more interesting as the respondents were mainly blue collar.[9] In a survey conducted by Professor Lawrence Schlemmer of the University of Natal's Institute for Social Research similar findings seem evident, although not without qualifications. In response to the question as to whether Africans should be allowed to form legally recognized unions, some sixty percent of English-speakers and forty-five percent of Afrikaans-speaking agreed. Once the dangers were stressed, however, attitudes changed somewhat. Faced with a question of this sort, those who *rejected* African unions increased by ten percent among the English-speaking and fourteen percent among the Afrikaans.[10] The differences indicated are reflected in the failure of TUCSA and the Afrikaans trade union coordinating body, the Confederation of Labour, to agree on African unions. There is, it seems, substantial support in the Confederation for African unions but as decisions must be unanimous a minority has been able to block any effective action.[11]

Despite the support which some unions have indicated and the (albeit qualified) support for African trade unions, all is not sweetness and light. The government, for one, is deadset against African unions offering its Wage Boards as a substitute.[12] Speaking at a meeting of employers, the Minister of Labour, Mr. Marais Viljoen, said: "Due, *inter alia*, to the way certain elements have abused Bantu trade unions in the past for political purposes—instead of using a union for its primary function as a negotiating body—the government is not willing to consider Bantu trade unions as a useful channel of employer/employee communication. To put it beyond any doubt, I wish to state quite unequivocally that *the government will not consider the recognition of Bantu trade unions or their organization or affiliation in a way which is tantamount to recognition.*"[13] (Emphasis added). The organizers of African trade unions thus have a difficult task in the face of government discouragement in a country where government power is very strong. Both the more liberal unions and the employers have, as a result, been half-hearted in their dealings with African unions or in organizing or recognizing these unions.

Although employers are, it seems, in principle in favor of African unions, they have shown reluctance in dealing with these unions though it is not unlawful to do so. A spokesman for the African union for the metal trade, the Metal and Allied Workers' Union, for instance, confirmed that five British-owned companies refused to deal with the union.[14] A large automobile company, when approached, said that workers' representation through trade unions would not be necessary, claiming that effective communication already existed. The workers wish to be represented by the union which has ninety percent of the workers organized, but the management does not wish to recognize the union. The same held for the other companies, all of whom, the spokesman said, evidenced hostility or indifference. Even the Wage Boards, the express instrument of the Government to regulate wages, have aroused the suspicions of some employers.[15] Africans, it is alleged, who demanded their rights in terms of the legislation were victimized and sometimes lost their jobs.

It may be appropriate, at this point, to take a brief look at the Wage Board idea without going too deeply into the technicalities. Briefly, then, the Bantu Labour (Settlement of Disputes) Act of 1953, as amended in 1955, defines the term "employee" to exclude Africans. It provides separate industrial conciliation machinery, excluding certain services and the mining industry. African workers can be represented in Works Committees in factories with more than twenty African workers if the African workers so wish. The Committee is convened and chaired by a Bantu Labour Officer appointed by the government who is to act in the interests of African workers. There is, in addition, a Regional Bantu Labour Committee in a number of regions consisting mainly of appointed African members. A central Bantu Labour Board consisting of white members appointed by the Minister of Labour settles disputes which cannot be settled by the committees, or if it is unsuccessful, disputes are referred to the Wage Board which has the final say. This machinery only works when the African workers are not covered by an Industrial Conciliation Act agreement. These agreements are arrived at by negotiations between government, employers and registered trade unions, and cover African wages as well as white, though African workers are not directly represented.[16] Where such an agreement is in force disputes would be settled under the machinery of the Conciliation Act rather than the Bantu Labour Act. This legislation is complicated, but complication has been compounded in response to the Natal strikes. Responding to pressures from employers and unions, and to the flow of events, the government has introduced new machinery for settlement of disputes for African workers. In addition, to the statutory Works Committees, an unofficial series of bodies, Liaison Committees, had come into being on which African workers and their white employers were represented. The amendments to the Bantu Labour Act have in effect given legal footing to these committees. Works Committees can now only be established in factories where no Liaison Committee exists: the committee is to consist of at least half of workers elected by their peers. The representation of employers and the direct participation of employer representatives has, according to some sources, given the employer virtual control over decision making, and does not begin to approach a system to collective bargaining.[17] This, then, is the background to the actions some employers have been taking in relation to their black workers.

The *Rand Daily Mail*—a liberal newspaper by South African standards—drew attention to the enthusiasm for Works Committees among Africans, which they found surprising, and the "almost paranoiac distrust" for these committees among some employers and the Security Police who are taking an intense interest in these bodies.[18] The article gives instances of African workers who claim victimization because they insisted on their legal rights by demanding the establishment of Works Committees, and the equally vigorous denials from employers. Admitting that the facts are difficult to establish, the *Rand Daily Mail* points out that employers refusing to establish Works Committees when these are legally demanded can face imprisonment or fines. However, two workers with good records, having worked with their respective firms for fourteen and nineteen years were fired on demanding Works Committees rather than Liaison Committees. The firms who had employed them adduced other reasons; however, the element of strong doubt remains. The figures indicate that most Africans would prefer Works Committees where they are aware of their rights, but most employers would, naturally, prefer Liaison Committees. At the South African Pulp and Paper Mills, for instance, some 1,200 African workers opted for the former and only 30 for the latter, nevertheless employer preference, given the relative powerlessness of African workers, seems dominant. An indication of the preference is the establishment of some 588 Liai-

son Committees compared with only 139 Works Committees. In
this, employers despite their desire for African unions, as often
expressed, seem tempered by fears even of the legal Works Committee.

In a sense, of course, it is the difficulties that Liaison Committees can cause even well-intentioned employers that raises employer
fears. A reported case is that of the *Toyota* assembly plant outside
Durban. This factory had been losing money and in hopes of improving this situation employed a veteran *Ford* administrator
Geoffrey Graves. Graves and his industrial relations manager saw
that wages were a problem and raised these before the strike wave
of 1972, increasing wages yet further after the big strikes which hit
other factories, the wage increases being altogether some 63 percent. Nevertheless the African work force struck the plant demanding
a wage increase of R1 per hour (the Rand is the South African
currency equivalent to $1.40 approximately at the time of writing)
an exceptionally high amount by South African standards, representing an increase of more than 180 percent. Now this plant *had*
a Liaison Committee. The Committee consisted of eight Africans
and four men from management. There was, in addition, an *Induna*
(an African term for "warrior" but used to indicate an African
designated as link between management and workers) for every
twenty Africans who were employed. Although management
believed that the workers were bringing their grievances to the
Liaison Committee, they were faced with the unexpected strike.[19]

Two things seem clear from this brief description: firstly, the
Liaison Committee and the Indunas cannot control the workers;
and secondly, that the worker's expectations go far beyond what
management conceives them to be. It also indicates that Works
Committees will not stop strikes.

The Works Committees, whether they work well or badly, are
not trade unions and lack many of the advantages of unions.[20]
The committees cannot, for instance, give workers membership
rights; they are not responsible to a body of members as unions
are. "The leaders of trade unions are directly responsible to their
members for their decisions and actions but Works Committee
representatives do not have to report back." Works Committees,
unlike unions, do not operate independently of the firm, and cannot
muster the collective strength of workers to act against an incon-

siderate or exploiting employer. Unions, on the other hand, can bargain collectively on a collective basis with employers' associations. Trade unions can build up administrative systems, provide research, legal aid, and education in their rights for workers. Nevertheless, it has been suggested that, as Works Committees and Liaison Committees seem permanent, their possibilities should be utilized as far as this is possible. African unions might, under these conditions, work within the Works Committee structure. This allows two questions to be raised: first, what is being done to establish African unions now; and second, what use is being made of the Works Committees to further the interests of African workers?

White Unions and African Unions—Further Considerations

In considering the actions of white unions, let us consider the coordinating bodies as the principal sources of collective policies. There are essentially three of these, two of which have already been mentioned earlier. The two already met are TUCSA and the South African Confederation of Labour (SACOL). The last, and most recently formed, is the Confederation of Metal and Building Unions (CMBU) which represents particularly the Amalgamated Engineering Union, the Electrical Workers' Association, the Iron Moulders' Society, and the Amalgamated Society of Wood Workers.[21] The largest are TUCSA which today has a largely non-white (Indian and coloured) membership, and SACOL with a largely white Afrikaner membership. The Metal and Building confederation involves both white and non-white members with white predominant.

If we divide the coordinating bodies along the "left-right" spectrum, unsatisfactory though this usually is, one can place SACOL on the right, TUCSA on the left, and CMBU in the center. The positions are, of course, relative positions only, for most trade unionists would find even TUCSA quite conservative. The position of SACOL on African unions is fairly unambiguous. It is not opposed to such African trade unions as exist, but is satisfied to see these remain both unrecognized and uninfluential. It recognizes that Africans would, in time, become more experienced, but did

not expect this time to be soon, and is reluctant to urge movement
in this direction.[22] CMBU has varied in its attitude. More recently
the Amalgamated Engineering Union had given an undertaking to
the International Metalworkers Federation to help form a parallel
African union, but progress to this end has seemed slow. This leaves
TUCSA, which has pursued a more active policy towards African
unions.

As the delegation from the British TUC has pointed out, TUCSA
and SACOL both see the facts of the labor situation in the same
way. They both see whites declining in numbers in the industrial
work force, but judge the pace differently. TUCSA had realized
some years ago that Africans made up as much as four-fifths of
the labor force in some industries and that if a responsible union
movement were to develop it would have to be led by the existing
unions. To this end TUCSA had established an African Affairs
Section financed by the German trade union congress Deutscher
Gewerkschaftsbund (DGB) of which more will be said when African
trade unionism is discussed below. This had, however, to be abandoned a year or two later. Indeed, the issue of African unions has
split TUCSA itself and has threatened at different times to split
it further. The most recent threat was in 1968 when the constituent
unions fought over the issue, and in hopes of preventing breakup
it was decided to exclude African unions from membership. Nevertheless, certain unions, subsequently principals in forming the
CMBU split off from TUCSA.[23] This has left TUCSA with about
200,000 members, of whom 90,000 are white, the rest being Coloured or Indian. TUCSA has, however, been continuously interested in African trade unionism in one or another way.

Although the white union leaders claim to favor the creation
of African trade unions, they have done little effective work to
further them. Three TUCSA unions stand out in their efforts:
the clothing workers, the leather workers, and the tobacco workers.
To use the clothing industry as an example, 15,000 Africans are
organized in the Clothing Workers' Union, an unregistered union
as it has exclusively African membership, which works closely
with the Garment Workers' Union which, having no African members, is registered. There is effective collaboration between the
two during wage negotiations, both organizations sharing the
same headquarters. In reaching agreement with employers all
means are used to extend any benefits gained to all workers with-

out regard to race. This shows that even under difficult conditions it is possible to create genuine representation for the African worker majority. TUCSA is, however, fully committed to setting up African trade unions.[24] The majority of TUCSA unions favor organizing Africans and have resolved to do this. They also favor the plan of the opposition United Party. This plan, should it ever be implemented, would divide African workers into three broad groupings: the first would consist of professionals—doctors and journalists for example—who would immediately be granted trade union rights; the second would consist of skilled workers who would be organized in parallel unions; and the third would consist of unskilled workers who would remain in Works Committees with some improvements in their structure.[25] Although the chances of an electoral victory for the United Party seem slim, the endorsement of this scheme, albeit with reservations, is indicative of TUCSA thinking in the matter.

Part of the reasoning on African unions seems to stem from the character of white unions in South Africa and part from difficulties that can arise from precipitate action on the part of overeager organizers.

The success of the Industrial Conciliation Act among white and non-white workers who could operate within registered trade unions has tended to make the functions of the unions on the shop floor somewhat artificial. The unions became remote from the shop floor, and the impression grew, both among white and non-white workers—as well as among many Africans—that unions were not vitally necessary. The working on the Act did, indeed, throw the greatest emphasis on the union headquarters. To the workers the union was identified mainly with the benefit schemes that they operated. The level and extent of public social security was often inadequate, and so trade unions acted to supplement them and to supply such benefits as were not available. The trade unions thus became, in effect, benefit societies, at least in part. The thinking of TUCSA was thus influenced when they thought of African unions, and it perceived the approach to African unions through the establishment of benefit societies. Fees for such societies could be deducted from wages legally, unlike African trade union dues, making establishment of such societies a practical proposition.

Against this some of the younger firebrands have sought to

influence the more conservative TUCSA leadership in a militant trade unionism. The "young Turks" under Harriet Bolton were associated with the Textile Workers Industrial Union, a Coloured and Indian union which came in conflict with South Africa's most powerful textile manufacturer, Phillip Frame. Needing support, the union appealed to the older TUCSA leadership for support which, after initial hesitation, was given. The meeting between Frame and the union was disastrous. The manufacturer was able to produce irrefutable evidence that the union's claims, which had received wide press publicity, were either exaggerated or false, though Frame had not bothered to deny them at the time they were trumpeted abroad. Despite this setback, the TUCSA leaders were able to gain some concessions, but at the price of a statement criticizing the press for its inaccurate reporting of the Frame Group's activities. The problems of the union were compounded when, at a meeting of angry pressmen, they tried to place responsibility for the falsifications on the TUCSA leadership. A rift in TUCSA was the inevitable result. The TUCSA leadership refused to attend a protest meeting called in response to the banning of four young trade unionists of the radical wing. The Textile Workers Industrial Union—a TUCSA affiliate— threatened to disaffiliate in response. The more traditional unions who are attempting to organize parallel unions seem very concerned at the danger of having a subversive label attached to their efforts.[26] The Textile Workers Union, in the meantime, have formed an African union, the National Union of Textile Workers, which although not officially restricted to Africans would initially be concerned largely with them.[27]

The trade unions were not, of course, the only white bodies concerned with organizing African unions. A considerable role was also adopted by the students and staffs of the Universities of Natal and Cape Town. Much of this activity centered on an organization known as Central Administration Services (CAS), which was backed by the clothing workers of Durban, that any union could join, and which was supported by interested persons in the University of Natal and by those from the National Union of Students Welfare Organization (NUSWEL), associated with the National Union of South African Students. CAS employed organizers to establish unions in particular factories, in some cases using membership of a benefit fund associated with CAS as a starting point. There was, in addition, an associated project to provide training, initially by correspondence and subsequently through weekend schools, for active trade unionists. This was supported by the neighboring Zulu homeland and various persons in the University of Natal as well as CAS and its associated unions. The role of NUSWEL seems to be more that of providing information, largely specific and factual, in the case of determination by Wage Boards and into the organization of benefit societies among black workers which could form the basis of African unions of the future.[28]

Even more interesting, perhaps, is the Urban Training Project (UTP) in Johannesburg. This has few academic links, and its aim is to educate African workers in union consciousness. The training is on a fairly elementary level and directed towards workshop representatives. Its aims are, in other words, more practical and less ambitious that the organizations already mentioned. The staff of the project and four African unions share premises in a building in Johannesburg. The project does not seek publicity, indeed it goes out of its way to avoid it. Heading the UTP is Erin Tyacke a man with ten years experience in promoting African unions, who was the organizer originally appointed for this purpose by TUCSA when African unions could still be affiliated to it. Tyacke is careful to point out that the UTP is an educational body and stays in the background in the battle between the African workers, and the twin forces of employers and officialdom. The UTP which was started in 1972 has organized three of the unions that share its premises: the Transport and Allied Workers' Union with 800 members; the Laundry and Dry Cleaning Workers' Union with 600; and the African Chemical Workers' Union with 500. The other union involved, the Engineering and Allied Workers' Union was established eleven years ago and now has a membership of 1,250 but this is only some 0.6 percent of the workers it seeks to represent. The UTP seeks to familiarize Africans with the workings of the Works Committee and Liaison Committee systems and to ensure that Africans obtain their rights.[29] The main way it does this is through a Workers' Calendar of which some 20,000 copies have been distributed. The calendar has aroused the suspicion of the authorities because it has a "Chinese look," which is vaguely the case, although the UTP is even more cautious and legal in its approach than other groups, cautious and legal as these are in their turn. On the East Rand, for instance, the UTP is run by Catholic priests, through the Young Christian Workers' Movement, who have been conducting classes for Africans interested in unions and in their legal rights under the laws.[30] Indeed, the UTP has been active in teaching, having taught some 700 Africans in Saturday courses, and a further 200 odd in residential seminars in the main urban centers.[31]

UTP has recently reported on the mixed results it has had in its approaches to sixteen of the leading South African employers.[32] Generally, the companies were not unsympathetic but were unwilling to make any commitment. All maintained that the Liaison Committee and Works Committee systems were working well. They were cautious about recognizing African unions because of the government's stand against such unions. Loet Douwes Dekker, the chairman of UTP, however, said that this could lead to trouble: "union members are beginning to get impatient at the lack of progress. Most employers are not treating the situation with the urgency it demands." He pointed out, and as our case earlier illustrated (see p. 182 above), that executives are unaware of the expectations of their workers.

> Most of the companies have kept the door open . . . some are actively preparing for the recognition of the unions, which we acknowledge cannot be done overnight. It involves not only the approval of top management but also middle management and supervisors. But I also believe that most of the companies are stalling, hoping to lie low until a confrontation with the unions is forced on them.

The approach of the UTP has been that the Works Committees should complement the unions, for the Works Committees cannot be a substitute for trade unionism.

Other bodies have, regularly or intermittently, entered into efforts at Black unionism, and the reaction seems to be mixed. Some of the more militant Black unionists seem to resent white entry into the organizing of Africans. In general, however, the reaction is one of welcoming combined with a measure of suspicion. One of the Black unionists put it in this form:

> black workers' unions welcome cooperation with any willed and well-intentioned organizations or individuaꞮꞌ, reject domination. We welcome material assistance with no strings attached. Our stand is based on the principle of self-determination.[33]

Africans are trying to organize unions with white help or without. They are organizing them in the teeth of government hostility or suspicion and with employers paying lip service to the idea of African unions while uncomfortably facing the idea of their usually subservient African workers making demands that go against the employers' ideas of what is best for their workers. African unions could make progress, for, as the Natal Employers' Association has pointed out, it is legal for employers to meet with representatives of African unions, negotiate with them, and conclude a collective agreement which could be written and made binding.[34] Nevertheless, the problems African unions face are daunting.

African Unions and Their Problems

The problems of African unions were summarized by Mr. Erin Tyacke when he was administrative assistant for African affairs at TUCSA.[35] Writing in 1964, he said that very few African workers belonged to any union and that many were hostile to the idea of unions. Many who had joined at one or another time said that the union had done nothing for them, was more interested in politics than in the workers, and that monies were collected from new members after which the organizers failed to appear at the factories. This hardened the attitude of Africans towards anyone canvassing for anything where money was involved. Experience of dishonesty and incompetence made Africans suspicious of unions, although unions honestly run and efficiently administered could have helped African workers in many important ways. There was, for instance, much underpayment of African workers, sometimes for five to six years, but most workers were ignorant of any laws covering their wages or working conditions. They knew that whites were paid more than they were, but thought this a matter of color rather than category of work. Had they known that payment often was by category, they could have improved their wages. Even fewer knew how to get the law enforced, even if they knew what the law was, and few were brave enough to risk victimization if they resorted to law. At that time (1964) no form of representative body or committee was found to exist through which grievances could reach the employer. Grievances had to be handled through a "boss-boy," or *Induna*, who often was even more disliked than a bad employer.

The extent of the difficulties in communication of often complex legislation can be gauged from a survey conducted by TUCSA in 1965 through Tyacke's committee.[36] Discussing the results for the Sheetmetal Workers' Union, he pointed out the following: out of the 182 members of the union who completed the questionaire twenty-three percent could neither read nor write. Some seventy-seven percent could read or write an African language, forty-five percent the English language, and nine percent the Afrikaans language. Of the members, forty-one (or twenty-three percent) had never been to school, and fifty-six percent had received an education to third grade or less. Of the membership fourteen did not know if they believed in trade unionism or not, and one was against unions, in spite of the fact that fifty-one claimed to have been cheated by unions at one or another time. Of the members 105 had heard of TUCSA, thirty of SACTU, twenty-one of FOFA-TUSA, and forty-nine (or twenty-seven percent) did not know of any of these bodies. When asked which was strongest, ninety-four said it was TUCSA, four said SACTU, and two mentioned FOFA-TUSA. Some sixty-two, or thirty-four percent, did not know. Yet there was hope in these numbers, for all questioned said they would be willing to attend classes on trade unionism, half were prepared to attend at night, and seventy-five percent at the weekend. The hunger for knowledge that has so often been found typical of Africans was present here also. This hunger had, of course, provided a basis for organization then as now. It is significant indeed that most of the problems outlined ten years ago have remained problems today.

Discussion of the difficulties of African unions may be illuminated both by indicating something of their organization and something of their working.

One of the best established and most interesting of the African unions is the National Union of Clothing Workers. It is most interesting not only for its structure but also for the way it came into being.[37] Although the intention of the 1937 Industrial Conciliation Act had been to exclude all Africans, by a strange quirk it was so drawn that African women *could* be treated as "employees" under the Act while African men could not be. The result was that the Garment Workers' Union could be a mixed union, of all races, and could secure the same benefits to members regardless of race. This continued until passage of the Native Labour (later renamed Bantu Labour) (Settlement of Disputes) Act of 1953 which forbade all mixed unions of whites and Africans. The leadership of the Garment Workers' Union then set about helping organize the African women and amalgamating it with the (male) African Clothing Workers' Union—an amalgamation which involved great difficulty, for the male union was highly political while the women wanted a nonpolitical union such as the Garment Workers' Union. The National Union of Clothing Workers' is now the best organized of African unions, with some 17,000 paid-up members. The union, in addition to assisting in finding employment for its members, has established a death benefit fund insurance and participates jointly with the white union in a loan fund and a welfare fund. It also contributes to the union's weekly paper, *Garment Worker*, which is the only weekly trade union paper in South Africa and the only one for African workers.

The general secretary of the union, Lucy Mvubelo, in many senses typifies the best of African trade union leaders.[38] Educated partly at the Inanda High School run by the American Board of Missions in Natal, almost immediately after leaving school she married a teacher and had two children. Her husband was later attacked by thugs and has been in a mental institution for years, and she had had the task of bringing up her children and earning a living for the family. To help feed and clothe her children she took a job at one of the first clothing factories in South Africa ever to employ African women. She started as a tablehand doing hand sewing at about $3.50 a week. Her abilities in organization and negotiation were recognized, and in a few years she was at the head of the union. She was employed by the Garment Workers' Union as an organizer in 1944 on the same terms and conditions as white organizers.[39] She has since emerged as a significant international figure in labor as well as an important spokeswoman for African workers.

The difficulties facing African unions, then, are best conceptualized if we consider them in terms of a union as well established as the National Union of Clothing Workers. The negotiations of 1973 in the garment industry throw them up in strong relief.

A few weeks after the strikes of 1973 had subsided in the clothing industry, officials of the white union were to meet the employers for talks about cost-of-living increases.[40] As relations between the two sides were cordial, no real problem was expected, and neither objected to a suggestion from the African union that they should join the negotiations. The negotiations were to be conducted, as usual in these cases, with representatives of the employers' association, the union, and representatives from the government who were there to speak, *inter alia*, for the interests of the Africans. When the African union representatives appeared, the Department of Labour representative threatened to walk out claiming that *he* was the Africans' representative. Although the African unionists said that they were going to act only as observers, the official would not even allow that to happen but insisted that the African unionists leave. This meant, in effect, that the African union with 17,000 members—72 percent of the work force in the industry—was barred from taking part in a conference, the results of which would be vital to its members. The workers were compelled to accept as their representative a white official, appointed by the government, who was not working alongside the people he claimed to represent. There has, however, been a recent modification of the law which now allows certain African representatives to attend meetings of industrial councils, but this has changed the actual situation little. The officials of African unions still cannot present the views of their members to the meetings.

An example (of the changed situation) which is not illegal but generally outside the framework of legislated conciliation is the meeting of African unionists and white employers which takes place in the garment industry. Before the formal meetings of the industrial council, employers and the representatives of African unions sit down and talk about wages and conditions of work. The talks are not official and could be ended at any time by either side. There is, however, a built-in safeguard in that if either side un-

reasonably breaks off the talks, they would appear in a bad light
not only to others in the trade but to the country at large. The
clothing industry seems unique in this initiative at the moment,
but it may be pointing the way to the future. A key to its position
is, of course, that it is well organized, that it enjoys total support
of the African workers in the industry and has the wholehearted
backing of the white union with which it is associated. This cannot,
unfortunately, be said of the other African unions whose situation
is very different.

As Mr. Cyril Plant, a member of the British TUC delegation to
South Africa pointed out, the African trade union movement in
South Africa was, on the whole, immature, weak, diffused and
pathetic and needed assistance.[41] Given the situation in which
African unions must function, a situation in which unions lack
legal recognition and can find their activities easily curbed by
employers and officials who do not favor their development, this
is not surprising. Nevertheless it is significant that unions have
formed and have maintained themselves in some cases. The figures
given by Muriel Horrell in 1969 are of some fourteen African
unions with a combined membership of about 16,000 and a later
newspaper report speaks of ten unions with "less than 22,000 members." If one recalls that the bulk of this membership is that of the
National Union of Clothing Workers, the miniscule membership
of the other unions is only too apparent.[42] Many of the unions of
1969 have vanished without trace; others have appeared, though
not necessarily in the same trades. The figures cited are, therefore,
not necessarily indicative of growth.

African unions have, nonetheless, gained in stature and in increasing self-confidence in part because of a growing awareness of African economic strength and in part because of overseas support.
African union leaders seem to be gathering experience in the conduct of negotiations with employers and the use of the law to aid their
members, matters in which they are assisted by the white groups indicated earlier.[43] The Transport and Allied Workers' Union provides an example. It was established in 1973 with the aid of the
Urban Training Project and grew out of a strike of African bus driv-
ers of the large PUTCO bus company. The Urban Training project
did the initial work in forming the union and trained Mr. John Hoffman, an African, as general secretary so that he can now function

independently of UTP though its general line closely follows that laid down by the parent organization. The union does not concern itself with politics but only with bread and butter issues. "We are not for disrupting anything," Hoffman has said, "just for improving the labor situation . . . .Trade unions to be successful [in South Africa] must keep out of politics." The union is now affiliated with the International Transport Workers' Federation.

Among the other recently formed African unions are the Metal and Allied Workers' Unions of Durban and Pietermaritzburg in Natal. The Durban body, the first to be founded, was formed on April 28, 1973, and the latter, at Pietermaritzburg, on June 9 of the same year. Both branches seem well established, with Durban employing three full-time officials and Maritzburg two.[44] Both have large memberships for African unions, about 2,300 and 1,500 respectively, though these are only a fraction of the African workers in the metal industries. The experiences of the two branches has, however, been somewhat different. The Durban branch, which could participate in Industrial Council meetings only with the consent of the Boilermakers Union and the Steel and Engineering Federation of South Africa (the employers' association) has been unable to obtain agreement. The Pietermaritzburg branch, on the other hand, has been able to establish collaboration with the Boilermakers' Union because much of the membership of both the African and the white union comes from Hullet's Aluminium. The branch was also aided in its organization by the secretary of the white Amalgamated Engineering Union, but the union itself was unwilling to collaborate with its African counterpart. Contact has also been made with the employers, and negotiations are underway to secure recognition from the owners. The union is also trying to gain acceptance at other plants. The union is, in other words, on its way though it still has a hard path to travel. The Durban branch has still further to go, having met blank resistance from employers. The unions are faced with a problem that is almost unique. Often when they have improved conditions of members, members lose interest in membership.

Certain statements about African unions in general can be amplified. The first is that the attitudes of African workers are the key to organizational capabilities.[45] Lack of legal recognition has to be made up in mass membership combined into strong organizations. Crucial to the attitude of African workers to African unions has been: the attitude of employers, the policy of the Homeland governments, the experience of Coloured or white unions, and indirect knowledge of the trade union movement. Attitudes may be clarified through trade union propaganda, but they crystallize during a dispute, which can serve as a severe test for the union itself.

The employers' attitude makes itself felt through the presence of victimization of African trade union leaders or of Africans who join unions and demand legal rights. The newness and weakness of many African unions make it simple for employers to repress the unions. Few unions have the funds to benefit those who are victimized, which weakens their appeal to prospective members in the face of determined employer opposition. Even where such funds exist, however, troubles are not over. Those who have received victimization benefits tend to become wards of the union and disinterested in fighting for themselves. Also, if not operated on a contributive basis, the victimization fund can become extremely expensive. Clearly, the best way would be for the union to find another and better job for the worker involved; however, this would require a high degree of cooperation among different African unions.

Another difficulty confronting African unions is the high paper membership. It is no exaggeration to state that at least forty percent of the membership of any African union is not paid up to within two weeks, and this is probably higher in old unions. This problem is, of course, intimately linked with the difficulties in collecting dues. One can easily imagine the difficulties of collecting dues where management is hostile, where there are a number of factories in the industry, and where these are at a considerable distance from each other. What is more, this is to say nothing of different shifts and of overtime worked. An analysis indicates that some fifty percent of an African organizer's time is taken up with recruiting and collecting subscriptions, thirty percent in meeting members and taking complaints, and the remainder in administrative work. This places a heavy burden on the organizer and defeats the purposes of the union. The organizers are well aware of complaints, but because they visit each factory relatively seldom, they tend to put off handling the complaints in favor of other administrative work. As the union "lives by results," members tend to lose interest.

The importance of management in all this must again be stressed, for the settlement of grievances, which means the attainment of results, requires a sympathetic management in the absence of legal recognition.[46] And, as we have seen, managements are more willing to give lip-service to the idea of African unions than to negotiate with unions that exist.

Difficulties in establishing committees that can determine union policy and exercise financial control are also a vexing question. There tends to be an inverse relationship between the degree of centralization and the difficulties faced at the periphery. Branch executive committee members are all too often inexperienced in committee procedure and in handling fairly substantial funds, and yet it is imperative for the success of the unions that these committees exercise control over policy and finance. African unions, much like white unions, tend to develop structures around the trade union secretary, and the committees tend to be uncritical towards secretaries who act without specific authority in financial and policy matters, seeming to trust these officials to an unhealthy extent. This leads, in turn, to frequent disappointment and declining interest in unions among workers who have been "burned" by dishonest or incapable secretaries.

Works Committees and Liaison Committees which were discussed earlier (see p. 180-81) also bedevil the organization of African unions. Workers' representatives on the Works Committees often see their relation with African trade unions as one of adversaries. The representatives on the committees, then, define their interests in opposition to those of the union leadership. The proliferation of Works Committees and Liaison Committees creates doubts in workers' minds as to what constitutes effective representation. Doubtless were these institutions absent, the trade union would be the logical source of representation, but this is not now the case.

The legal bodies established by the government to represent workers are not the only obstacles. It seems that the Security Police (i.e. the political police) do pay close attention to the affairs of African trade unions. Police investigation of an organizer or of a secretary clearly creates the impression that the union is possibly illegal and that the secretary is in some kind of difficulty. It erodes worker willingness to engage in action and lowers their morale, There is, of course, not much that the African unions or their organizers can do about this.

In spite of these difficulties, and they are considerable, there seems to be a firm belief among employers and white labor leaders that African unions are bound to come and bound sooner or later to be effective. The reasons for this will emerge as we discuss the present labor market and what it holds for the African workers.

The Future of African Unions

Two factors give rise to optimism for the future of the African trade unions: (1) the white labor shortage, which seems likely to grow increasingly serious, and (2) the need for continued economic growth to maintain the society.

The class subject to the most rapid growth with economic development is the "professional class," which includes all professional, technical, managerial, administrative, and clerical workers. The numbers of all races employed in this class in 1970 made up 17.3 percent of all who were gainfully employed, and of this percentage some 70 percent were white. The class had grown by about 1.6 percent per year between 1960 and 1970, and further increases in the rate of growth may be expected if other industrialized societies were any guide. In the same ten years the professional class grew to 18.0 percent in the United States and 18.5 percent in Canada. On this basis the professional class could make up 20 percent of the South African labor force by the year 2000. Now, given their projected growth rate, whites could not even staff the professional class, let alone white or blue collar ranks. Assuming with reputable demographers that the white population of South Africa will number some seven millions by the end of the century, and assuming that the proportions of working to non-working population remain roughly the same as they now are, there should be some 2.8 million whites in the labor force—about 40 percent of their numbers. According to conservative estimates the whole population will number about twenty millions, hence the professional class will need to include about four million people. It therefore seems to follow that whites will be unable to staff the advanced positions in the economy, given a random distribution of abilities.[47] These shortages are not envisaged for a distant future. The year 2000 is, after all, only some 26 years away.

The labor shortage is already being felt, and barring some economic crisis in the near future is bound to worsen. Unfilled vacancies for white workers in industry have grown from year to year, rising from 41,000 in 1969 to 53,000 in 1971 for skilled workers alone. The shortfall for artisans in the same period rose from 11,000 to 17,000—roughly from 7.6 to 9.5 percent of all vacancies of this kind.[48] Efforts have been bent towards meeting the labor shortage by using Indians and Coloureds, but their numbers are limited and they have themselves begun climbing the white-collar ladder. The hope that they will relieve the shortage among blue-collar ranks seems doomed to frustration. With the white labor force declining at the rate of about ten percent per decade, this leaves only the African. Either that, or to slow industrial growth.

There are important reasons why economic growth cannot be halted or retarded without serious hardship and risk. These have been fully set forth by Professor W. F. J. Steenkamp, and can be briefly restated.[49] Steenkamp begins by pointing to the two besetting problems in the modern world: the rapid spread of new wants in both old and new nations; and second, the explosive growth of populations—problems to which South Africa is also subject. Because of these problems it would be impossible to sustain existing white standards of consumption, let alone satisfy new wants without industrial growth. Growth is also necessary to internal peace and stability. Africans obviously wish to escape their benumbing poverty and to share more in the fruits of industry. As South Africa has been able to outrun the low pitched revolution of rising expectations among Africans so far, she has enjoyed a comparatively long period of industrial peace. This peace was shaken in 1972 and the shock waves are still spreading. Africans and whites are thus interested in industrial expansion. Industrial expansion would satisfy some white cravings for a still higher living standard, but for Africans it means far more, it means access to more promising jobs and to a brighter future. The discontent among Africans, smoldering below the surface might be set aflame were industrialization to be retarded.

Industrialization would allow time for a gradual improvement in African social and political statuses to be smoothly effected, and would offer hope for their growing numbers. The numbers are impressive. Some seventy-five to ninety-five thousand new job-seekers are expected each year without counting the labor reserves of Botswana, Lesotho, and Swaziland. The government hopes to provide work for most of these in the "Bantu Homelands"—autonomous areas in which Africans would be free of legal bars under their "own" rulers—but such homelands cannot meet the needs of this growing population which is estimated to number twenty-four millions at the end of this century. Satisfactory living standards call for a level of industrialization in the Homelands that has not been possible before. Advanced industries would need to be established in one generation among people who, through no fault of theirs, lack the attitudes and aptitudes such massive change demands. The homelands would, thus, be doomed to permanent poverty unless their inhabitants could, at different times, work in industry in the white areas. This depends, in its turn, on continued industrial growth. Failure to provide work for the growing numbers of Africans would mean large numbers of impoverished and resentful people—a continuous invitation to revolt and a standing source of revolutionaries.

Finally, economic growth is needed for the survival of South Africa itself. In a world hostile to its present social setup, South Africa needs ties to other countries independent of ideological considerations. Economic strength combined with the strategic importance of the Cape route has served to save South Africa from sanctions in the past. Good customers, as always, have many friends as have suppliers of vital materials. Friendship of this sort depends on the continued ability to produce and consume, again underlining the importance of continued growth.

Reasons such as these militate against any substantial slowing of industrial development which has been continuing at a rate of some six percent every year in real terms. The emptying of the white labor pool, already evident, means that industrial advance—which ensures whites the good life—can only be maintained and enlarged by the increasing use of blacks in a broadening range of work.

The effects of the labor shortage can already not be gainsaid. New industries, large and small, using new technologies, in which labor patterns have not been hardened, are using Africans in a growing range of work. These industries have greatest growth potential, comprising as they do electronics, computers, and newer office machinery. In the more traditional industries Africans are being moved into more skilled and better paid work either by stealth or through very costly agreements with the white trade unions, while the government tends to turn a blind eye. Indeed, the government has taken a more active role lately, adopting a tougher attitude to white unions that resist changes in the labor pattern, often punishing recalcitrant unions by establishing apprenticeship programs in the homelands beyond the unions' jurisdictions. The white unions, in their turn are, as we have seen, increasingly considering the advantages of unionizing Africans themselves in the interests of their members and in the interests of the white unions themselves.

Although the government is set against African unions at the moment the outlook for unions seems promising. As Africans become more diversified in their skills their value to employers must increase and their opportunities for organization multiply. Once a worker has ceased to be a "labor unit" and has independent value to his employers, he is in a better position to bargain with them. As Anna Scheepers put it, when African unions are strong and well-organized, only then will legislation be amended giving the *cachet* of recognition to the African unions and allowing their presence as full partners in Industrial Councils.[51]

Many white trade unions, even some who had previously opposed the idea, would today support the organization of Africans. This is for a number of reasons variously advanced: African workers seem bound to organize unions and are moving in that direction; industry depends increasingly on African workers and realizes that this is so; and some employers, though not sufficient, have found that they can work with such African unions as exist. Finally, the parliamentary opposition in South Africa has come around to support of African unionism, as it has not done in the past. Given these trends, and assuming nothing untoward happens to upset developments, Africans may cease to be workers without weapons.

Notes

Notes to Introduction

1. Francis Wilson, *Labour in the South African Gold Mines 1911-1969* (Cambridge, Eng.: Cambridge University Press, 1972).

2. Sheridan W. Johns III, "The Birth of Non-White Unionism in South Africa," *Race*, IX(1967), 173-192.

3. See for instance Clements Kadalie, *My Life and the ICU: the Autobiography of a Black Trade Unionist in South Africa*, London, Frank Cass, 1970; H. J. and R.E. Simons, *Class and Colour in South Africa 1850-1950* (Baltimore: Penguin Books, 1969).

4. Herbert Blumer, "Industrialization and Race Relations," in *Industrialization and Race Relations: A Symposium*, Guy Hunter (ed.) (London: Oxford University Press, 1965), pp. 220-253.

5. Blumer, *Industrialization*, p. 232.

6. C. S. Richards, "Problems of Economic Development of the Republic of South Africa," in *Economic Development of Africa South of the Sahara*, E.A.G. Robinson (ed.) (London: Macmillan, 1964), p. 265.

7. See for instance Francis Wilson, *Migrant Labour in South Africa*, Johannesburg, South African Council of Churches - Spro-Cas, 1972; and G. M. E. Leistner, "Patterns of Urban Bantu Labour: Some Findings of a Sample Survey in the Metropolitan Area of Pretoria," *South African Journal of Economics*, XXXII(1964) 275.

8. For a discussion of white trade unionism see Ralph Horwitz, *The Political Economy of South Africa* (London: Weidenfeld & Nicholson, 1967) especially chs. 11-13; Ernest Gitsham and J. F. Trembath, *A First*

Account of Labour Organization in South Africa (Durban: E.P. & Commercial Printing, 1926); Ivan L. Walker and Ben Weinbren, *2,000 Casualities* (Johannesburg: South African Trade Union Council, 1961).

9. Jeffrey Lever, "White Organized Labour and the Socio-Economic Development of Non-White South Africans," presented at the Third Research Workshop of the Abe Bailey Institute of Inter-racial Studies, University of Cape Town, January 29-31, 1972.

10. Much of this section is based on Johns, *The Birth of Non-White Unionism* virtually the only scholarly treatment of this subject at that stage of development.

11. Neither Simons and Simons, *Class and Colour*, nor Edward Roux, *Time Longer Than Rope* (London: Victor Gollancz, 1948), which are the principal sources on the ICU have much to say of that year.

12. Roux, *Time Longer Than Rope*, pp. 157-58.

13. Simons and Simons, *Class and Colour*, pp. 354-59, Roux, *Time Longer Than Rope*, pp. 161-68.

14. Simons and Simons, *Class and Colour*.

15. Roux, *Time Longer Than Rope*, p. 160.

16. Simons and Simons, *Class and Colour*, pp. 356-57.

17. Roux, *Time Longer Than Rope*, p. 171.

18. Simons and Simons, *Class and Colour*, pp. 357-58, Roux, *Time Longer Than Rope*, p. 160.

19. Roux, *Time Longer Than Rope*, p. 164.

20. Ibid.

21. See for instance Edward Feit, *African Opposition in South Africa* (Stanford: Hoover Institution, 1967).

22. Simons and Simons, *Class and Colour*, p. 359.

23. Roux, *Time Longer Than Rope*, pp 164, 167. The argument that the breach with the Communists caused the downfall of the ICU is still, it seems the Communist Party line, according to their official history, see A. Lerumo, *Fifty Fighting Years: The South African Communist Party, 1921-1971* (London: Inkululeko Publications, 1971), p. 62, though Lerumo fairly assesses the strength of the government and its forces in bringing about the downfall of the ICU.

24. Roux, *Time Longer Than Rope*, p. 169.

25. Ibid., p. 171.

26. Ibid., p. 172.

27. Simons & Simons, *Class and Colour*, p. 362.

28. Roux, *Time Longer Than Rope*, p. 172.

29. Ibid., pp. 173-74, Simons & Simons, *Class and Colour*, pp. 365-66.

30. Simons & Simons, *Class and Colour*, p. 366.

31. Roux, *Time Longer Than Rope*, p. 177.

32. Ibid., p. 178.

33. Ibid., p. 176.

34. Ibid., p. 178 Simons & Simons, *Class and Colour*, p. 373.

35. Simons & Simons, *Class and Colour*, p. 374.

36. *Ibid.*, p. 374, Roux, *Time Longer Than Rope*, p. 179.

37. Roux, *Time Longer Than Rope*, pp. 184-85.

38. Ibid., p. 188.
39. Ibid., pp. 194-96.
40. Lerumo, *Fifty Fighting Years*, p. 62.
41. Ibid.
42. Simons and Simons, *Class and Colour*, pp. 376-77.
43. Roux, *Time Longer Than Rope*, pp. 264-65, see also Lerumo, *Fifty Fighting Years*, pp. 63-5 who handles this topic rather delicately.
44. Roux, *Time Longer Than Rope*, p. 335.
45. Ibid.
46. Ibid., p. 337.
47. Ibid., pp. 338-39.
48. Ibid., pp. 341-342.
49. South Africa, *Report of the Industrial Legislation Commission of Enquiry* UG 62-1951 (Pretoria: Government Printer), p. 203. The organization of African unions in the '40s is also dealt with in chapter 1.
50. Roux, *Time Longer Than Rope*, pp. 344-45.
51. *Legislation Commission*, p. 207.

Notes to Chapter I

1. South African whites are also termed "Europeans," blacks are called "Natives" and "Bantu" in South Africa and these terms will be used where appropriate. "Coloureds" so named by themselves and others, are people of mixed descent. The Indians are also called Asiatics.
2. The best history of the African National Congress to 1952 is Peter Walshe, *The Rise of African Nationalism in South Africa: The African National Congress 1912-1952*, (Berkeley: University of California Press, 1971). For subsequent years see Edward Feit, *South Africa: The Dynamics of the African National Congress*, (London: Oxford University Press, 1962), *African Opposition in South Africa: The Failure of Passive Resistance*, (Stanford, Calif: Hoover, 1967), and *Urban Revolt in South Africa 1960-1964*, (Evanston, Ill.: Northwestern University Press, 1971).
3. "Battle in the Factories," *Fighting Talk*, October 1961.
4. Muriel Horrell (comp.) *South African Trade Unionism: A Study of a Divided Working Class*, (Johannesburg: Inst. of Race Relations, 1961), p. 89.
5. According to the Industrial Legislation Commission of 1951 the ethnic distribution of the trade unions was as follows: 38 whites; 54 registered as multi-racial but actually all white; 14 non-white; 22 registered as multi-racial but with only non-white members; and 8 who furnished no information as to racial composition; 63 had both white and non-white members. As of December 31, 1948, the membership of these unions stood at 269,397 for the whites, 70,427 for Coloureds and Asians, and some 2,344 Africans.
6. Muriel Horrell (comp.), *South African Trade Unionism*, (Johannesburg, Institute of Race Relations, 19X), p. 17.

7. Minutes of the Meeting of the Interim Committee of the Dissenting Trade Unions held in Durban on 7th October 1954, typewritten.

8. Ibid.

9. Quoted in Edward Roux, *Time Longer than Rope*, (Madison, Wis.: University of Wisconsin Press, 196), p. 300.

10. An example is the case of an amount of about $65 paid to the CNETU in respect of arrears of a worker's wages. This sum was not paid to the worker concerned, but kept in the union as office expenses. The worker took his case to court and recovered the money.

11. Coordination Committee, 10/19/1954. The initials mean International Labor Organization, International Confederation of Free Trade Unions, and World Federation of Trade Unions.

12. *Workers' Unity*, Vol. 1, No. 1. April 1955, pp. 2, 7, mimeo.

13. The secretary was then and later L. Masina; the acting secretary at the time under consideration was O. A. Olssen. Masina seems to have been absent from a number of meetings at that time.

14. Ibid., January 2, 1955.

15. Credentials Committee Report to the Conference Organized by the Trade Union Coordinating Committee, held at the Trades Hall, Johannesburg, March 5-6, 1955, handwritten.

16. The members of the National Executive Committee of that time were as President, P. Beyleveld; Vice-President, L. Mvubelo and C. Sidande; General Secretary, L. Masina; Treasurer, Leon Levy; ordinary members, S. Damons, C. Jassen, M. Lee, D. Mateman, B. January, P. G. Mei, A. Mahalangu, B. Nair, V. M. Pillay, C. Mayekiso. Of these Leon Levy eventually became president, and Billy Nair was to play a particularly significant part when the Congress Alliance went underground.

17. Minutes of the National Executive Committee of the South African Congress of Trade Unions held on Monday, 27th June, at 11 a.m. at Somerset House, 110 Fox Street, Johannesburg, typewritten.

18. South African Congress of Trade Unions: Annual Report and Balance Sheet, February 1956, mimeographed.

19. Ibid.

20. The major unions affiliated with SACTU were: the Textile Workers' Industrial Union (registered); African Textile Workers' Industrial Union; National Union of Laundering, Cleaning, and Dyeing Workers (registered), National Union of African Laundering Cleaning and Dyeing Workers; Food and Canning Workers' Union (registered), the African Food and Canning Workers' Union. Among the more local unions were the Natal Aluminum Workers' Union; the Toy Workers' Union; the Municipal Workers' Union; the Transport Workers' Union; and the Bag Workers' Union.

21. Correspondence National Secretary, National Union of Distributive Workers to Joint Secretary SACTU, March 1 and 5. Coordination Committee Report, March 1, 1955. See also *New Day* (not to be confused with *New Age*) March and October issues, 1955.

22. Coordination Committee, October 19, 1954.

23. Ibid., November 24, 1954.

24. Ibid., December 21, 1954 and January 13, 1955.

25. Trade Union Coordination Committee, Financial Statement to January 31, 1955. The conversion from South African pounds (then the currency) to dollars is by the author.

26. National Executive Committee, June 27, 1955 and General Secretary's Report, June 27, 1955.

Notes to Chapter II

1. *World Trade Union Movement*, January 1961.

2. The S.A. Congress of Trade Unions and the Organizing of the Unorganized, typewritten, n.d. Much of the following paragraphs is drawn from this document.

3. Ibid.

4. Report of the Secretariat Presented to the Fifth Annual National Conference of the South African Congress of Trade Unions, October 1960, mimeographed.

5. Muriel Horrell (comp.), *A Survey of Race Relations in South Africa, 1958-1959*, Johannesburg, Institute of Race Relations, 1960, pp. 130-140.

6. South African Congress of Trade Unions: Sixth Annual National Conference held at Durban, 1-2 April, 1961. Report. Proceedings, mimeo.

7. Ibid., A campaign launched to raise African wages to about $2.80 per day. This is treated later in this book.

8. South African Congress of Trade Unions: Seventh Annual National Conference, held at Johannesburg, 21-22 April, 1962, Report. Mimeo.

9. Minutes, National Executive Committee, June 9-10, 1956.

10. Seventh Annual Conference, report, 1962.

11. Special Conference, 1956.

12. Ibid.

13. Report of the Secretariat to the Fifth National Conference of the South African Congress of Trade Unions, 1960, mimeo.

14. Minutes, Management Committee, December 7, 1960.

15. Minutes, Fourth National Conference, 1959.

16. Minutes, Fifth National Conference, 1960.

17. Minutes, National Executive Committee, November 11-12, 1961.

Notes to Chapter III

1. Report of Dulcie Hartwell to the International Conference of Free Trade Unions, n.d.

2. September 12, 1957.

3. Hartwell report.

4. VI (2) Nov. 1961-Jan. 1962, p. 11.

5. Muriel Horrell, *South African Trade Unionism*, (Johannesburg: South African Institute of Race Relations, 1961) and her *South Africa's Workers*, (Johannesburg, South African Institute of Race Relations, 1969).

6. Minutes, Fifth Annual Conference, 1960.

7. Minutes, NEC, November 11-12, 1961.

8. Minutes, Sixth Annual Conference, 1961.

9. Minutes, Management Committee, July 20, 1961.

10. Report, Seventh National Conference, 1962.

11. Minutes, Management Committee, November 30, 1961. Bantu is the official term for African.

12. Horrell, *South Africa's Workers*, p. 73.

13. See annual reports SACTU, and Horrell, Survey 1955+.

14. In South Africa a Registered Nurse is usually referred to as "Sister." A "Sister-tutor" is a Registered Nurse Instructor.

15. Seventh Annual Conference Report, 1962.

16. Seventh Annual Conference, Report, 1962. Much of the material on these strikes comes from that Report and from Horrell, *Survey* 1961, pp. 211-213.

17. Minutes, NEC, June 9-10, 1957.

18. Minutes, Second Annual Conference, April 12-14, 1957.

19. Ibid.

20. Minutes, Management Committee, November 30, 1961.

21. Minutes, Management Committee, November 5, 1958.

22. Minutes, Fourth Annual Conference, March 26-29, 1959.

23. Minutes, Management Committee, May 5, 1962.

24. Report, Seventh Annual Conference, April 21-22, 1962.

25. Minutes, Management Committee, October 30, 1962.

Notes to Chapter IV

1. *The Politics of Despair* (New York: Collier, 1962).

2. *The Organizational Weapon* (New York: Free Press, 1960), p. 183.

3. Minutes, Management Committee, August 5, 1959.

4. Minutes, Management Committee, August 5, 1959.

5. Minutes, Management Committee, August 12, 1959.

6. Ibid.

7. Report, Sixth National Conference, 1962.

8. *New Age*, August 15, 1957.

9.

10. *New Age*, August 11, 1955.

11. Minutes, Management Committee, April 7, 1962.

12. Report, Seventh Annual Conference, 1962 and minutes, Management Committee, April 7, 1962.

13. Ibid.

14. Statement with Regard to SACTU, an ICFTU document, type-written, undated. Also *New Age*, August 29, 1957.

15. See pp. 00 and 00 above.

16. *Workers' Unity*, VII (1) Feb.-Oct. 1962.

17. Ibid.

18. Minutes, Management Committee, July 28, 1962.

19. The decline in the activities of the railway unions is also evident from Minutes, Management Committee, August 11, September 1, and September 22, 1962.

20. Minutes, Management Committee, December 7, 1960.

21. Report, Sixth Annual Conference, 1961; and *New Age* October 12, 1961.

22. *Modernizing Racial Domination: The Dynamics of South African Politics* (Berkeley: University of California Press, 1971), p. 105.

23. Sheila T. van der Horst, "Labour," *Handbook on Race Relations in South Africa*, Ellen Hellman (ed.) (London: Oxford University Press, 1949), p. 145.

24. Minutes, NEC, November 11-12, 1961.

25. Minutes, Management Committee, September 1, 1962.

26. For details of these actions see Edward Roux, *Time Longer Then Rape*, pp. 336-342, and Alex Hepple, *The African Workers in South Africa* (London: 1956), pp. 16-17.

27. *The Industrial Colour Bar in South Africa* (London: Oxford University Press, 1961), p. 32.

28. Report, Sixth Annual Conference, 1961.

29. Minutes, NEC, November 11-12, 1961.

30. Report, Seventh Annual Conference, 1962.

Notes to Chapter V

1. *New Age*, March 6, 1958, p. 6.

2. *New Age*, March 21, 1957.

3. *New Age*, March 28, 1957.

4. *New Age*, April 4, 1957.

5. *Minutes*, NEC, April 11, 1957.

6. See Jordan K. Ngubane, *An African Explains Apartheid* (New York: Praeger, 1963), pp. 162-190.

7. *Report*, Second Annual Conference, April 12-14, 1957.

8. *New Age*, May 30, 1957.

9. *New Age*, September 5 and October 10, 1957.

10. *New Age*, November 28, 1957.

11. Quoted from *New Age*, December 5, 1957 which reproduces the contents of the leaflet.

12. *New Age,* January 2, 1958.

13. Ibid.

14. *New Age*, February 20, 1958.

15. *New Age*, February 13, 1958.

16. *New Age*, February 20, 1958.

17. *New Age*, February 27, 1958.

18. *New Age*, March 20, 1958.

19. *New Age,* April 17, 1958.

20. *New Age,* April 17, 1958.

21. *New Age*, March 27, 1958.

22. "The Campaign for 20,000 New Trade Union Members, A National Minimum Wage of £1-a-Day and Increases for All Workers Receiving More", Mimeo, (Feb. 1957?)

23. J. Peters, *The Communist Party—A Manual on Organization* (New York: Workers' Library, 1935).

24. *Minutes*, Fourth Annual Conference, March 26-29, 1959.

25. Mimeographed, April 23, 1958.

26. *New Age*, August 28, 1958.

27. *New Age*, October 23, 1958.

28. *Draft Resolutions*, Fourth Annual Conference, March 28-29, 1959.

29. *Minutes*, Management Committee, July 22, 1959.

30. *Report of the Secretariat*, Fifth National Conference, October 1960.

31. *Minutes*, Management Committee, October 20, 1960.

32. *New Age*, October 27, 1960.

33. *New Age*, November 3, 1960.

34. *Minutes*, NEC, November 11-12, 1961.

35. *Minutes*, Management Committee, November 30, 1961.

36. *Minutes*, Management Committee, November 30, 1961.

37. Mrs. Helen Suzman was the only candidate of the Progressive Party elected to the South African Parliament, as she still is at the time of writing. She and the Progressive Party have no connection with the Congress Alliance. The Progressive Party program calls for the gradual enfranchisement of Africans on the basis of education and/or income and/or property ownership. The aim is to allow for sufficient flexibility and to promote education with sufficient speed so that the majority of Africans can be enfranchised in a reasonable time.

38. *Minutes*, Management Committee, February 1, 1962.

39. *New Age*, February 15, 1962.

40. Ibid.

41. *Minutes*, Management Committee, May 5, 1962.

42. *Minutes*, Management Committee, May 5, 1962.

43. *New Age*, February 22, 1962.

44. Mimeographed, July 12, 1962.

45. *Minutes*, Management Committee, September 22, 1962.

46. *Minutes*, Management Committee, October 30, 1962.

47. Signed Edward M. Davoren, Assistant General Secretary, November 1, 1963.

48. *Spark*, January 10 and February 14, 1963.

Notes to Chapter VI

1. *New Age*, March 8, 1962.
2. *Report*, Fourth Annual Conference, March 28-29, 1959.
3. *Report*, General Secretary to NEC SACTU, February 4-5, 1961.
4. *Report*, Seventh Annual Conference, April 21-22, 1962.
5. *ICFTU Information*, mimeographed.
6. *Workers Unity*, I (2).
7. *Report of the Secretary*, Fifth Annual Conference, SACTU, October 1960.
8. Meynaud and Salah Bey, *Trade Unionism in Africa*, pp. 125-26.
9. Ibid., p. 126.
10. November 26, 1959.
11. *New Age*, April 20, 1961.
12. *New Age*, August 3, 1961.
13. *New Age*, August 10, 1961.
14. *Minutes*, National Executive Committee SACTU, November 11-12, 1961.
15. *Report*, Seventh Annual Conference, April 21-22, 1962.
16. *Trade Unionism in Africa*, p. 141.
17. *Minutes*, National Executive Committee SACTU, November 11-12, 1961.
18. *African Trade Unions*, (Baltimore, Md.: Penguin, 1966), p. 194.
19. *African Trade Unions*, p. 156.
20. Ibid., p. 195.
21. *ICFTU Information*.
22. *Letter*, signed Leslie Masina, to Secretary-General ICFTU, May 9, 1959.
23. *State vs Willie Mbolompo and 44 Others*, RC/460-64, typewritten.
24. See for instance *New Age*, May 21, 1959.
25. *Letter* from Reeves to C. H. Millard, June 19, 1959.
26. August 13, 1959.
27. "An Open Letter to the Delegates and Observers at the ICFTU African Regional Conference being held in Tunis," signed Leon Levy and Leslie Masina, October 31, 1960, typewritten.
28. *Report*, Third Annual Conference SACTU, March 17-18, 1958.
29. *Report*, Fourth Annual Conference SACTU, March 28-29, 1959.
30. *New Age*, May 21, 1959, p. 3.
31. *Minutes*, Management Committee SACTU, July 22, 1959.
32. *Report*, Sixth Annual National Conference, April 1-2, 1961.
33. *Report*, Seventh Annual Conference SACTU, April 21-22, 1962.
34. *South Africa's Workers*, pp. 31-32.

Notes to Chapter VII

1. *South African Trade Unionism*, pp. 54-55.

2. Ibid., p. 89.

3. *Minutes*, Second Annual Conference SACTU, April 13, 1957.

4. Ibid.

5. *Organizational Weapon*, p. 136.

6. October 1, 1961.

7. February 6, 1960. The same letter denied that ICFTU had influenced the formation of FOFATUSA, and a letter from Millard in the same issue confirms this.

8. *New Age* (Johannesburg) January 5, 1961.

9. Edward Feit, *Urban Revolt in South Africa 1960-1964: A Case Study* (Evanston, Illinois: Northwestern University Press, 1972).

10. *Minutes*, Management Committee, March 9, 1961.

11. *Minutes*, Management Committee, April 7, 1962.

12. Ibid.

13. *Minutes*, Management Committee, May 6, September 1, 1962.

14. *Minutes*, Management Committee, September 1, 1962.

15. *New Age*, June 7, 1962.

16. *Minutes*, Management Committee, October 30, 1962.

17. *South Africa's Workers*, p. 30.

18. February 23, 1963.

19. *South Africa's Workers*, pp. 34-35.

20. Ibid., p. 37.

Notes to Chapter VIII

1. For a detailed discussion see Edward Feit, *Urban Revolt in South Africa 1960-1964: A Case Study* (Evanston, Ill: Northwestern University Press, 1972).

2. *Minutes*, Management Committee, July 28, 1962.

3. *Minutes*, National Executive Committee, SACTU, July 28, 1962.

4. *Minutes*, Management Committee, November 4, 1961.

5. *Report*, Fifth Annual Conference, April 1-2, 1961.

6. *Minutes*, Management Committee, July 28, 1962.

7. Bruno Mtolo, *Umkonto we Sizwe: The Road to the Left* (Durban: Drakensburg Press, 1966).

8. "The Case for the Persecution," *African Communist*, No. 33, Second Quarter, 1968, pp. 25-26.

9. Bruno Mtolo, *Umkonto we Sizwe*, pp. 11-12, also p. 5.

10. Ibid., pp. 13-14.

11. See the case of Rowley Arenstein in the *Star* (Johannesburg) of September 14 and October 21, 1966.

12. Bruno Mtolo, *Umkonto we Sizwe*, p. 24.

13. Ibid., p. 25.

14. Ibid., pp. 27-28.

15. Ibid., pp. 58-59.

16. Ibid., pp. 59-61.

17. Ibid., p. 65.

18. *Cape Times*, (Cape Town), April 24, 1966.

19. Bruno Mtolo, *Umkonto we Sizwe*, p. 66.

20. Ibid., p. 77.

21. Ndhlovu is mentioned by Mtolo on p. 196 of *Umkonto we Sizwe*. The information given here is from the *Natal Mercury* (Durban) February 13, 1964.

22. *Eastern Province Herald*, (Port Elizabeth), January 23, 1965.

23. Evidence in State vs Fischer.

24. Philip Selznick, *The Organizational Weapon: A Study of Bolshevik Strategy and Tactics* (New York: Free Press, 1960), pp. 118-19. It is interesting how "nineteenth century" the conception of "transmission belts" is.

25. *African Worker in South Africa*, p. 6.

26. Philip Selznick, *Organizational Weapon*, pp. 176-77.

Notes to Conclusion

1. Horrell,   *South Africa's Workers: Their Organizations and Patterns of Employment* (Johannesburg: South African Institute of Race Relations, 1969), p. 73.

2. ——————, *A Survey of Race Relations in South Africa* (Johannesburg: South African Institute of Race Relations, 1964 and 1965), pp. 215 and 266 respectively.

3. P. J. van der Merwe, "Labour Policy," *Economic Policy in South Africa: Selected Essays* (Cape Town: HAUM, 1974), p. 173.

4. South Africa, *House of Assembly Debates (Hansard)*, Vol. L, col. 7 Questions.

5. *Hansard*, L. col. 346.

6. *Rand Daily Mail* (Johannesburg) April 12, 1974.

7. Ibid., April 16, 1974.

8. Ibid., March 19, 1974.

9. *Star* (Johannesburg) July 21, 1973. The survey was conducted by the official opposition United Party in the Nationalist-held Northern Peninsula constituency of the Cape.

10. Lawrence Schlemmer, *Privilege, Prejudice and Parties: A Study of Political Motivation Among White Voters in Durban* (Johannesburg, Institute of Race Relations, 1973), pp. 22-3.

11. *Star* (Johannesburg) May 29, 1974.

12. Wage Boards are discussed on p. 000 below.

13. Address by the Honorable Marais Viljoen, Minister of Labour, at a Conference Organized by the National Development and Management Foundation and the Productivity and Wage Association on March 1st 1973 at 8:30 a.m. in the Carlton Hotel, Johannesburg, mimeographed.

14. *Rand Daily Mail*, December 17, 1973.

15. *Rand Daily Mail*, April 18, 1974.

16. Muriel Horrell, *South Africa's Workers*, pp. 16-17.

17. _____, *Survey of Race Relations, 1973*, pp. 280-81.

18. April 18, 1974.

19. *Rand Daily Mail* (Johannesburg) February 15, 1974.

20. Loet Douwes-Dekker, "Are Works Committees in Other Countries Effective?" *South African Labour Bulletin*, I (June 1974) p. 35.

21. Much of what follows is drawn from the Trades Union Congress (Great Britain) "Visit of the General Council Delegation to South Africa, October 6-20, 1973," I.C. 3/1, December 10, 1973, mimeographed. This is a perceptive survey of labor problems and trade unionism in South Africa.

22. See for instance, *Friend* (Bloemfontein) March 5, 1973.

23. Trade Union Council of South Africa, *Special Conference 1967: Report of Proceedings*, and *Fourteenth Annual Conference held at Cape Town, April 1968: Report of Proceedings*.

24. *Rand Daily Mail* (Johannesburg) March 3, 1973.

25. *Star* (Johannesburg) February 8, 1974.

26. *Star* (Johannesburg) February 12, 1974.

27. *Daily News* (Pietermaritzburg, Natal) September 9, 1973.

28. Once again the useful report of the British Trade Union Congress must be acknowledged.

29. *Sunday Times* (Johannesburg) February 3, 1974.

30. *Rand Daily Mail* (Johannesburg) April 18, 1974.

31. *Sunday Times* February 3, 1974.

32. *Sunday Times* (Johannesburg) December 8, 1974.

33. Trades Union Congress (Great Britain) Report.

34. Ibid.

35. Trade Union Council of South Africa, *Tenth Annual Conference held at Cape Town, April, 1964*, pp. 81-2.

36. Trade Union Council of South Africa, *Eleventh Annual Conference held at East London, March, 1965: Report of Proceedings*, p. 70.

37. Unless otherwise mentioned most of the material on this union is from "An Address Delivered by Miss Anna Scheepers, President of the Garment Workers' Union of South Africa and Vice-President of the Trade Union Council of South Africa, at the Third Research Workshop of the Abe Bailey Institute of Interracial Studies, University of Cape Town; January 1973 entitled 'Trade Unions Face Challenge' " (mimeo).

38. *Star* (Johannesburg) July 18, 1973.

39. Scheepers, "*An Address . . .*"

40. Most of the description that follows is derived from *Sunday Times* (Johannesburg) February 17, 1974.

43. *Sunday Times* (Johannesburg) February 24, 1974.

44. Linda Ensor, "A Look at the Open Trade Unions," *South African Labour Bulletin*, June 1974, Vol. 1. pp. 17-21.

45. Linda Ensor, "The Problems of African Unions," *South African Labour Bulletin* I (May) 1974, pp. 35-38.

46. *Ibid.*, Indeed much of this and the following paragraphs is derived from this source.

47. W. F. J. Steenkamp, "Labour Management in Industrial Relations," *South African Journal of Economics*, XXXXI (December 1973) 401-437.

48. Republic of South Africa, Department of Labour, *Manpower Survey Nr. 9*, Pretoria 1971.

49. W. F. J. Steenkamp, "Labour Policies for Growth during the Seventies," *South African Journal of Economics*, XXXIX (June 1971) 97-111.

50. Merle Lipton, "South Africa: Authoritarian Reform?" *World Today*, XXX (1974) 247-59.

51. Anna Scheepers, "*An Address* . . ."

Bibliography

Adam, Heribert. *Modernizing Racial Domination: The Dynamics of South African Politics.* Berkeley: University of California, 1971.

Anonymous, "The Fight for a Living Wage in South Africa," *Free Labour World*, 138(1961) 507-10.

——— ,"The Free Trade Unions of South Africa's Fight for Existence," *Free Labour World*, 68(1956) 20-4.

Arkin, Marcus. "Strikes, Boycotts and the History of their Impact in South Africa," *SAJE* 28(1960) 303-18.

Babs, M. "The WFTU and the Struggles in South Africa," *World Trade Union Movement*, 11(1963), 17-18.

Backer, W. *Motivating Black Workers*, Johannesburg: McGraw-Hill, 1973.

Blumer, Herbert. "Industrialization and Race Relations," in *Industrialization and Race Relations: A Symposium*, London: OUP, 1965.

Braunthal, Julius and A. J. Forrest (eds.), *Yearbook of the International Free Trade Union Movement: Volume 2: 1961-2.* Appendix: "The Rise of Trade Unionism in South Africa." London: Lincolns-Prager, 1961-62.

Cantril, Hadley. *The Politics of Despair.* New York: Collier, 1962.

Clark, Garfield. "Industrial Peace in South Africa," *British Journal of Industrial Relations*, I(1963) 94-106.

Devyver, Frank T. "South African Labour Relations," *Labor Law Journal*, XI(1960) 837-46, 855.

Diamond, Charles. "The Native Grievances Enquiry 1913-1914" *SAJE*, 36(1968).

Douwes-Dekker, Loet. "Are Works Committees in other Countries Effective?" *South African Labour Bulletin*, June 1974.

Doxey, G. V. *The Industrial Colour-Bar in South Africa*, London: OUP, 1961.

Drugis, Hans. "Rassenkampf und Gewerkschaften in Südafrika," *Gewerkschaftliche Monatshefte*, March 1957, 182-85.

Ensor, Linda. "A Look at the Open Trade Unions," *South Africa Labour Bulletin*, June 1974.

――――――, "Problems of African Unions," *South African Labour Bulletin*, May 1974.

Feit, Edward. *South Africa: The Dynamics of the African National Congress*, London: OUP 1962.

――――――, *African Opposition in South Africa: The Failure of Passive Resistance*, Stanford: Hoover Institution, 1967.

――――――, *Urban Revolt in South Africa 1960-1964: A Case Study*. Evanston: Northwestern University, 1971.

First, Ruth, Jonathan Steele, and Christabel Gurney. *The South African Connection: Western Investment in Apartheid*, London: Temple Smith, 1972.

Gitsham, Ernest and James F. Trembath, *Labour Organization in South Africa*, Durban: Commercial Printing, 1926.

Graham, G. C. V. "Increased Non-European Semi-Skilled and Unskilled Wages," *Race Relations Journal*, 28(1961) 3-17.

Hartmann, Heinz. *Enterprise and Politics in South Africa*, Princeton: Princeton University, 1962.

Hepple, Alex *The African Worker in South Africa: A Study in Trade Unionism,* London: Africa Bureau, 1956.

――――――, *South Africa: Workers under Apartheid*, London: International Defence and Aid, 1969.

Hobart, D. Houghton, *The South African Economy*, London: OUP, 1964.

――――――, "Economic Development 1865-1965," in *Oxford History of South Africa, Volume II 1870-1966*, London: OUP, 1964.

Horrell, Muriel (comp.), *South African Trade Unionism: A Study of a Divided Working Class*, Johannesburg: SAIRR, 1961.

—————, *A Survey of Race Relations in South Africa*, issued annually, Johannesburg: SAIRR.

—————, *South Africa's Workers: Their Organizations and Patterns of Employment*, Johannesburg, SAIRR, 1969.

Horwitz, Ralph. *The Political Economy of South Africa*, London: Weidenfeld and Nicholson, 1967.

International Metalworkers' Federation, *Report of the IMF Delegation on Their Visit to South Africa in 1972*, Geneva: International Metalworkers Federation, 1972.

Johns III, Sheridan W. "The Birth of Non-White Unionism in South Africa," *Race* IX(1967) 173-192.

Jones, J. D. R. "Industrial Relations in South Africa," *International Affairs*, 39(1953) 43-51.

Johnstone, R. "White Prosperity and White Supremacy in South Africa Today," *African Affairs*, 69(1970) 124-140.

Kadalie, Clements. *My Life and the ICU: The Autobiography of a Black Trade Unionist in South Africa*, London: Frank Cass, 1970.

Kahn, Ellison. "The Right to Strike in South Africa: An Historical Analysis," *SAJE* 11(1943) 24-47.

Key, A. C. "The Strike in the Gold Mines of South Africa," *International Labour Review*, 6(1922) 892-916.

Legassick, M. "Development and Underdevelopment in South Africa," unpublished seminar paper for the Southern Africa Group, Royal Institute of International Affairs, Chatham House, London 1971, mimeographed.

Leistner, G. M. E. "Patterns of Urban Bantu Labour: Some Findings of a Sample Survey in the Metropolitan Area of Pretoria," *SAJE* 32(1964).

Lerumo, A. *Fifty Fighting Years: The South African Communist Party 1921-1971*, London: Inkululeko Publications, 1971.

Lever, Jeffrey. "White Organized Labour and the Socio-Economic Development of the Non-White South Africans," presented at the Third Research Workshop of the Abe Bailey Institute of Interracial Studies, University of Cape Town, January 29-31, 1972, mimeographed.

Levy, Leon. "African Trade Unionism in South Africa," *Africa South in Exile*, V(1961) 32-43.

_____, "The Battle in the Factories," *Fighting Talk*, October 1961.

Lewin, Julius. "The Recognition of African Trade Unions," *Race Relations*, IX(1942) 111-116.

Lipton, Merle. "South Africa: Authoritarian or Reform?" *World Today*, 30(1974) 247-259.

Lombard, J. A. "The Determination of Racial Income Differentials in South Africa," in *Problems in Transition*, J. Knox, J. W. Mann, and K. A. Heard (eds.), Durban, Institute for Social Research, University of Natal, 1964.

_____.(ed.) *Economic Policy in South Africa: Selected Essays*, Cape Town: HAUM, n.d.

Mabhida, Moses. "End the Suffering of Millions," *World Trade Union Movement*, March 1962. 29-31, 34.

Meynaud, Jean and Anisse Salah Bey, *Trade Unionism in Africa*, London: Methuen, 1967.

Mtolo, Bruno. *Umkonto we Sizwe: The Turn to the Left*, Durban: Drakensberg Press, 1966.

Natal, University of, Department of Economics, *The African Factory Worker: A Sample Study of the Life and Labour of the Urban African Worker*, Cape Town: OUP, 1950.

Naude, C. F. Beyers, Wolfgang H. Thomas, et. al. *Management Responsibility and African Employment*, Johannesburg: Ravan Press, 1973.

Ngubane, Jordan K. *An African Explains Apartheid*, New York, Praeger, 1963.

Peters, J. *The Communist Party: A Manual on Organization*, New York: Workers' Library, 1935.

Pursell, Donald E. "Bantu Real Wages and Employment Opportunities," *SAJE*, 36(1958)

Randall, Peter (ed.), *Power, Privilege and Poverty: Report of the Spro-Cas Economics Commission*, Johannesburg: Christian Institute of South Africa, 1972.

Rheinhallt-Jones, J. D. "The Effects of Urbanization in South and Central Africa," *African Affairs*, 52(1953) 37-44.

Rhoodie, N. J. *Apartheid and Racial Partnership in South Africa*, Pretoria, Academica, 1969.

Richards, C. S. "Problems of Economic Development of the Republic of South Africa," in *Economic Development of Africa South of the Sahara*, E. A. G. Robinson (ed). London: Macmillan, 1964.

Ringrose, H. G. *Trade Unions in Natal*, Cape Town: OUP, 1951.

Routh, Guy. *Industrial Relations and Race Relations*, Johannesburg: SAIRR, n.d.

——————, "Industrial Relations in South Africa," *SAJE* 20(1952) 1-11.

——————, "State Intervention in the Regulation of Wages and Working Conditions in Great Britain and South Africa," *SAJE* 17(1949) 289-305.

Roux, Edward. *Time Longer Than Rope*, Madison: University of Wisconsin, 1964.

Rudkin, W. C. "Industrial Relations in South Africa," *SAJE*, 20(1952) 280-83.

Sadie, J. L. "The White Labour Force of South Africa," *SAJE*, 28(1960) 87-101.

——————, "Population and Economic Development in South Africa," *SAJE*, 36(1968) 205-234.

——————, "An Evaluation of the Demographic Data Pertaining to the Non-White Population of South Africa," *SAJE* (1970) 171-191.

Schlemmer, Lawrence. *Privilege, Prejudice and Parties: A Study of Political Motivation among White Voters in Durban*, Johannesburg, SAIRR, 1973.

Selznick, Philip. *The Organizational Weapon*, New York: Free Press, 1960.

Simons, H. J. "Trade Unions," in *Handbook on Race Relations in Race Relations in South Africa*, Ellen Hellman (ed.), Cape Town: OUP, 1949.

——————, and R. E. Simons, *Class and Colour in South Africa 1850-1950*, London and Baltimore: Penguin African Series, 1969.

Smith, R. H. "Some Reflections on the Economics of Wage Fixation in South Africa," *SAJE* 8(1940) 91-116.

South Africa, Department of Labour, *Manpower Survey #9*, Pretoria, 1971.

——————, *Report of the Industrial Legislation Commission of Enquiry* UG 62-1951, Pretoria, Government Printer, 1952.

Springbok, A. (Psued.), "South African Labour and its Problems," Free Trade Union News, V(1960) 6-7.

Steenkamp, W.F.J. "The Bantu Wage Problems," *SAJE*30 (1962) 93-118.

_____ , "Labour Management in Industrial Relations," *SAJE* 31(1973) 401-437.

_____ , "Labour Policies for Growth in the Seventies," *SAJE* 39(1971) 97-111.

Thomas, Wolfgang H. (ed.) *Labour Perspectives on South Africa*, Cape Town: David Phillip, 1974.

Tinley, J. M. *The Native Labour Problem of South Africa*, Chapel Hill, University of North Carolina, 1942.

Trades Union Congress Delegation to South Africa, *Trades Unions in South Africa*, London: TUC, 1954.

_____ , Report, mimeographed, 1973.

Trade Union Council of South Africa, *Reports of Proceedings*.

_____ , Special Conferences, 1967 and 1969, *Reports of Proceedings*.

Transvaal Chamber of Mines, *Tribal Natives and Trade Unionism*, Johannesburg, Transvaal Chamber of Mines, 1956.

Trapido, S. "South Africa: A Comparative Study in Industrialization," *Journal of Development Studies,* 7(1971) 309-320.

van der Horst, Sheila T. "Equal Pay for Equal Work," *SAJE,* 22(1954) 187-209.

_____ , *Native Labour in South Africa*, London: OUP, 1942.

_____ , "Some Aspects of Industrial Legislation in the Market for Native Labour in South Africa," *SAJE* 3 (1935) 481-501.

_____ , *African Workers in Town*, London and Cape Town, OUP, 1964.

_____ , "Labour" in *Handbook on Race Relations in South Africa*, Ellen Hellman (ed.), Cape Town and London: OUP, 1949.

van der Merwe, P. J. "Labour Policy," in *Economic Policy in South Africa: Selected Essays*, Cape Town: HAUM, 1974.

_____ , unpublished Ph.D. thesis *Die Bantoe Arbeidsmark in Suid-Afrika*, University of Pretoria, 1971.

Walker, Ivan L. and Ben Weinbren, *2000 Casualties: A History of the Trade Unions and the Labour Movement in the Union of South Africa*, Johannesburg: Trade Union Council of South Africa, 1961.

Walshe, Peter. *The Rise of African Nationalism in South Africa: The African National Congress 1912-1952*, Berkeley, University of California, 1971.

Wilson, Francis. *Labour in the South African Gold Mines 1911-1969*, Cambridge: at the University Press, 1972.

——————, *Migrant Labour in South Africa*, Johannesburg: South African Council of Churches, 1972.

Index